a soup a day

a soup a day

365 delicious soups
for every day of the year

hamlyn

An Hachette UK Company
www.hachette.co.uk

First published in Great Britain in 2018
by Hamlyn, a division of
Octopus Publishing Group Ltd
Carmelite House
50 Victoria Embankment
London EC4Y 0DZ
www.octopusbooks.co.uk

This material was previously published
in *200 Super Soups*, *200 Fast Vegetarian Recipes*,
200 One Pot Meals and *Soups*

Distributed in the US by
Hachette Book Group
1290 Avenue of the Americas
4th and 5th Floors
New York, NY 10104

Distributed in Canada by
Canadian Manda Group
664 Annette St.
Toronto, Ontario, Canada M6S 2C8

ISBN 978 0 600 63540 6

A CIP catalogue record for this book is available from
the British Library.

Printed and bound in China

10 9 8 7 6 5 4 3 2 1

Standard level spoon measurements are used in all
recipes.
1 tablespoon = one 15 ml spoon
1 teaspoon = one 5 ml spoon

Both imperial and metric measurements have been
given in all recipes.

Use one set of measurements only and not a mixture
of both.

Eggs should be medium unless otherwise stated. This
book contains dishes made with raw or lightly cooked
eggs. It is prudent for more vulnerable people such as
pregnant and nursing mothers, older people, babies
and young children to avoid uncooked or lightly
cooked dishes made with eggs.

This book includes dishes made with nuts and nut
derivatives. It is advisable for customers with known
allergic reactions to nuts and nut derivatives and
those who may be potentially vulnerable to these
allergies, such as pregnant and nursing mothers,
invalids, the elderly, babies and children, to avoid
dishes made with nuts and nut oils. It is also prudent
to check the labels of pre-prepared ingredients for the
possible inclusion of nut derivatives.

contents

introduction

We are all being encouraged to eat more vegetables. Current guidelines recommend eating five portions of vegetables and fruit a day, but nutritionists would rather it was nearer seven, yet the reality is that many people don't even eat two portions! Soup is an easy way to up our consumption of vegetables without it feeling worthy. Soup is also the ultimate comfort food, warming, revitalizing, energizing and full of good things – the culinary equivalent of a hug.

The key to a healthy diet is variety, and given that such a mixture of ingredients can be added to soups, it is easy to include a wide range of essential vitamins, minerals, protein, complex carbohydrates and healthy fats, which are all vital for energy, growth, repair, immunity and key metabolic processes.

The more colourful the vegetables are that you add to your soups, the more cancer-protecting antioxidants and phytochemicals they contain. And adding wholegrains such as brown rice, pearl barley, lentils and dried or canned beans not only keeps us feeling fuller for longer but boosts fibre, which in turn can help to lower cholesterol levels.

In this book you will find a huge range of soups, from super-speedy to slow-cooked; light and summery to winter warmers; budget busters to soups to impress; chunky broths to smooth bisques – something for every occasion.

Some recipes include 'next time' ideas, a twist on the previous day's soup, so the chances are that you will have the core ingredients already

in your cupboard, saving on shopping, and it's a good way of ringing the changes with a favourite soup.

The secret of a good soup is the stock that you use. Homemade chicken stock is the easiest to make, but you will also find recipes for beef, fish and vegetable stocks (see pages 9–10). For times when you don't have homemade stock to hand, choose reduced-salt stock cubes for a quick and easy solution, or for luxury soups, buy cartons of ready-made stock from the supermarket chiller cabinet (see page 11).

With flavours from around the world, you can choose from American fish chowders, Indian spiced lentil soups and Far Eastern clear hot and sour soups, to Russian borscht, French classics and nostalgic flavours of childhood.

Raw, natural ingredients bought locally, transformed into a heart-warming soup is home cooking at its easiest and simplest.

These soups are perfect to serve at a relaxed weekend lunch or as a smart starter for friends; to enjoy as lunch for one or as a late supper after a long day at work; or to provide a speedy kids' supper grabbed between school and dashing to a sports club. With 365 recipes to choose from, there really is a soup for everyone every day.

soup basics

types of soup

Bisques These rich soups are always made with fish and puréed at the end of cooking, then generally mixed with cream or a mixture of milk and cream.

Broths These chunky, clear soups are really a complete meal in a bowl and can be thickened with rice, potatoes or pulses and mixed with lots of diced or shredded vegetables. They can be made even more substantial with the addition of tiny dumplings or pasta towards the end of cooking.

Chowders These chunky soups originated in the USA and contain lightly fried onions and diced potatoes simmered gently with smoked or white fish, or a mixture of flat fish and shellfish in fish stock, then finished with milk or milk and cream.

Consommés Ultra-clear soups that are rather out of vogue now. They are made with a concentrated beef stock that is then filtered through a jelly bag with eggshells and egg white to remove any scum.

Potages A French term used to describe unstrained soups either poured over bread or topped with a bread croûte. They can also contain rice or pasta.

Purées Probably the most popular, these soups can be made with a huge variety of ingredients gently simmered with stock, then blended in the pan with a stick blender or in a blender or food processor at the end of cooking for a smooth, silky texture.

Veloutés These smooth soups are thickened with a mixture of egg yolks and cream to enrich the soup at the end of the cooking time. To prevent the eggs from curdling, a ladleful of hot soup is mixed with the eggs and cream before adding to the main pot of soup. It is crucial that these soups are then heated gently and not boiled, just as you would when making a sweet custard, stirring constantly, so that the eggs thicken the soup rather than scramble.

homemade stock

The best soups are those made with homemade stock. Traditionally this was made from the bones of the Sunday roast and flavoured with a few vegetable trimmings and herbs as a way of making use of every part of a joint or bird, including the scraps of leftover meat, to create a hearty and filling meal. In today's age of recycling and war on wastage, it still makes perfect sense to use that chicken carcass and its remnants as the base for a delicious lunch or supper. And don't chuck out those oddments in the refrigerator and vegetable basket either – that slightly wrinkled carrot, those last few slightly bendy celery sticks and the stems from that bunch of parsley or coriander can all be put into the stock. Add the odd bay leaf from the garden or green leek or spring onion tops that are rather strong tasting and a sprinkling of peppercorns for extra flavour. The more you add, the better your stock will be.

The secret is to add all the ingredients and bring the stock just to the boil, then reduce the heat to a very gentle simmer so that the water barely shudders and cook with the lid half on, half off the pan for 2 hours, or longer if you have the time. Keep the heat very low, as if it is too high you will produce a thick, muddy-looking stock.

At the end of the cooking time, taste the stock. If it seems a little thin, remove the lid and simmer for a further hour or two to reduce the liquid and concentrate the flavours. Strain and leave to cool. Skim any fat off the surface of meat stocks and refrigerate the stock until needed, for up to 3 days.

Alternatively, you can freeze the stock in a plastic box or loaf tin lined with a large plastic bag for use later. Seal, label and freeze for up to 3 months. Defrost at room temperature, or in a microwave oven if preferred, minus the bag tie if used.

chicken stock

PREPARATION TIME 10 MINUTES
COOKING TIME 2–2½ HOURS
MAKES ABOUT 1 LITRE (1¾ PINTS)

1 leftover cooked chicken carcass
1 onion, quartered
2 carrots, thickly sliced
2 celery sticks, thickly sliced
1 bay leaf or 1 small bunch of mixed herbs
½ teaspoon roughly crushed black peppercorns
¼ teaspoon salt
2.5 litres (4 pints) cold water

Put the chicken carcass and vegetables into a large saucepan. Add the herbs, peppercorns and salt, pour over the measured water and bring slowly just to the boil. Skim off any scum with a slotted spoon. Reduce the heat, half-cover and simmer gently for 2–2½ hours until the liquid has reduced by about half. Strain through a large sieve into a jug and leave to cool. Remove any chicken pieces still on the carcass, pick out the meat pieces from the sieve and reserve for the soup, but discard the vegetables. Cover and chill the stock in the refrigerator for several hours or overnight. Skim any fat off the surface, re-cover and store in the refrigerator for up to 3 days.

A duck, pheasant or guinea fowl carcass or a ham knuckle can also be made into stock in just the same way. If you have a turkey carcass, then double up the vegetable and water quantities specified above.

If you have a chicken carcass but don't have time to make it into stock straight away, you can freeze it for up to 3 months closely wrapped in clingfilm, then packed into a plastic bag. Defrost it at room temperature, then make into stock as above.

beef stock

PREPARATION TIME 10 MINUTES
COOKING TIME 4 HOURS 20 MINUTES–
5 HOURS 20 MINUTES
MAKES ABOUT 1 LITRE (1¾ PINTS)

2 kg (4 lb) beef bones, such as ribs or shin
2 smoked streaky bacon rashers, diced
2 onions, quartered but with the inner brown
    layer still on
2 carrots, thickly sliced
2 celery sticks, thickly sliced
1 turnip, diced (optional)
2 bay leaves or 2 rosemary or sage sprigs
½ teaspoon roughly crushed black peppercorns
¼ teaspoon salt
3.6 litres (6 pints) cold water

Put the bones and bacon into a large saucepan and heat gently for 10 minutes until the marrow begins to run from the centre of the bones, turning the bones occasionally. Add the vegetables and fry for a further 10 minutes, stirring the vegetables and turning the bones until browned. Add the herbs, peppercorns and salt, pour over the measured water and bring slowly just to the boil. Skim off any scum with a slotted spoon. Reduce the heat, half-cover and simmer gently for 4–5 hours until the liquid has reduced by about half. Strain through a large sieve into a jug and leave to cool. Cover and chill the stock in the refrigerator for several hours or overnight. Skim any fat off the surface, re-cover and store in the refrigerator for up to 3 days.

If you're not in the habit of roasting large beef joints on the bone, you can obtain the beef bones from your local butcher; they may even give them to you for free. Use the bones raw when preparing your stock. Lamb stock can be made in the same way from cooked or uncooked lamb bones.

fish stock

PREPARATION TIME 10 MINUTES
COOKING TIME 45 MINUTES
MAKES ABOUT 1 LITRE (1¾ PINTS)

1 kg (2 lb) fish trimmings, such as heads,
    backbones, tails, skins and prawn shells
1 onion, quartered
2 green leek tops, sliced
2 carrots, thickly sliced
2 celery sticks, thickly sliced
a few thyme sprigs
1 bay leaf
a few parsley stems
½ teaspoon roughly crushed white peppercorns
¼ teaspoon salt
1.5 litres (2½ pints) cold water
300 ml (½ pint) dry white wine or extra water

Put the fish trimmings in a large sieve, rinse
with cold water, drain and then put them
into a large saucepan with all the remaining
ingredients. Bring slowly just to the boil and
skim off any scum with a slotted spoon. Reduce
the heat, cover and simmer for 30 minutes.
Strain through a large sieve, return the stock
to the pan and then simmer it, uncovered, for
about 15 minutes until reduced by half. Leave to
cool, then cover and store in the refrigerator for
up to 3 days.

If you are adding fish heads, don't cook them
for longer than 30 minutes before straining, or
they will begin to add a bitter taste.

vegetable stock

PREPARATION TIME 10 MINUTES
COOKING TIME 1 HOUR 5 MINUTES
MAKES ABOUT 1 LITRE (1¾ PINTS)

1 tablespoon olive oil
2 onions, roughly chopped
2 green leek tops, roughly chopped
4 carrots, roughly chopped
2 celery sticks, thickly sliced
100 g (3½ oz) cup mushrooms, sliced
4 tomatoes, roughly chopped
1 small bunch of mixed herbs
½ teaspoon roughly crushed black peppercorns
¼ teaspoon salt
1.8 litres (3 pints) cold water

Heat the oil in a large saucepan, add the
onions, green leek tops, carrots, celery and
mushrooms and fry for about 5 minutes,
stirring occasionally, until softened and just
beginning to turn golden around the edges.
Add the tomatoes, herbs, peppercorns and salt,
pour over the measured water and bring slowly
just to the boil. Reduce the heat, half-cover
and simmer gently for 1 hour. Strain through
a large sieve into a jug and leave it to cool.
Cover and store in the refrigerator for up to
3 days.

If you have some opened dry white wine or dry
cider, you can replace 150 ml (¼ pint) water
with either.

Mix and match vegetables depending on what
you have – chopped fennel or peeled and diced
celeriac make a flavourful addition. Half a red
or orange pepper, cored, deseeded and chopped,
and a few dried mushrooms are also ideal.

stock cubes & ready-made stock

In our grandmothers' day, it would have been unheard of to make soup with a stock cube; nowadays, juggling work with family life means that time-saving short cuts are a must. Very few people make enough stock for all their cooking needs, and while it is great to have a few bags of stock in the freezer, most of us cheat and use shop-bought products.

While there is nothing wrong with using stock cubes, there are some soups for which homemade stock is crucial such as the light, delicate-tasting Chilled Lettuce Soup (see page 56), Vichysoisse-style soups (see page 149) or clear consommé-style broths such as Italian Tortellini in Brodo (see page 137) or Chicken Soup with Lockshen (see page 133). The strength of flavour varies hugely in shop-bought stock cubes, so choose cubes or powder that are low in salt and make them up with a little extra water than instructed on the packet so that their flavour is not overpowering.

More and more supermarkets now sell tubs of chilled ready-made stocks and for a special-occasion soup such as Crab Bisque (see page 87) or French Onion Soup (see page 148) they give a much more authentic taste. They are more expensive, but much closer to the taste of homemade stock.

get ahead

Soups make such a warming, satisfying lunch that it is well worthwhile freezing portions in individual plastic boxes or plastic bags for occasions when you don't have time to cook from scratch. So, rather than always having a sandwich at work, why not take a frozen pack of soup with you so that it defrosts while you work, then give it a quick blast in the microwave at lunchtime.

If you don't have many plastic boxes, line a rectangular loaf tin with a freezer bag, fill with soup and seal, squeezing out as much air as possible. Freeze until solid, then remove the bag from the tin, rinsing with cold water to loosen the bag from the tin if needed. The frozen block then makes for an easy stacking shape in your freezer. Just remember to label and date it so that you will know what it is when you come to defrost it. There is nothing more frustrating than defrosting an item expecting it to be savoury, only to find it is fruit purée or something else sweet instead.

reheating

Only ever reheat foods once. If your family is planning to tuck into a batch of soup at different times, then ladle the amount required at any one time into a smaller saucepan or microwaveable bowl and then reheat thoroughly, leaving the remaining soup in the refrigerator until needed. Don't add extra liquid until the soup is heated through, as many will thin again once hot. Keep a watchful eye on the heat if eggs and cream were used in the recipe; the soup needs to be thoroughly reheated but not boiled rapidly, or it will curdle. Stir frequently so that the soup heats up evenly.

finishing touches

A swirl of cream This always looks special, yet what could be simpler than to drizzle a tablespoon or two of double cream or natural yogurt over a bowlful of puréed soup? Alternatively, you can drop small spoonfuls of cream into the soup and then run a cocktail stick through them for a teardrop effect, or add a spoonful of thick Greek yogurt or crème fraîche into the centre of the soup and then sprinkle it with a few snipped herbs.

Herb garnishes A few finely chopped herbs can be all that is needed to liven up a pale puréed soup, such as Fennel Vichyssoise (see page 149). For a crispy herb topping, shallow-fry a handful of sage, basil or parsley leaves for a few seconds. For a topping with punch, try a sprinkling of gremolata – a mix of chopped parsley, grated lemon rind and chopped garlic – or salsa verde – a mix of chopped herbs, anchovies, garlic and olive oil. You could make up some herb-infused oil, store in a bottle and drizzle over the soup at the last minute, or cheat and add a spoonful of ready-made pesto.

Citrus curls Tiny lemon, lime or orange curls can be sprinkled over the top of the soup for a delicate zing. Use a zester, or the finest holes on a grater.

Spicy sprinkles Try a little freshly grated nutmeg, a few roughly crushed peppercorns, a few chilli flakes for extra heat or a little paprika or ground turmeric for added colour.

Flavoured butters and mayo-based sauces Mix a little butter with chopped blue cheese, anchovies and chilli, garlic, grated lemon rind or freshly chopped herbs. Roll the butter up in clingfilm or foil into a log and chill until firm, then cut off a slice and add to the hot soup just before serving. Alternatively, make up some mayonnaise-based sauces and flavour with garlic to make aïoli, chilli for rouille or lemon rind and juice for a citrus burst.

Ice cubes For chilled soups, add a few whole or roughly crushed ice cubes for added texture and impact.

Croûtons Fry diced or sliced bread (half a slice per serving of soup) in a mixture of butter and sunflower oil or just olive oil until golden. Drain on kitchen paper and then float on bowls of soup just before serving. Croûtons can also be flavoured with garlic or spices. For French bread or ciabatta, rub the fried bread with a cut garlic clove or spread with a little olive tapenade, pesto or crumbled blue cheese. For a lower-fat option, bake croûtons sprayed with a little olive oil on a baking sheet in the oven until crisp.

01

broad bean & chorizo soup

SERVES 6

2 tablespoons olive oil
1 large onion, roughly chopped
500 g (1 lb) potatoes, diced
150 g (5 oz) chorizo, diced
4 tomatoes, diced
300 g (10 oz) frozen broad beans
1.5 litres (2½ pints) chicken stock
   (see page 9)
salt and pepper
small basil leaves, to garnish

OLIVE TAPENADE TOASTS

6 slices of baguette
4 tablespoons green or black
   olive tapenade

Heat the oil in a large saucepan, add the onion, potatoes and chorizo and fry for 5 minutes, stirring frequently, until just beginning to soften.

Stir in the tomatoes, broad beans and stock, season to taste with salt and pepper and bring to the boil. Reduce the heat, cover and simmer for 15 minutes until the vegetables are tender.

Mash some of the potatoes roughly with a fork to thicken the soup slightly, and then taste and adjust the seasoning if needed.

Toast the slices of baguette, then spread with the tapenade. Ladle the soup into bowls, top each serving with a tapenade toast and sprinkle with small basil leaves to garnish.

02

tomato & balsamic vinegar soup

SERVES 6

750 g (1½ lb) large tomatoes on the vine
2 tablespoons olive oil
1 onion, roughly chopped
1 baking potato, about 200 g (7 oz), diced
2 garlic cloves, finely chopped (optional)
750 ml (1¼ pints) vegetable or chicken stock
    (see pages 10 and 9)
1 tablespoon tomato purée
1 tablespoon brown sugar
4 teaspoons balsamic vinegar
1 small bunch of basil
salt and pepper

Cut the tomatoes in half, place them cut-side down in a foil-lined grill pan and drizzle with some of the oil. Cook under a hot grill for 4–5 minutes until the skins have split and blackened, then leave to cool slightly.

Meanwhile, heat the remaining oil in a large saucepan, add the onion, potato and garlic and fry for 5 minutes, stirring occasionally, until softened and turning golden around the edges.

Skin and roughly chop the tomatoes, then add to the saucepan with the grill pan juices. Stir in the stock, tomato purée, sugar and vinegar. Add half the basil, season to taste with salt and pepper and bring to the boil. Reduce the heat, cover and simmer for 15 minutes.

Leave to cool slightly, then purée half the soup, in batches if necessary, in a blender or food processor until smooth. Return to the pan and reheat. Taste and adjust the seasoning if needed, then ladle into bowls, garnish with the remaining basil leaves.

03

celeriac & apple soup

SERVES 6

25 g (1 oz) butter
1 celeriac, about 500 g (1 lb), peeled and coarsely
    grated
3 dessert apples, peeled, cored and chopped
1.2 litres (2 pints) vegetable or chicken stock
    (see pages 10 and 9)
pinch of cayenne pepper, or more to taste
salt

Melt the butter in a large saucepan, add the celeriac and apples and cook over a medium heat for 5 minutes, stirring occasionally, or until they have begun to soften.

Add the stock and cayenne pepper and bring to the boil. Reduce the heat, cover and simmer for 15–20 minutes, or until the celeriac and apples are very soft.

Leave to cool slightly, then purée in batches in a blender or food processor until very smooth, transferring to a clean saucepan. Reheat gently, season to taste with salt and more cayenne if needed and serve in individual bowls.

04

next time...

For celeriac & roasted garlic soup, halve 2 whole, unpeeled garlic bulbs, put into a roasting tin, drizzle with 2 teaspoons olive oil and roast in a preheated oven, 200°C (400°F), Gas Mark 6, for 15 minutes. Fry the celeriac with 1 onion, chopped, in place of the apples as in the recipe above. When cool enough to handle, squeeze the roasted garlic flesh into the celeriac, add 1 litre (1¾ pints) vegetable stock with salt and cayenne pepper to taste and simmer as above. Purée, reheat with 150 ml (¼ pint) milk and serve swirled with a little double cream in each bowl.

05

black bean soup
with soba noodles

SERVES 4

200 g (7 oz) dried soba noodles
2 tablespoons groundnut or vegetable oil
1 bunch of spring onions, sliced
2 garlic cloves, roughly chopped
1 red chilli, deseeded and sliced
4 cm (1½ inch) piece of fresh root ginger, peeled and grated
125 ml (4 fl oz) ready-made black bean sauce or black bean stir-fry sauce
750 ml (1¼ pints) vegetable stock (see page 10)
200 g (7 oz) pak choi or spring greens, shredded
2 teaspoons soy sauce
1 teaspoon caster sugar
50 g (2 oz) raw, unsalted peanuts

Cook the noodles in a saucepan of boiling water for about 5 minutes, or until just tender.

Meanwhile, heat the oil in a saucepan, add the spring onions and garlic and fry gently for 1 minute.

Add the chilli, ginger, black bean sauce and stock and bring to the boil. Stir in the pak choi or spring greens, soy sauce, sugar and peanuts, then reduce the heat and simmer gently, uncovered, for 4 minutes.

Drain the noodles and then pile into serving bowls. Ladle the soup over the noodles and serve immediately.

06

next time...

For beef & black bean soup, cook 125 g (4 oz) dried soba noodles in boiling water as in the previous recipe. Meanwhile, fry the spring onions and garlic, then add the chilli, ginger, black bean sauce and stock as before. Bring to the boil and add the pak choi or spring greens, soy sauce and sugar, then simmer gently for 2 minutes. Quickly trim the fat off a 250 g (8 oz) sirloin steak, cut into thin slices and add to the soup. Simmer for a further 2 minutes until the steak is cooked, then ladle over the drained cooked noodles in bowls.

07

cheesy cauliflower & cider soup

SERVES 6

40 g (1½ oz) butter
1 onion, finely chopped
200 g (7 oz) potato, coarsely grated
1 cauliflower, cut into small florets, woody core discarded, about 500 g (1 lb) when prepared
900 ml (1½ pints) vegetable or chicken stock (see pages 10 and 9)
300 ml (½ pint) dry cider
2 teaspoons wholegrain mustard
75 g (3 oz) mature Cheddar cheese, grated
cayenne pepper, to taste
salt
chopped chives, to garnish

Melt the butter in a saucepan, add the onion and fry gently for 5 minutes, stirring frequently, or until just beginning to turn golden around the edges. Stir in the potato and cook briefly, then mix in the cauliflower florets, stock, cider and mustard. Season to taste with cayenne and salt and bring to the boil. Reduce the heat, cover and simmer for 15 minutes, or until the vegetables are tender.

Mash the soup roughly to thicken it slightly, then stir in the Cheddar and heat gently, stirring, until melted. Taste and adjust the seasoning if needed.

Ladle the soup into bowls, garnish with chopped chives and serve with croûtons (see page 13).

08

broccoli & almond soup

SERVES 6

25 g (1 oz) butter
1 onion, roughly chopped
500 g (1 lb) broccoli, cut into florets, stems sliced
40 g (1½ oz) ground almonds
900 ml (1½ pints) vegetable or chicken stock (see pages 10 and 9)
300 ml (½ pint) milk
salt and pepper

TO GARNISH
15 g (½ oz) butter
6 tablespoons natural yogurt
3 tablespoons flaked almonds

Melt the butter in a saucepan, add the onion and fry gently for 5 minutes until beginning to soften. Stir in the broccoli, then add the ground almonds, stock and salt and pepper to taste. Bring to the boil, then reduce the heat, cover and simmer for 10 minutes until the broccoli is just tender and still bright green. Leave to cool slightly, then purée in batches in a blender or food processor until speckled green.

Return the purée to the saucepan and stir in the milk. Reheat, then taste and adjust the seasoning if needed. Melt the butter for the garnish in a frying pan and fry the almonds for a few minutes, stirring, until golden. Ladle the soup into bowls, drizzle a spoonful of yogurt over each and sprinkle with the almonds.

09

next time...

For broccoli & Stilton soup, make the soup as in the recipe above, omitting the ground almonds and adding 125 g (4 oz) Stilton cheese, crumbled, stirring until melted. Ladle into bowls and sprinkle with a little extra cheese and coarsely crushed black peppercorns.

10

cream of leek & pea soup

SERVES 6

2 tablespoons olive oil
375 g (12 oz) leeks, finely sliced
375 g (12 oz) shelled fresh or frozen peas
900 ml (1½ pints) vegetable or chicken stock
    (see pages 10 and 9)
1 small bunch of mint
150 g (5 oz) full-fat mascarpone cheese
grated rind of 1 small lemon
salt and pepper

Heat the oil in a saucepan, add the leeks and toss in the oil, then cover and fry gently for 10 minutes, stirring occasionally, until softened but not browned. Mix in the peas and cook briefly, stirring.

Pour the stock into the pan, add a little salt and pepper and bring to the boil. Reduce the heat, cover and simmer gently for 10 minutes.

Leave to cool slightly, then ladle half the soup into a blender or food processor, add all the mint, reserving a few leaves for garnishing, and blend until smooth. Return the purée to the pan.

Mix the mascarpone with half the lemon rind, reserving the remainder for garnishing. Spoon half the mascarpone mixture into the soup, then reheat gently, stirring until the mascarpone has melted. Taste and adjust the seasoning if needed.

Ladle the soup into bowls and top with spoonfuls of the remaining mascarpone, a few mint leaves and a sprinkling of the reserved lemon rind.

11

next time...

For cream of leek, pea & watercress soup, fry the leeks in the oil as in the previous recipe, then add 175 g (6 oz) peas along with a roughly chopped bunch of watercress. Pour in 600 ml (1 pint) vegetable or chicken stock and bring to the boil, then simmer gently for 10 minutes. Purée as before, then stir in 150 ml (¼ pint) milk and 150 ml (¼ pint) double cream instead of the mascarpone, reheat gently and check the seasoning. Ladle into bowls, drizzle with a little extra cream and top with some crispy grilled and chopped bacon to garnish.

12
garden herb
soup

SERVES 4

50 g (2 oz) butter
1 onion, roughly chopped
1 baking potato, about 250 g (8 oz), diced
1 litre (1¾ pints) ham, chicken or vegetable
    stock (see pages 9 and 10)
75 g (3 oz) mixed parsley and chives, roughly
    torn into pieces
salt and pepper

Melt the butter in a saucepan, add the onion and fry gently for 5 minutes, stirring occasionally, until softened but not browned. Add the potato and toss in the butter, then cover and fry gently for 10 minutes, stirring occasionally, until just turning golden around the edges.

Add the stock, season to taste with salt and pepper and bring to the boil. Reduce the heat, cover and simmer for 10 minutes, or until the potato is tender. Leave the soup to cool slightly, then purée in batches in a blender or food processor with the herbs.

Return to the pan, reheat and taste and adjust the seasoning if needed. Serve in mugs with toasted bacon sandwiches, if liked.

13
next time...

For Italian herb soup, heat 2 tablespoons of oil in a saucepan, add the onion and fry until softened. Mix in 150 g (5 oz) potato, diced, cover and fry gently for 10 minutes. Add the stock and salt and pepper to taste, then cook as in the recipe above. Purée the soup, replacing the herbs with 75 g (3 oz) rocket leaves and adding 25 g (1 oz) ground pine nuts or almonds and 40 g (1½ oz) freshly grated Parmesan. Reheat and serve topped with toasted pine nuts.

14
leek & potato
soup

SERVES 4–6

25 g (1 oz) butter
2 large leeks, finely sliced
250 g (8 oz) potatoes, roughly diced
1 onion, roughly chopped
750 ml (1¼ pints) vegetable or chicken stock
    (see pages 10 or 9), or water
300 ml (½ pint) milk
salt and pepper
1 tablespoon snipped chives, to garnish

Melt the butter in a large saucepan, add the leeks, potatoes and onion and stir well to coat with the butter. Cover tightly with a piece of greaseproof paper and cook over a very gentle heat for about 15 minutes, or until the vegetables have softened, stirring frequently to prevent them from browning.

Add the stock or water and milk and season to taste with salt and pepper. Bring to the boil, then reduce the heat and simmer gently, uncovered, for about 20 minutes, or until the vegetables are tender.

Leave the soup to cool slightly, then purée in batches in a blender or food processor until smooth, transferring to a clean saucepan.

Taste and adjust the seasoning if needed and reheat until very hot, then pour the soup into warmed bowls. Garnish with the chives and serve immediately.

15

turkey & vegetable soup

SERVES 8

1 large turkey drumstick, about 750 g (1½ Ib)
2.5 litres (4 pints) water
1 small unpeeled onion, studded with 4 cloves,
    plus 1 large onion, peeled and chopped
2 parsley sprigs
1 bouquet garni
1 teaspoon salt
1 thyme sprig or ¼ teaspoon dried thyme
1 marjoram sprig or ½ teaspoon dried
    marjoram
3 carrots, chopped
2 celery sticks, sliced
250 g (8 oz) dried red lentils, rinsed and drained
250 g (8 oz) potatoes, cut into 1 cm (½ inch) cubes
3 turnips, cut into 1 cm (½ inch) cubes
3 leeks, sliced
2 tablespoons light soy sauce
pepper
3–4 tablespoons finely chopped parsley,
    to garnish

Put the drumstick into a large saucepan. Add the measured water, the clove-studded onion, parsley sprigs, bouquet garni, salt, thyme and marjoram. Bring to the boil, then reduce the heat, half-cover and simmer for 45 minutes, stirring occasionally.

Add the chopped onion, carrots and celery, half-cover again and cook over a low to medium heat for 30 minutes, stirring occasionally. Stir in the lentils, potatoes, turnips and leeks, cover and cook for 20 minutes, or until all the vegetables and lentils are tender.

Lift the drumstick out and leave it to cool. Remove and discard the bouquet garni, the clove-studded onion and any herb stems.

Cut the turkey meat off the bone, discarding the skin. Carefully remove any small bones. Cut the meat into small pieces and return it to the soup. Add the soy sauce and season to taste with pepper. Reheat the soup thoroughly and serve in a soup tureen, garnished with the parsley.

16

heart of artichoke soup with dill

SERVES 4–6

50 g (2 oz) butter
1 onion, chopped
1 garlic clove, chopped
1 celery stick, sliced
425 g (14 oz) can artichoke hearts, drained
1.2 litres (2 pints) vegetable or chicken stock
    (see pages 10 and 9)
1 tablespoon lemon juice
3 tablespoons chopped dill
2 tablespoons plain flour
150 ml (¼ pint) single cream
salt and white pepper
4–6 dill sprigs, to garnish

Melt the butter in a saucepan, add the onion, garlic and celery and toss in the butter. Cover and cook over a medium heat for 10–12 minutes or until soft, stirring occasionally.

Add the artichoke hearts, re-cover and cook for about 3 minutes. Pour in 1 litre (1¾ pints) of the stock and stir in the lemon juice and 1 tablespoon of the chopped dill, then re-cover and cook for a further 15 minutes.

Leave the soup to cool slightly, then purée the in batches in a blender or food processor until smooth, transferring to a clean saucepan.

Mix the flour with the remaining stock in a small bowl until smooth, adding a little water if necessary. Reheat the soup, whisk in the flour mixture and cook, stirring, until the soup thickens slightly. Add the remaining chopped dill, season to taste with salt and pepper and then stir in the cream. Heat the soup thoroughly, but don't allow it to boil, or it will curdle. Serve in warmed bowls, garnished with the dill sprigs.

17

red chicken
& coconut broth

SERVES 4

1 tablespoon sunflower oil
250 g (8 oz) skinless chicken thigh fillets, diced
4 teaspoons ready-made red Thai curry paste
1 teaspoon ready-made galangal paste
3 dried kaffir lime leaves
400 ml (13 fl oz) can full-fat coconut milk
2 teaspoons Thai fish sauce
1 teaspoon light muscovado sugar
600 ml (1 pint) chicken stock (see page 9)
4 spring onions, thinly sliced, plus 2 to garnish
50 g (2 oz) mangetout, sliced
100 g (3½ oz) bean sprouts, rinsed
1 small bunch of coriander, leaves only

Heat the oil in a saucepan, add the chicken and curry paste and fry for 3–4 minutes, stirring frequently, until just beginning to colour. Stir in the galangal paste, lime leaves, coconut milk, fish sauce and sugar, then add the stock.

Bring to the boil, then reduce the heat, cover and simmer for 15 minutes, stirring occasionally, or until the chicken is cooked.

Meanwhile, create spring onion curls by cutting very thin strips from the 2 spring onions for garnishing. Soak in cold water for 10 minutes, then drain.

Add the remaining spring onions, the mangetout and bean sprouts to the broth and cook for 2 minutes.

Ladle the broth into bowls and scatter the spring onion curls over the top. Serve the coriander leaves separately for diners to tear and add to the soup.

18

next time...

For red fish & coconut broth, heat 1 tablespoon sunflower oil in a saucepan, add the curry paste as in the previous recipe and fry for 1 minute, stirring. Add the galangal paste, lime leaves, coconut milk, fish sauce and sugar, then pour in the stock and bring to the boil as before. Add a 250 g (8 oz) salmon fillet, cover and simmer for 10 minutes. Lift the fish out with a slotted spoon and flake it into pieces, discarding the skin and any stray bones. Return the salmon to the broth and add the vegetables as before, along with 125 g (4 oz) cooked peeled small prawns, defrosted, rinsed with cold water and drained if frozen. Cook for 2 minutes, then serve with the coriander leaves as before.

19

sweetcorn & celery soup

SERVES 6

50 g (2 oz) butter
1 onion, chopped
4 corn on the cob, green leaves and
   silky threads removed, then
   kernels cut from the cobs
3 celery sticks, sliced
2 garlic cloves, finely chopped
1 litre (1¾ pints) vegetable or
   chicken stock (see pages 10 and 9)
2 bay leaves
cayenne pepper, to taste
salt
chilli and tomato chutney, to garnish

Melt the butter in a saucepan, add the onion and fry gently for 5 minutes until just beginning to turn golden around the edges, stirring occasionally. Add the corn, celery and garlic and fry for 5 minutes, stirring.

Pour in the stock, add the bay leaves and season to taste with salt and cayenne. Bring to the boil, then reduce the heat, cover and simmer for 20 minutes.

Remove and discard the bay leaves. Leave the soup to cool slightly, then purée in the pan with a stick blender or in batches in a blender or food processor until smooth, returning to the pan. Reheat, then taste and adjust the seasoning if needed.

Ladle the soup into bowls and top each serving with a spoonful of chilli and tomato chutney.

20

ghanaian groundnut
soup

SERVES 6

1 tablespoon sunflower oil
1 onion, finely chopped
2 carrots, diced
500 g (1 lb) tomatoes, skinned if liked and
    roughly chopped
½ teaspoon piri piri seasoning or chilli flakes
100 g (3½ oz) roasted, salted peanuts, plus
    extra, roughly chopped, to garnish
1 litre (1¾ pints) fish or vegetable stock (see
    page 10)
chilli flakes, to garnish

Heat the oil in a large saucepan, add the onion
and carrots and fry gently for 5 minutes until
softened and just turning golden around
the edges, stirring occasionally. Stir in the
tomatoes and the piri piri seasoning or chilli
flakes and cook for 1 minute.

Grind the peanuts in a food processor or spice
grinder until the texture of ground almonds.
Stir into the tomato mixture, add the stock and
bring to the boil. Reduce the heat, cover and
simmer for 30 minutes.

Leave to cool slightly, then purée half the soup
in batches in a blender or food processor until
smooth. Return to the pan, reheat and taste
and adjust the seasoning if needed.

Ladle the soup into bowls, garnish with chilli
flakes and chopped peanuts and serve.

21

next time...

**For Ghanaian squash & groundnut soup with
foo foo**, make the soup as in the previous
recipe, replacing the tomatoes with 500 g (1 lb)
butternut squash, sliced, deseeded, peeled and
diced. Meanwhile, for the foo foo, cook 750 g
(1½ lb) yams or potatoes, peeled and cut into
chunks, in a saucepan of boiling water for
20 minutes until tender. Drain and mash
with 3 tablespoons milk and salt and pepper
to taste. Shape into balls. Ladle the soup into
bowls and serve the foo foo separately for
dunking into the hot soup.

22

chilli, bean & pepper
soup

SERVES 6

2 tablespoons sunflower oil
1 large onion, finely chopped
4 garlic cloves, finely chopped
2 red peppers, cored, deseeded and diced
2 red chillies, deseeded and finely chopped
900 ml (1½ pints) vegetable stock (see page 10)
750 ml (1¼ pints) tomato juice or passata
1 tablespoon tomato purée
1 tablespoon sun-dried tomato paste
2 tablespoons sweet chilli sauce, or more
    to taste
400 g (13 oz) can red kidney beans, rinsed
    and drained
2 tablespoons finely chopped coriander
75 ml (3 fl oz) soured cream, plus extra to serve
    (optional)
salt and pepper
zested lime rind, to garnish (optional)

Heat the oil in a large saucepan, add the onion and garlic and fry gently for 5 minutes, stirring frequently, or until soft but not browned. Add the red peppers and chillies and fry for a few minutes, stirring occasionally.

Stir in the stock and tomato juice or passata, tomato purée and paste, chilli sauce, beans and coriander. Bring to the boil, then reduce the heat, cover and simmer for 20 minutes.

Leave the soup to cool slightly, then purée in the pan with a stick blender or in batches in a blender or food processor until smooth, returning to the pan. Taste and adjust the seasoning, adding a little extra chilli sauce if needed. Reheat the soup thoroughly.

Pour the soup into bowls and swirl a little soured cream into each. Serve with tortilla chips and extra soured cream, garnished with a little zested lime rind, if liked.

23

next time...

For **chilli, aubergine & pepper soup**, heat 2 tablespoons sunflower oil in a large saucepan, add 1 aubergine, diced, along with the onion and garlic as in the previous recipe and fry until the aubergine is very lightly browned. Add the red peppers and chillies as before, then stir in 600 ml (1 pint) vegetable stock (see page 10) along with the tomato juice or passata, tomato purée and paste and chilli sauce. Omit the red kidney beans and add a small bunch of basil instead. Simmer and then purée and reheat as before, adjusting the consistency if necessary with a little extra stock.

24

pea, lettuce & lemon
soup

SERVES 4

25 g (1 oz) butter
1 large onion, finely chopped
425 g (14 oz) frozen peas
2 Little Gem lettuces, roughly chopped
1 litre (1¾ pints) vegetable or chicken stock (see
   pages 10 and 9)
grated rind and juice of ½ lemon
salt and pepper

SESAME CROÛTONS
2 thick slices of bread, cubed
1 tablespoon olive oil
1 tablespoon sesame seeds

Brush the bread cubes for the croûtons with the oil and put into a roasting tin. Sprinkle with the sesame seeds and bake in a preheated oven, 200°C (400°F), Gas Mark 6, for 10–15 minutes, or until golden.

Meanwhile, melt the butter in a large saucepan, add the onion and fry gently for 5 minutes, stirring frequently, until softened. Add the peas, lettuce, stock, lemon rind and juice and salt and pepper to taste. Bring to the boil, then reduce the heat, cover and simmer for 10–15 minutes.

Leave the soup to cool slightly, then purée in the pan with a stick blender or in batches in a blender or food processor until smooth, returning to the pan. Reheat, then taste and adjust the seasoning if needed.

Spoon the soup into bowls and sprinkle with the sesame croûtons.

25

next time...

For pea, spinach & lemon soup, make the soup as in the previous recipe, replacing the lettuces with 125 g (4 oz) baby spinach leaves. Cook and then purée and reheat as before, adding a little grated nutmeg to taste. Ladle the soup into bowls and top with 2 teaspoons natural yogurt per serving.

26

prawn & noodle soup

SERVES 4

900 ml (1½ pints) vegetable or chicken stock
    (see pages 10 and 9)
2 dried kaffir lime leaves
1 lemon grass stalk, lightly bruised
150 g (5 oz) dried egg noodles
50 g (2 oz) frozen peas
50 g (2 oz) frozen sweetcorn
100 g (3½ oz) raw large king prawns in their
    shells, cooked, peeled and deveined; if
    frozen, defrost, rinse with cold water and
    drain before cooking
4 spring onions, sliced
2 teaspoons soy sauce

Pour the stock into a saucepan, add the lime
leaves and lemon grass and bring to the boil.
Reduce the heat and simmer, uncovered, for
10 minutes.

Add the noodles to the stock and cook
according to the packet instructions until just
tender. Two minutes from the end of the noodle
cooking time, stir in the peas, sweetcorn,
prawns, spring onions and soy sauce.

Remove and discard the lemon grass, then
serve the soup in bowls.

27

next time...

For chicken & noodle soup, pour the stock
into a saucepan and add the lime leaves and
lemon grass as in the previous recipe, then add
2 skinless chicken breast fillets, diced, and
bring to the boil. Reduce the heat and simmer,
uncovered, for 10 minutes, then finish making
the soup as before.

28

mediterranean garlic soup

SERVES 4

2 tablespoons olive oil
2–3 garlic cloves, finely chopped
125 g (4 oz) chorizo, diced
6 tablespoons red wine
1 litre (1¾ pints) beef or game stock (see page 9)
2 teaspoons tomato purée
1 teaspoon brown sugar
4 eggs
salt and pepper
chopped parsley, to garnish

Heat the oil in a saucepan, add the garlic and chorizo and fry gently for 3–4 minutes, stirring frequently. Add the wine, stock, tomato purée and sugar, season to taste with salt and pepper and simmer for 5 minutes.

Reduce the heat to a very gentle simmer, then drop the eggs, one at a time, into the hot liquid, leaving a little space between them. Poach for 3–4 minutes until the whites are just set and the yolks are cooked to your liking.

Taste and adjust the seasoning if needed, then lift the poached eggs out of the soup carefully with a slotted spoon and place in the bowls, cover with the soup and sprinkle with a little chopped parsley. Serve with croûtons (see page 13).

29

next time...

For garlic & potato soup, add 375 g (12 oz) potato, diced, when frying the garlic and chorizo as in the recipe above. Add the wine, stock, tomato purée, sugar and salt and pepper to taste as before, then simmer for 30 minutes. Ladle the soup into bowls and serve with garlic croûtes topped with grated Gruyère cheese.

30

pesto & lemon soup

SERVES 6

1 tablespoon olive oil
1 onion, finely chopped
2 garlic cloves, finely chopped
2 tomatoes, skinned and chopped
1.2 litres (2 pints) vegetable stock (see page 10)
3 teaspoons pesto, plus extra to serve
grated rind and juice of 1 lemon
100 g (3½ oz) broccoli, cut into small florets, stems sliced
150 g (5 oz) courgettes, diced
100 g (3½ oz) frozen soya (edamame) beans
65 g (2½ oz) dried small pasta shapes
50 g (2 oz) spinach leaves, shredded
salt and pepper
basil leaves, to garnish (optional)

Heat the oil in a large saucepan, add the onion and fry gently for 5 minutes, stirring frequently, until softened. Stir in the garlic, tomatoes, stock, pesto, lemon rind and a little salt and pepper, then simmer gently for 10 minutes.

Add the broccoli, courgettes, soya beans and pasta shapes, then simmer for 6 minutes, stirring frequently. Stir in the spinach and lemon juice and cook for a further 2 minutes until the spinach has just wilted and the pasta is just tender.

Ladle into bowls, top with extra spoonfuls of pesto and garnish with a sprinkling of basil leaves, if liked. Serve with warm olive or sun-dried tomato focaccia or ciabatta bread.

31

hot & sour soup

SERVES 4

750 ml (1¼ pints) vegetable or fish stock (see
   page 10)
4 dried kaffir lime leaves
2.5 cm (1 inch) piece of fresh root ginger, peeled
   and grated
1 red chilli, deseeded and sliced
1 lemon grass stalk, lightly bruised
125 g (4 oz) mushrooms, sliced
100 g (3½ oz) dried rice noodles
75 g (3 oz) baby spinach leaves
125 g (4 oz) cooked peeled tiger prawns,
   defrosted, rinsed with cold water and
   drained if frozen
2 tablespoons lemon juice
pepper

Put the stock, lime leaves, ginger, chilli and
lemon grass into a large saucepan. Cover and
bring to the boil. Add the mushrooms, reduce
the heat and simmer for 2 minutes. Break the
noodles into short lengths, drop into the soup
and simmer for 3 minutes.

Stir in the spinach and prawns and simmer for
2 minutes until the prawns are heated through,
then add the lemon juice.

Remove and discard the lemon grass. Season
the soup to taste with pepper before serving.

32

next time...

For hot coconut soup, make the soup as in
the recipe above, but using 450 ml (¾ pint)
stock along with a 400 ml (14 fl oz) can full-fat
coconut milk, and adding 2 teaspoons ready-
made red Thai curry paste. Serve sprinkled
with chopped coriander.

33

spring vegetable broth

SERVES 4

2 teaspoons olive oil
2 celery sticks with their leaves, chopped
2 leeks, chopped
1 carrot, finely diced
50 g (2 oz) pearl barley
1.2 litres (2 pints) vegetable stock (see page 10)
1 teaspoon English mustard
125 g (4 oz) mangetout, diagonally sliced
   (optional)
salt and pepper

Heat the oil in a saucepan, add the celery, leeks
and carrot and cook over a medium heat for
5 minutes, stirring occasionally.

Stir in the pearl barley, stock and mustard,
season to taste with salt and pepper and bring
just to the boil. Reduce the heat, cover and
simmer for 20–25 minutes. Add the mangetout
(if using) and simmer for a further 5 minutes.

Ladle the broth into bowls and serve piping hot.

34

next time...

For winter vegetable broth, make the soup
as above, but using 1 leek, chopped, and
adding 125 g (4 oz) swede, finely diced. After
simmering for 20 minutes, add 125 g (4 oz)
green cabbage, finely shredded, instead of
the mangetout and simmer for a further
10 minutes. Ladle the soup into bowls and
top with diced crispy grilled bacon.

35

stracciatella

SERVES 6

1.2 litres (2 pints) chicken stock (see page 9)
4 eggs
25 g (1 oz) Parmesan cheese, freshly grated, plus
extra to serve
2 tablespoons fresh white breadcrumbs
¼ teaspoon grated nutmeg
handful of basil leaves
salt and pepper

Pour the stock into a large saucepan and bring
to the boil, then reduce the heat and simmer for
2–3 minutes.

Beat the eggs, Parmesan, breadcrumbs
and nutmeg together in a bowl and season
generously with salt and pepper. Gradually
pour 2 ladlefuls of the hot stock into the egg
mixture, whisking constantly.

Reduce the heat under the saucepan, then
slowly stir the egg mixture into the stock until
smooth, making sure that the temperature
remains moderate, as the egg will curdle if the
soup boils. Gently simmer for 2–3 minutes,
stirring, until piping hot.

Tear the basil leaves into pieces and add to the
pan, then ladle the soup into bowls. Serve with
extra Parmesan to grate over the soup to taste.

36

next time...

For egg drop soup, heat the stock in a large
saucepan as in the previous recipe, then add
½ teaspoon caster sugar and 1 tablespoon
soy sauce. Beat 2 eggs together in a small bowl.
Stir the hot stock with a fork in a circular
motion, then drizzle the beaten egg through
the prongs of the fork held high over the soup
so that it sets in droplets in the swirling stock.
Leave to cook for 1–2 minutes until the egg has
set, then ladle into bowls. Garnish with sliced
green spring onion tops and a little chopped
coriander or green chilli.

37

courgette soup with gremolata

SERVES 6

25 g (1 oz) butter
1 onion, finely chopped
250 g (8 oz) courgettes, diced
1 celery stick, diced
2 garlic cloves, finely chopped
75 g (3 oz) risotto rice
1.2 litres (2 pints) hot vegetable or chicken
  stock (see pages 10 and 9)
150 ml (¼ pint) dry white wine
2 eggs, beaten
4 tablespoons freshly grated Parmesan cheese
salt and pepper

GREMOLATA

1 small bunch of basil, finely chopped
1 small bunch of flat leaf parsley, finely
  chopped
2 teaspoons capers, finely chopped
grated rind of 1 lemon

Melt the butter in a large saucepan, add
the onion and fry gently for 5 minutes,
stirring frequently, until softened. Stir in the
courgettes, celery and garlic and fry briefly,
then stir in the rice.

Pour in the stock and wine, season to taste
with salt and pepper and simmer, stirring
occasionally, for 15 minutes, or until the rice
is just tender.

Meanwhile, mix all the ingredients for the
gremolata together in a small bowl.

Remove the pan from the heat and leave
the soup to cool slightly. Beat the eggs and
Parmesan together in a bowl, then gradually
pour in a ladleful of the hot soup, whisking
constantly. Slowly stir the egg mixture into the
pan. Heat gently, stirring, until the soup has
thickened slightly, but don't allow it to boil, or
the eggs will scramble.

Ladle the soup into bowls and sprinkle the
gremolata on top.

38

next time...

For courgette, lemon & salmon soup, make the
soup as in the previous recipe, adding 375 g
(12 oz) salmon steak for the last 10 minutes of
the cooking time. Lift the fish out with a slotted
spoon and flake it into pieces, discarding the
skin and any stray bones. Beat 2 eggs with
the juice of ½ lemon in a bowl, then gradually
pour in a ladleful of the hot soup, whisking
constantly. Slowly stir the egg mixture into the
pan. Heat gently, stirring, until the soup has
thickened slightly. Divide the salmon among
bowls, ladle the soup over and sprinkle a little
chopped parsley on top.

39

39

red pepper soup
& pesto stifato

SERVES 6

4 red peppers, halved, cored and deseeded
3 tablespoons olive oil, plus extra to garnish
1 large onion, roughly chopped
2–3 garlic cloves, finely chopped
400 g (13 oz) can chopped tomatoes
900 ml (1½ pints) vegetable or chicken stock
  (see pages 10 and 9)
2 tablespoons balsamic vinegar
salt and pepper
handful of basil leaves, to garnish

PESTO STIFATO
2 stifato sticks or long thin bread rolls
2 tablespoons pesto
50 g (2 oz) Parmesan cheese, grated

Arrange the peppers skin-side up in a foil-lined grill pan, brush with 2 tablespoons of the oil and cook under a hot grill for about 10 minutes until the skins are blackened and the peppers are softened. Wrap the foil around the peppers, then leave them to cool for 10 minutes.

Meanwhile, heat the remaining oil in a saucepan, add the onion and fry gently for 5 minutes, stirring occasionally, until softened and just beginning to brown. Add the garlic and cook for 1 minute, then stir in the tomatoes, stock and vinegar and season to taste with salt and pepper.

Peel the blackened skins off the peppers, then roughly chop the peppers. Add to the saucepan and bring to the boil, then reduce the heat, cover and simmer for 30 minutes.

Leave the soup to cool slightly, then purée in the pan with a stick blender or in batches in a blender or food processor until smooth, returning to the pan. Reheat and then taste and adjust the seasoning if needed.

Cut the stifato sticks or bread rolls into strips, then lightly toast on both sides. Spread the sticks with the pesto, sprinkle with the Parmesan and cook under a hot grill until just melting.

Ladle the soup into bowls, then garnish with a swirl of olive oil, the basil leaves and a grinding of pepper. Serve with the stifato.

40

next time...

For roasted red pepper & cannellini bean soup, grill the peppers as in the previous recipe, then skin and finely chop. Fry the onion and then the garlic in the oil as before, then stir in the roasted peppers with the tomatoes and stock. Omit the balsamic vinegar and add 3 large pinches of saffron threads and a rinsed and drained 410 g (13½ oz) can cannellini beans. Season to taste with salt and pepper, then cover and simmer for 30 minutes. Serve the soup chunky, without puréeing, with garlic bread.

41

roasted aubergine soup

SERVES 4–6

1 kg (2 lb) aubergines
3 tablespoons olive oil
1 red onion, finely chopped
2 garlic cloves, crushed
1.2 litres (2 pints) vegetable or chicken stock
(see pages 10 and 9)
200 g (7 oz) crème fraîche or Greek yogurt
2 tablespoons chopped mint, plus extra sprigs
to garnish
salt and pepper

Prick each aubergine just below the stalk and cook under a hot grill for about 20 minutes, turning occasionally, until the skin is well blackened and the flesh has softened. Leave to cool slightly. Cut the aubergines in half and use a spoon to scoop out the soft flesh from the blackened skins, then chop.

Heat the oil in a saucepan, add the onion and garlic and fry gently for 5–6 minutes, stirring frequently, until softened but not browned. Add the chopped aubergine and stock, bring to a simmer and cook for 10–15 minutes.

Leave the soup to cool slightly, then purée in batches in a blender or food processor. Pass the purée through a fine sieve back into the pan, reheat and season to taste with salt and pepper.

Mix the crème fraîche or Greek yogurt with the chopped mint in a small bowl and season to taste with salt and pepper.

Serve the soup in bowls topped with a spoonful of the minted cream and garnish each serving with mint sprigs.

42

miso soup with tofu

SERVES 4

2 tablespoons red or white miso
1 small leek, cut into fine julienne strips
125 g (4 oz) firm tofu, cut into small cubes
1 tablespoon wakame seaweed
1 small bunch of chives

DASHI STOCK
15 g (½ oz) kombu seaweed
1.8 litres (3 pints) water
2 tablespoons dried tuna (bonito) flakes

Wipe the kombu seaweed for the dashi stock with a damp cloth and put it into a saucepan with the measured water. Bring to a simmer, skimming off any scum that rises to the surface with a slotted spoon. When the soup is clear, add 1½ tablespoons of the dried tuna flakes and simmer, uncovered, for 20 minutes.

Remove the pan from the heat and add the remaining dried tuna flakes. Set aside for 5 minutes, then pour the dashi through a sieve back into the saucepan.

Mix the miso with a little of the warm dashi in a small bowl, then add 1 tablespoon at a time to the dashi in the pan, stirring constantly, until the miso has dissolved. Remove from the heat until ready to serve.

Warm the miso soup and stir in the leek, tofu and wakame seaweed.

Blanch the chives briefly in boiling water, then drain, tie them into a bundle and float them on the top of the soup. Serve immediately in bowls.

43

split pea soup
with chorizo

SERVES 6–8

375 g (12 oz) dried yellow split peas, soaked in
    cold water overnight
2 tablespoons olive oil
3 cooking chorizo sausages, thinly sliced
1 onion, chopped
2 garlic cloves, finely chopped
1.2 litres (2 pints) chicken stock (see page 9)
900 ml (1½ pints) water
1 bay leaf
1 thyme sprig or ¼ teaspoon dried thyme
3 carrots, quartered lengthways and thinly
    sliced
salt

Drain the soaked split peas in a colander, rinse
under cold running water and drain again.

Heat the oil in a large saucepan, add the chorizo
and fry over a medium heat for 5 minutes,
stirring. Using a slotted spoon, transfer the
slices to kitchen paper to drain. Pour off all but
1 tablespoon of the fat in the pan.

Add the onion and garlic to the pan and fry
gently for a few minutes, stirring frequently,
until softened. Add the drained split peas,
stock, measured water, bay leaf and thyme.
Bring to the boil, skimming off the scum as
it rises to the surface with a slotted spoon.
Reduce the heat, half-cover and simmer for
1¼ hours, stirring occasionally.

Add the carrots, half-cover the pan again and
simmer for a further 30 minutes, or until
tender. Season to taste with salt. Remove and
discard the bay leaf, stir in the fried chorizo
and cook for another 10 minutes. Serve the
soup in bowls.

44

green lentil soup
with spiced butter

SERVES 4

2 tablespoons olive oil
2 onions, chopped
2 bay leaves
175 g (6 oz) dried green lentils, rinsed and
    drained
1 litre (1¾ pints) vegetable stock (see page 10)
½ teaspoon ground turmeric
small handful of coriander leaves, roughly
    chopped
salt and pepper

SPICED BUTTER
50 g (2 oz) lightly salted butter, softened
1 large garlic clove, crushed
1 tablespoon chopped coriander
1 teaspoon paprika
1 teaspoon cumin seeds
1 red chilli, deseeded and finely chopped

Heat the oil in a large saucepan, add the onions
and fry gently for 3 minutes. Add the bay
leaves, lentils, stock and turmeric. Bring to the
boil, then reduce the heat, cover and simmer for
20 minutes, or until the lentils are tender and
turning mushy.

Meanwhile, to make the spiced butter, beat
the butter with the garlic, coriander, paprika,
cumin and chilli in a bowl. Transfer the
mixture to a small serving dish.

Stir the chopped coriander into the soup,
season to taste with salt and pepper and serve
in soup bowls with the spiced butter separately
for stirring into the soup.

45

minestrone

SERVES 4

2 tablespoons olive oil
1 onion, chopped
1 garlic clove, crushed
2 celery sticks, chopped
1 leek, finely sliced
1 carrot, chopped
400 g (13 oz) can chopped tomatoes
600 ml (1 pint) vegetable or chicken stock (see
    pages 10 and 9)
1 courgette, diced
½ small cabbage, shredded
1 bay leaf
75 g (3 oz) rinsed and drained canned haricot
    beans
75 g (3 oz) dried spaghetti, broken into small
    pieces, or small pasta shapes
1 tablespoon chopped flat leaf parsley
salt and pepper
freshly grated Parmesan cheese, to serve

Heat the oil in a large saucepan, add the
onion, garlic, celery, leek and carrot and fry
over a medium heat for 5 minutes, stirring
occasionally. Add the tomatoes, stock, courgette,
cabbage, bay leaf and beans. Bring to the boil,
then reduce the heat and simmer, uncovered, for
10 minutes.

Add the pasta, season to taste with salt and
pepper and stir well. Cook for 8 minutes,
stirring frequently to prevent the soup sticking
to the base of the pan.

Just before serving, add the parsley and stir
well. Ladle into soup bowls and serve with
grated Parmesan.

46

next time...

For minestrone with rocket & basil pesto, make
the soup as in the previous recipe. Meanwhile,
for the pesto, finely chop 25 g (1 oz) each rocket
and basil leaves, 1 garlic clove, peeled, and 25 g
(1 oz) pine nuts. Mix with 2 tablespoons freshly
grated Parmesan, a little salt and pepper and
125 ml (4 fl oz) olive oil in a bowl. Alternatively,
put all the pesto ingredients into a blender or
food processor and whizz together. Ladle the
finished soup into bowls and top with
spoonfuls of the pesto.

47

gazpacho

SERVES 6

2 garlic cloves, roughly chopped
¼ teaspoon salt
3 slices of thick white bread, crusts removed
375 g (12 oz) tomatoes, skinned and coarsely
   chopped
½ large cucumber, peeled, deseeded and
   coarsely chopped
1 large red pepper, cored, deseeded and coarsely
   chopped
2 celery sticks, quartered
5 tablespoons olive oil
4 tablespoons white wine vinegar
1 litre (1¾ pints) water
pepper

TO GARNISH
2 tomatoes, deseeded and diced
½ red onion, diced
¼ cucumber, diced

Put the garlic and salt in a mortar and pound with a pestle until smooth. Alternatively, crush the garlic with the salt on a chopping board with the flattened blade of a knife.

Cover the bread with cold water in a bowl and leave to soak for 5 seconds, then drain and squeeze out the moisture.

Add the tomatoes, cucumber, red pepper, celery and oil along with the garlic paste and bread to a blender or food processor and purée the ingredients until very smooth.

Pour the mixture into a large bowl and stir in the vinegar and measured water. Season to taste with pepper. Cover closely and chill in the refrigerator for at least 3 hours.

Serve the soup very cold in chilled glasses, garnished with a sprinkling of the diced tomatoes, red onion and cucumber.

48

next time...

For chillied gazpacho, make the soup as in the previous recipe, adding 1 large mild red chilli, deseeded and finely chopped, along with the other vegetables. Serve garnished with a scattering of finely chopped mint and a drizzle of olive oil.

49

yogurt, walnut & cucumber soup

SERVES 4

½ cucumber
25 g (1 oz) walnut pieces, plus extra to garnish
1 garlic clove
4 dill sprigs, plus extra to garnish
½ slice of white bread, torn into pieces
2 tablespoons olive oil, plus extra to garnish
400 g (13 oz) low-fat natural yogurt
4 tablespoons cold water
2 teaspoons lemon juice
salt and pepper

Peel off half the skin from the cucumber, then roughly chop the cucumber. Put on to a plate, sprinkle with a little salt and leave to stand for 20 minutes.

Rinse the cucumber in cold water and drain well in a sieve.

Put the walnuts, garlic, dill, bread and oil into a blender or food processor and whizz until finely chopped. Add the cucumber and yogurt and whizz until the cucumber is finely chopped.

Pour the mixture into a large bowl and stir in the measured water and lemon juice. Season to taste with salt and pepper. Cover and chill in the refrigerator for at least 3 hours.

Ladle into glasses. Drizzle with a little extra olive oil, sprinkle over a few walnut pieces and add a dill sprig or two to garnish. Serve with strips of toasted pitta bread.

50

next time...

For minted yogurt, almond & cucumber soup, make the soup as in the previous recipe, but replace the walnuts and dill with 25 g (1 oz) ground almonds and 2 mint sprigs, omitting the garlic. Ladle the well-chilled soup into bowls and garnish with a swirl of olive oil, a few toasted flaked almonds and some tiny mint leaves before serving.

51

chilled almond
& grape soup

SERVES 6

100 g (3½ oz) stale ciabatta bread, crusts
   removed
600 ml (1 pint) chicken stock (see page 9)
100 g (3½ oz) blanched almonds
1–2 garlic cloves, sliced
2 tablespoons olive oil
2 tablespoons sherry vinegar
salt and pepper

TO GARNISH
150 g (5 oz) seedless grapes, halved
3 tablespoons flaked almonds, toasted

Tear the bread into pieces into a bowl, pour over
150 ml (¼ pint) of the stock and leave to soak
for 5 minutes until softened.

Put the almonds and garlic into a blender or
food processor and whizz until finely ground.
Add the soaked bread with its stock, the oil,
vinegar and a little salt and pepper and blend
together. With the motor running, gradually
mix in the remaining stock.

Pour the mixture into a large bowl, cover and
chill in the refrigerator for at least 3 hours.
Taste and adjust the seasoning if needed, then
ladle into small bowls and sprinkle with the
grapes and flaked almonds to garnish. Serve
with fresh ciabatta.

52

next time...

For chilled tomato & almond soup, make the
soup as in the previous recipe, but soak the
bread in 150 ml (¼ pint) vegetable stock (see
page 10) instead of chicken stock and then
mix in 150 ml (¼ pint) passata along with the
remaining 450 ml (¾ pint) stock. Garnish the
well-chilled soup with the toasted flaked
almonds, adding 4 pieces of sun-dried tomato
in oil, drained, and some basil leaves in place
of the grapes.

53

beetroot & apple soup

SERVES 6

1 tablespoon olive oil
1 onion, roughly chopped
500 g (1 lb) raw beetroot, peeled and diced
1 large cooking apple, about 375 g (12 oz),
   quartered, cored, peeled and diced
1.5 litres (2½ pints) vegetable or chicken stock
   (see pages 10 and 9)
salt and pepper

TO FINISH
6 tablespoons soured cream
1 red dessert apple, cored and diced
seeds from ½ pomegranate
4 tablespoons maple syrup, plus extra to serve

Heat the oil in a large saucepan, add the onion and fry gently for 5 minutes, stirring occasionally, until softened. Add the beetroot and cooking apple, pour in the stock and season to taste with salt and pepper. Bring it to the boil, then reduce the heat, cover and simmer for 45 minutes, stirring occasionally, until the beetroot is tender.

Leave the soup to cool slightly, then purée in batches in a blender or food processor until smooth. Pour into a large jug and taste and adjust the seasoning if needed. Cover and chill in the refrigerator for 3–4 hours or overnight.

Pour the soup into bowls to serve and top each with a spoonful of soured cream, sprinkle with the dessert apple and pomegranate seeds and drizzle with the maple syrup. Serve extra maple syrup in a small jug to add as required and accompany with sliced rye bread.

54

next time...

For beetroot & orange soup, make the soup as in the previous recipe, but omit the cooking apple. After puréeing the soup, mix in the grated rind and juice of 2 large oranges. Serve the chilled soup finished with a swirl of soured cream, a drizzle of honey and some orange rind curls made with a zester.

55

caldo verde

SERVE 6

2 tablespoons olive oil
1 large onion, chopped
2 garlic cloves, chopped
500 g (1 lb) potatoes, cut into 2.5 cm (1 inch)
   cubes
1.2 litres (2 pints) water or vegetable stock (see
   page 10)
250 g (8 oz) spring greens, finely shredded
2 tablespoons chopped parsley
salt and pepper

Heat the oil in a large frying pan, add the onion and fry gently for 5 minutes, stirring occasionally, or until softened but not browned. Add the garlic and potatoes and cook for a few minutes, stirring occasionally.

Transfer the vegetables to a large saucepan. Add the water or stock, season to taste with salt and pepper. Cover and simmer for 15 minutes until the potatoes are tender.

Mash the potatoes roughly in the liquid, then add the spring greens, bring to the boil and continue boiling for 10 minutes. Stir in the parsley, reduce the heat and simmer for 2–3 minutes, or until heated through.

Serve the soup in bowls with croûtons, but made with strips of bread instead of cubes (see page 13).

56

beef & barley brö

SERVES 6

25 g (1 oz) butter
250 g (8 oz) boneless braising beef, trimmed of
   fat and cut into small cubes
1 large onion, finely chopped
200 g (7 oz) swede, diced
150 g (5 oz) carrots, diced
100 g (3½ oz) pearl barley
2 litres (3½ pints) beef stock (see page 9)
2 teaspoons English mustard powder (optional)
salt and pepper
chopped parsley, to garnish

Melt the butter in a large saucepan, add the
beef and onion and fry for 5 minutes, stirring,
until the beef is browned and the onion is just
beginning to colour.

Stir in the diced vegetables, pearl barley, stock
and mustard (if using). Season with salt and
pepper and bring to the boil. Reduce the heat,
cover and simmer for 1¾ hours until the
meat and vegetables are very tender, stirring
occasionally. Taste and adjust the seasoning
if needed.

Ladle the soup into bowls and sprinkle with a
little chopped parsley. Serve with warm potato
bannocks or farls.

57

next time...

For lamb & barley hotpot, replace the beef with
250 g (8 oz) boneless lamb, diced, and fry with
the onion as in the previous recipe. Add the
sliced white part of 1 leek and 175 g (6 oz) each
swede, carrot and potato, diced, then mix in
50 g (2 oz) pearl barley, 2 litres (3½ pints) lamb
stock (see page 9), 2–3 rosemary sprigs and salt
and pepper. Bring to the boil, then reduce the
heat, cover and simmer for 1¾ hours. Remove
and discard the rosemary, add the remaining
green part of the leek, thinly sliced, and
simmer for 10 minutes. Ladle the soup into
bowls and sprinkle with a little extra chopped
rosemary to serve.

58

avocado & soured cream soup

SERVES 6

1 tablespoon sunflower oil
4 spring onions, sliced, plus 2 to garnish
2 large ripe avocados
4 tablespoons soured cream
600 ml (1 pint) vegetable or chicken stock (see pages 10 and 9)
juice of 2 limes
a few drops of Tabasco sauce
salt and pepper

Heat the oil in a frying pan, add the spring onions and fry gently for 5 minutes, stirring occasionally, until softened.

Meanwhile, create spring onion curls by cutting very thin strips from the 2 spring onions for garnishing. Soak in cold water for 10 minutes, then drain.

Halve the avocados and remove and discard the stones. Scoop out the avocado flesh from the skins with a dessertspoon and add to a blender or food processor with the fried spring onions, the soured cream and about one-third of the stock. Purée until smooth and then, with the motor running, gradually mix in the remaining stock and lime juice. Season to taste with salt and pepper and Tabasco sauce.

Serve the soup immediately while the avocado is still bright green in cups or glass tumblers containing some ice. Scatter the spring onion curls over the soup and serve with breadsticks.

59

ham & pea soup

SERVES 4

250 g (8 oz) dried yellow or green split peas, soaked in cold water for 4–6 hours
50 g (2 oz) butter
1 large onion, roughly chopped
1 large carrot, roughly chopped
4 thick bacon rashers, about 175 g (6 oz), rinded and diced
1 small bay leaf
1 ham bone
1.2 litres (2 pints) water
2 tablespoons snipped chives
salt (if needed) and pepper

Drain the soaked split peas in a colander, rinse under cold running water and drain again.

Melt the butter in a saucepan, add the onion, carrot and two-thirds of the bacon and fry gently for about 15 minutes, or until soft, stirring occasionally. Add the split peas, bay leaf, ham bone and measured water. Bring to the boil, then reduce the heat, cover and simmer gently for 1 hour.

Remove the pan from the heat and lift out and discard the ham bone. Season the soup with pepper, and salt if needed. Return the pan to the heat to keep the soup hot.

Heat a dry frying pan, add the remaining bacon and cook until crisp, then add to the soup along with half the chives.

Serve the soup in bowls, garnished with the remaining chives.

60

spiced lamb & sweet potato soup

SERVES 6

1 tablespoon olive oil
500 g (1 lb) stewing lamb on the bone
1 onion, finely chopped
1–2 garlic cloves, finely chopped
2 teaspoons ras el hanout Moroccan spice blend
2.5 cm (1 inch) piece of fresh root ginger, peeled and grated
2 litres (3½ pints) lamb or chicken stock (see page 9)
75 g (3 oz) dried red lentils, rinsed and drained
300 g (10 oz) sweet potato, diced
175 g (6 oz) carrot, diced
salt and pepper
1 small bunch of coriander, leaves torn, to garnish (optional)

Heat the oil in a large saucepan, add the lamb and fry until browned on one side. Turn the lamb over, add the onion and cook until the lamb is browned all over and the onion is just beginning to colour.

Stir in the garlic, spice blend and ginger, then the stock, lentils and salt and pepper. Bring to the boil, then reduce the heat, cover and simmer for 1½ hours.

Add the sweet potato and carrot and bring back to a simmer, then re-cover and cook for a further 1 hour.

Lift the lamb out of the soup with a slotted spoon, put on to a plate and carefully take the lamb off the bones, discarding the excess fat. Break the lamb into small pieces and return to the soup, then reheat if necessary. Taste and adjust the seasoning if needed.

Ladle the soup into bowls and sprinkle with torn coriander leaves, if liked.

61

next time...

For herby lamb & mixed roots, fry the lamb and onion in the oil as in the previous recipe. Flavour with the leaves stripped and chopped from 2 rosemary sprigs and ½ teaspoon dried mixed herbs, omitting the garlic, spice blend and ginger. Add the stock, lentils and salt and pepper, then cover and simmer for 1½ hours as before. Mix in 175 g (6 oz) each potatoes, swede and carrots, diced, then re-cover and cook for a further 1 hour. Take the lamb off the bones and return to the soup as before, then serve sprinkled with chopped parsley.

62

tomato & orange soup

SERVES 6

2 tablespoons olive oil
1 onion, roughly chopped
2 garlic cloves, crushed
2 kg (4 lb) ripe tomatoes, skinned and chopped
2 tablespoons tomato purée
450 ml (¾ pint) vegetable or chicken stock (see
    pages 10 and 9)
grated rind of 1 large orange
75 ml (3 fl oz) orange juice
4 basil sprigs
1–2 teaspoons brown sugar
salt and pepper

TO GARNISH
2–3 tablespoons finely chopped basil, plus
    6 small basil sprigs
150 g (5 oz) low-fat Greek yogurt
thin strips of orange rind

Heat the oil in a large saucepan, add the onion
and garlic and fry for a few minutes, stirring
frequently, until the onion is softened. Add the
tomatoes, tomato purée, stock, grated orange
rind and juice and basil. Bring to the boil, then
reduce the heat, cover and simmer gently for
20–25 minutes until the vegetables are soft.

Leave the soup to cool slightly, then purée in
batches in a blender or food processor until
smooth. Press the purée through a nylon sieve
back into the rinsed-out pan to remove the
tomato seeds. Season to taste with salt and
pepper and add the sugar. Bring to the boil,
then add a little extra stock or orange juice if
necessary to achieve the desired consistency.

Stir the chopped basil gently into the Greek
yogurt. Pour the hot soup into bowls. Spoon a
little of the basil yogurt on each serving and
add a small basil sprig and a little orange rind
to garnish.

63

next time...

For tomato soup with crispy chorizo, make
the soup as in the previous recipe, replacing
the orange rind and juice with 75 ml (3 fl oz)
red wine. Purée the soup as before and serve
topped with 40 g (1½ oz) ready-sliced chorizo,
dry-fried until browned, then diced.

64

fennel seed root vegetable
soup

SERVES 6

1 tablespoon olive oil
1 onion, roughly chopped
2 garlic cloves, roughly chopped
2 teaspoons fennel seeds, roughly
    crushed
½ teaspoon smoked paprika
½ teaspoon ground turmeric
250 g (8 oz) carrots, diced
250 g (8 oz) parsnips, diced
250 g (8 oz) swede, diced
1 litre (1¾ pints) vegetable or
    chicken stock (see pages 10 and 9)
300 ml (½ pint) skimmed milk
salt and pepper

Heat the oil in a large saucepan, add the onion and fry for
5 minutes, stirring occasionally, until just beginning to
soften. Stir in the garlic, fennel seeds and ground spices
and cook for 1 minute to release their flavour.

Add the root vegetables and stock and season to taste
with salt and pepper. Bring to the boil, then reduce
the heat, cover and simmer, stirring occasionally, for
45 minutes until the vegetables are very tender.

Leave the soup to cool slightly, then purée in the pan with
a stick blender or in batches in a blender or food processor
until smooth, returning to the pan. Stir in the milk and
reheat gently. Taste and adjust the seasoning if needed.

Ladle the hot soup into bowls and serve sprinkled with
croûtons (see page 13).

65

harira

SERVES 8–10

250 g (8 oz) dried chickpeas, soaked in cold
    water overnight
2 chicken breast fillets, halved
1.2 litres (2 pints) chicken stock (see page 9)
1.2 litres (2 pints) water
2 x 400 g (13 oz) cans chopped tomatoes
¼ teaspoon crumbled saffron threads
    (optional)
2 onions, chopped
125 g (4 oz) long-grain white rice
50 g (2 oz) dried green lentils, rinsed and
    drained
2 tablespoons finely chopped coriander
2 tablespoons finely chopped flat leaf parsley
salt and pepper

Drain the chickpeas in a colander, rinse under
cold running water and drain again. Put them
into a saucepan, cover with 5 cm (2 inches) of
water and bring to the boil. Boil rapidly for
10 minutes, then reduce the heat, half-cover
and simmer until tender, adding more water
as necessary. This will take anything up to
1¾ hours. Drain the chickpeas and set aside.

Put the chicken, stock and measured water
into a separate, large saucepan and bring to
the boil. Reduce the heat, cover and simmer
for 10–15 minutes, or until the chicken is just
cooked. Lift the chicken out with a slotted
spoon and put it on a chopping board. Shred the
meat, discarding the skin, and set aside.

Add the chickpeas, tomatoes, saffron (if using),
onions, rice and lentils to the stock remaining in
the pan. Cover and simmer for 30–35 minutes,
or until the rice and lentils are tender.

Add the shredded chicken and herbs just
before serving and heat through for 5 minutes
without allowing the soup to boil. Season to
taste with salt and pepper and serve in bowls.

66

next time...

For budget harira, make the soup as in the
previous recipe, but omit the chicken and
and add ½ teaspoon ground turmeric and
½ teaspoon ground cinnamon instead of the
crumbled saffron.

67

onion, tomato
& chickpea soup

SERVES 6

2 tablespoons olive oil
2 red onions, roughly chopped
2 garlic cloves, finely chopped
2 teaspoons brown sugar
625 g (1¼ lb) tomatoes, skinned if liked and
    roughly chopped
2 teaspoons harissa paste
3 teaspoons tomato purée
400 g (13 oz) can chickpeas, rinsed and drained
900 ml (1½ pints) vegetable or chicken stock
    (see pages 10 and 9)
salt and pepper

Heat the oil in a large saucepan, add the
onions and fry over a low heat for 10 minutes,
stirring occasionally, until just beginning to
brown around the edges. Stir in the garlic
and sugar and cook for a further 10 minutes,
stirring more frequently as the onions begin
to caramelize.

Stir in the tomatoes and harissa paste and
cook for 5 minutes. Mix in the tomato purée,
chickpeas and stock, season to taste with salt
and pepper and bring to the boil. Reduce the
heat, cover and simmer for 45 minutes until
the tomatoes and onion are very soft. Taste and
adjust the seasoning if needed.

Ladle the soup into bowls and serve with warm
tomato ciabatta.

68

next time...

For chillied red onion & bean soup, make the
the soup as in the previous recipe, replacing the
harissa with 1 teaspoon smoked paprika and
1 dried red chilli, split, and the chickpeas with
a rinsed and drained 400g (13 oz) can red
kidney beans. Serve the soup with garlic bread.

69

cock-a-leekie soup

SERVES 6

1 tablespoon sunflower oil
2 chicken thigh and leg joints, about 375 g
  (12 oz)
500 g (1 lb) leeks, thinly sliced, white and green
  parts kept separate
3 rindless smoked streaky bacon rashers, diced
2.5 litres (4 pints) chicken stock (see page 9)
75 g (3 oz) pitted prunes, quartered
1 bay leaf
1 large thyme sprig
50 g (2 oz) long-grain white rice
salt and pepper

Heat the oil in a large saucepan, add the
chicken joints and fry on one side until golden.
Turn them over, add the white leek parts and
bacon and fry until the chicken is golden all
over and the leeks and bacon are just beginning
to colour.

Pour in the stock, add the prunes, bay leaf and
thyme, season to taste with salt and pepper and
bring to the boil. Reduce the heat, cover and
simmer for 1½ hours, stirring occasionally,
until the chicken is falling off the bones.

Lift the chicken, bay leaf and thyme sprigs out
of the soup with a slotted spoon, discard the
herbs and put the chicken on to a plate. Take the
chicken off the bones, discarding the skin, and
cut into pieces. Return the chicken to the soup
and add the rice and green leek parts. Re-cover
and simmer for 10 minutes until the rice and
leeks are tender. Taste and adjust the seasoning
if needed.

Ladle the soup into bowls and serve with warm
crusty bread.

70

next time...

For cream of chicken soup, make the soup
as in the previous recipe, but using 2 litres
(3½ pints) stock and omitting the prunes and
adding 250 g (8 oz) diced potato. Then omit the
rice and just return the chicken meat to the
finished soup. Leave the soup to cool slightly,
then purée in the pan with a stick blender
or in batches in a blender or food processor,
returning to the pan. Stir in 150 ml (¼ pint)
milk and 150 ml (¼ pint) double cream, reheat
and taste and adjust the seasoning if needed.
Serve with croûtons (see page 13).

71

honey-roasted parsnip
soup

SERVES 6

750 g (1½ lb) parsnips, cut into wedges
2 onions, cut into wedges
2 tablespoons olive oil
2 tablespoons clear honey
1 teaspoon ground turmeric, plus extra to
    garnish (optional)
½ teaspoon chilli flakes
3 garlic cloves, thickly sliced
1.2 litres (2 pints) vegetable or chicken stock
    (see pages 10 and 9)
2 tablespoons sherry or cider vinegar
150 ml (¼ pint) double cream
5 cm (2 inch) piece of fresh root ginger, peeled
    and grated
salt and pepper

Arrange the parsnips and onions in a large
roasting tin in a single layer, then drizzle with
the oil and honey. Sprinkle with the turmeric,
chilli flakes and garlic.

Roast in a preheated oven, 190°C (375°F), Gas
Mark 5, for 45–50 minutes, turning halfway
through, until a deep golden brown with sticky,
caramelized edges.

Transfer the roasting tin to the hob, add the
stock and vinegar and season to taste with salt
and pepper. Bring to the boil, scraping up the
juices from the base of the tin, then reduce the
heat and simmer for 5 minutes.

Leave the soup to cool slightly, then purée in
batches in a blender or food processor until
smooth. Pour into a saucepan and reheat, then
taste and adjust the seasoning and top up with
a little extra stock if needed.

Mix the cream, ginger and a little pepper
together in a small bowl. Ladle the soup into
soup bowls and drizzle the ginger cream over
the top, then garnish with a little turmeric,
if liked. Serve with croûtons (see page 13).

72

next time...

For honey-roasted sweet potato soup, make
the soup as in the previous recipe, but replace
the parsnips with 750 g (1½ lb) sweet potato,
cut into wedges, sprinkled with 1 teaspoon
roughly crushed cumin seeds in addition to
the turmeric and chilli. Serve ladled into soup
bowls topped with spoonfuls of natural yogurt
and a teaspoon of mango chutney drizzled over
each bowl.

73

oriental soup
with egg & greens

SERVES 4

4 spring onions
100 g (3½ oz) pak choi, roughly
chopped
2 tablespoons vegetable oil
2.5 cm (1 inch) piece of fresh root
ginger, peeled and finely grated
2 garlic cloves, finely chopped
200 g (7 oz) jasmine rice
100 ml (3½ fl oz) rice wine
2 tablespoons soy sauce
1 teaspoon rice wine vinegar
1 litre (1¾ pints) hot vegetable stock
(see page 10)
4 eggs
1 tablespoon chilli oil

Finely slice the spring onions, keeping the white and green parts separate. Combine the green parts with the pak choi in a bowl and set aside.

Heat the oil gently in a saucepan. When hot, add the spring onion white parts, ginger and garlic and stir-fry for 2–3 minutes. Stir in the rice, then add the wine and bubble for a minute or so. Add the soy sauce, vinegar and hot stock and simmer, stirring occasionally, for 10–12 minutes. Then stir in the green spring onion and pak choi mixture and cook for a further 2–3 minutes.

Meanwhile, poach the eggs in 2 batches in a saucepan of gently simmering water for 3–4 minutes. Remove with a slotted spoon and drain well on kitchen paper. Ladle the soup into 4 shallow soup bowls, then top each with a poached egg and drizzle over the chilli oil.

74

avgolemono

SERVES 4–6

1.5 litres (2½ pints) vegetable or chicken stock
(see pages 10 and 9)
50 g (2 oz) long-grain white rice
2 eggs
2–3 tablespoons lemon juice
salt and pepper
1 tablespoon chopped parsley, to garnish
(optional)

Combine the stock, ½ teaspoon salt and the
rice in a saucepan. Bring to the boil and stir,
then reduce the heat, cover and simmer for
20 minutes. Stir once more.

Beat the eggs together in a small bowl, then
whisk in the lemon juice. Add a ladleful of the
hot stock and beat in, then add another ladleful
of stock and beat again.

Bring the stock and rice mixture back to the
boil, then briefly remove from the heat, add
the egg and lemon mixture and stir well.
Reduce the heat and simmer gently for a
further 2 minutes. Season to taste with salt
and pepper. Serve immediately in warmed soup
bowls, sprinkled with the parsley to garnish,
if liked.

75

next time...

For salmon avgolomeno, simmer vegetable
or fish stock with salt and rice as in the recipe
above, while steaming 400 g (13 oz) or 3 salmon
steaks above the saucepan in a covered steamer
pan for 10 minutes of the simmering time.
Lift the salmon out and flake into bite-sized
pieces, discarding the skin and any stray bones.
Continue as above, adding the egg and lemon
mixture, then ladle into soup bowls, pile the
salmon flakes in the centre and sprinkle with
chopped parsley.

76

watercress soup with poached quails' eggs

SERVES 4

50 g (2 oz) butter
1 onion, finely chopped
250 g (8 oz) potatoes, cut into 1 cm (½ inch)
cubes
300 g (10 oz) watercress, roughly chopped
900 ml (1½ pints) vegetable or chicken stock
(see pages 10 and 9)
300 ml (½ pint) single cream
12 quails' eggs
50 g (2 oz) Parmesan cheese, finely grated
salt and pepper

Melt the butter in a large saucepan, add
the onion and fry gently for 8–10 minutes,
or until well softened but not browned,
stirring occasionally. Stir in the potatoes and
watercress, cover and cook for 3–5 minutes,
stirring once or twice, until the watercress has
just wilted.

Add the stock and season to taste with salt
and pepper. Bring to the boil, then reduce the
heat and simmer for 6–8 minutes, or until the
potatoes are tender.

Leave the soup to cool slightly, then purée in
batches in a blender or food processor until
smooth. Pass the purée through a fine sieve
back into the pan. Add the cream and reheat
without boiling, then taste and adjust the
seasoning if needed.

Poach the quails' eggs in a saucepan of gently
simmering water for 1–2 minutes, or until
cooked to your liking. Remove with a slotted
spoon and drain well on kitchen paper.

Place 3 poached eggs in each bowl. Ladle the
watercress soup over the eggs and serve
sprinkled with the grated Parmesan.

77

chilled lettuce soup

SERVES 6

25 g (1 oz) butter
4 spring onions, sliced
250 g (8 oz) shelled fresh or frozen peas
1 Cos (Romaine) lettuce heart, leaves separated
 and shredded
600 ml (1 pint) vegetable and chicken stock
 (see pages 10 and 9)
1 teaspoon caster sugar
6 tablespoons double cream
salt and pepper

TO SERVE

12 Little Gem lettuce leaves
1 small fresh prepared crab on the shell,
 about 150 g (5 oz)
2 tablespoons mayonnaise
1 tablespoon lemon juice
a little paprika

Melt the butter in a saucepan, add the spring
onions and fry for 2–3 minutes until softened.
Add the peas and cook for 2 minutes, then
stir in the lettuce. Pour over the stock, add the
sugar and a little salt and pepper and bring to
the boil. Reduce the heat, cover and simmer
gently for 10 minutes until the lettuce is wilted
but still bright green.

Leave the soup to cool slightly, then purée in
batches in a blender or food processor until
smooth. Pour into a large bowl, stir in the
cream and taste and adjust the seasoning if
needed. Cover and chill in the refrigerator for
at least 3 hours.

Ladle the chilled soup into small bowls set on
plates. Serve with the Little Gem lettuce leaves
topped with a small amount of the crab mixed
with the mayonnaise and lemon juice, and
sprinkled with paprika.

78

next time...

For chilled watercress soup, melt the butter
as in the previous recipe and stir in the sliced
white part of 1 small leek and 200 g (7 oz) potato,
diced. Cover and cook gently for 10 minutes,
stirring occasionally. Add 750 ml (1¼ pints)
chicken or vegetable stock and season to taste
with salt and pepper, then re-cover and simmer
for 10 minutes. Add the remaining green part
of the leek, sliced, and 2 bunches or 200 g (7 oz)
watercress, re-cover and simmer for 5 minutes
until the watercress has just wilted. Leave the
soup to cool slightly, then purée as before, pour
into a large bowl and stir in 150 ml (¼ pint) milk
and 150 ml (¼ pint) double cream. Cover and
chill as before. Serve in shallow bowls with a
swirl of double cream.

79

celery, carrot & apple soup

SERVES 6

50 g (2 oz) unsalted butter
500 g (1 lb) celery sticks, sliced
500 g (1 lb) carrots, chopped
250 g (8 oz) dessert apples, peeled, cored and
    roughly chopped
1.2 litres (2 pints) vegetable stock (see page 10)
1 teaspoon paprika, plus extra to garnish
cayenne pepper, to taste
1 tablespoon chopped basil leaves or 1 teaspoon
    dried basil
1 bay leaf
1 teaspoon peeled and grated fresh root ginger
salt and white pepper
chopped celery leaves, to garnish

Melt the butter in a large saucepan and stir
in the celery, carrots and apple. Cover with a
tight-fitting lid and cook over a low heat for
15 minutes, stirring occasionally.

Add the stock, paprika, cayenne, basil, bay leaf
and ginger. Bring to the boil, then reduce the
heat, half-cover and simmer for 40–45 minutes,
or until the vegetables and apple are very soft.

Leave the soup to cool slightly, then purée in
batches in a blender or food processor until
smooth. Pass the purée through a sieve back
into the pan, reheat and season to taste with
salt and pepper.

Serve the soup in bowls, garnishing each
serving with a few chopped celery leaves and a
light sprinkling of paprika.

80

mint, cucumber & green pea soup

SERVES 6

50 g (2 oz) butter
500 g (1 lb) cucumbers, peeled, deseeded
    and cut into 1 cm (½ inch) pieces
250 g (8 oz) shelled fresh or frozen peas
pinch of sugar
¼ teaspoon white pepper
3 tablespoons finely chopped mint
1.2 litres (2 pints) vegetable or chicken stock
    (see pages 10 and 9)
175 g (6 oz) potatoes, roughly chopped
150 ml (¼ pint) double cream (chilled if the
    soup is to be served cold)
salt

Melt the butter in a large saucepan, add the
cucumbers and cook over a medium heat for
5 minutes, stirring occasionally. Add the peas,
sugar, pepper and 2 tablespoons of the mint.
Pour in the stock, bring to the boil and stir in
the potatoes. Reduce the heat, half-cover and
simmer for about 20 minutes, or until the
potatoes are tender.

Leave the soup to cool slightly, then purée in
batches in a blender or food processor until
smooth. Pour into a clean saucepan or, if the
soup is to be served cold, a large bowl. Season to
taste with salt.

If the soup is to be served hot, add the cream
and reheat it gently without boiling. Serve in
bowls, garnishing each serving with a little of
the remaining chopped mint. If the soup is to be
served cold, cover the bowl closely and chill in
the refrigerator for at least 3 hours. Just before
serving, fold in the chilled cream. Serve in
chilled bowls, garnished with the remaining
chopped mint.

81

smooth carrot soup with mint

SERVES 6

2 tablespoons olive oil
1 onion, roughly chopped
750 g (1½ lb) carrots, diced
40 g (1½ oz) long-grain white rice
1 litre (1¾ pints) vegetable or chicken stock (see pages 10 and 9)
300 ml (½ pint) milk
salt and pepper

MINT OIL
15 g (½ oz) mint sprigs, plus extra leaves to garnish (optional)
¼ teaspoon caster sugar
3 tablespoons olive oil

Heat the oil in a saucepan, add the onion and fry for 5 minutes, stirring occasionally, until just beginning to soften and turn golden around the edges. Stir in the carrots and cook for 5 minutes.

Mix in the rice, stock and a little salt and pepper. Bring to the boil, then reduce the heat, cover and simmer for 45 minutes, stirring occasionally, until the carrots are tender.

Meanwhile, make the mint oil. Strip the leaves from the mint stems and add to a blender or food processor with the sugar and a little pepper. Whizz until finely chopped and then, with the motor running, gradually blend in the oil a little at a time. Spoon into a small bowl and stir before using.

Leave the soup to cool slightly, then purée in batches in the rinsed-out blender or food processor until smooth. Return to the pan and stir in the milk. Reheat and taste and adjust the seasoning if needed.

Ladle the soup into bowls, then drizzle with the mint oil and garnish with mint leaves if liked.

82

next time...

For smooth squash soup with mint, fry the onion in oil as in the previous recipe, then stir in 750 g (1½ lb) butternut squash, halved, deseeded, peeled and diced, instead of the carrots and cook 5 minutes. Mix in the rice, stock and salt and pepper, then continue as before, serving the puréed soup drizzled with the mint oil.

83

christmas special

SERVES 6

25 g (1 oz) butter
1 onion, roughly chopped
2 rindless smoked streaky bacon rashers,
    diced, plus 4 grilled and diced to garnish
250 g (8 oz) potato, diced
1 litre (1¾ pints) chicken or turkey stock (see
    page 9)
100 g (3½ oz) vacuum-packed peeled chestnuts
large pinch of grated nutmeg
250 g (8 oz) Brussels sprouts, sliced
salt and pepper

Melt the butter in a saucepan, add the
onion and fry gently for 5 minutes, stirring
occasionally, until softened. Add the raw diced
bacon and potato and toss in the butter, then
cover and fry for 5 minutes until just beginning
to brown.

Pour over the stock and crumble in the
chestnuts, then add the nutmeg and season
to taste with salt and pepper. Bring to the boil,
then reduce the heat, cover and simmer for
30 minutes. Stir in the Brussels sprouts, then
re-cover and simmer for 5 minutes until they
are tender but still bright green.

Lift out and reserve a few Brussels sprout
slices for garnishing. Leave the soup to cool
slightly, then purée in the pan with a stick
blender or in batches in a blender or food
processor until green specks can still be seen,
returning to the pan. Reheat, then taste and
adjust the seasoning if needed.

Serve the soup in bowls, garnished with the
reserved Brussels sprout slices and the diced
grilled bacon.

84

next time...

For chestnut & mushroom soup, fry the onion
and then the bacon and potato in the butter
as in the previous recipe, add 250 g (8 oz) cup
mushrooms, sliced, and fry, uncovered, for
2–3 minutes, stirring frequently. Continue
making the soup as before, but omit the
Brussels sprouts. Purée and reheat the soup,
then serve garnished with a swirl of double
cream and a little crumbled chestnut along
with the diced grilled bacon as before.

85

thai squash
& coriander soup

SERVES 6

1 tablespoon sunflower oil
1 onion, roughly chopped
3 teaspoons ready-made red Thai curry paste
1–2 garlic cloves, finely chopped
2.5 cm (1 inch) piece of fresh root ginger, peeled
   and finely chopped
1 butternut squash, about 750 g (1½ lb), halved,
   deseeded, peeled and diced
400 ml (14 fl oz) can full-fat coconut milk
750 ml (1¼ pints) vegetable or chicken stock
   (see pages 10 and 9)
2 teaspoons Thai fish sauce
1 small bunch of coriander
pepper

Heat the oil in a saucepan, add the onion and
fry gently for 5 minutes, stirring occasionally,
until softened. Stir in the curry paste, garlic
and ginger and cook for 1 minute. Add the
squash, coconut milk, stock, fish sauce and a
little pepper (do not add salt, as the fish sauce
is so salty), then bring to the boil. Reduce the
heat, cover and simmer for 45 minutes, stirring
occasionally, until the squash is soft.

Leave to cool slightly. Reserve a few sprigs
of coriander for garnishing, then tear the
remainder into pieces and add to the soup.
Purée the soup in batches in a blender or food
processor until smooth. Return to the pan and
reheat, tearing in the reserved coriander sprigs.
Ladle into bowls and serve.

86

next time...

For gingered squash soup, fry the onion in the
oil as in the previous recipe, then mix in the
garlic and a 3.5 cm (1½ inch) piece of fresh
root ginger, peeled and finely chopped. Add the
squash as before with 900 ml (1½ pints)
vegetable stock and a little salt and pepper,
omitting the curry paste, coconut milk, fish
sauce and coriander. Bring to the boil, then
cover and simmer for 45 minutes. Purée and
stir in 300 ml (½ pint) milk. Reheat and serve
with croûtons (see page 13).

87

chillied melon foam

SERVES 6

2 ripe Galia melons
freshly squeezed juice of 1 lime
½–1 large mild red chilli, deseeded and
    quartered
1 small bunch of coriander, plus 6 sprigs
    to garnish (optional)
300 ml (½ pint) pressed apple juice
6 lime wedges, to garnish (optional)

Cut the melons in half and scoop out and
discard the seeds. Scoop the flesh from
the skins and put it into a blender or food
processor. Add the lime juice and chilli, and
tear in the bunch of coriander. Pour in half the
apple juice and blend until smooth. With the
motor running, gradually mix in the remaining
juice until frothy.

Pour the soup into cups or glass tumblers half-
filled with ice, garnish each with a coriander
sprig and lime wedge, if liked, and serve
immediately before the soup loses its bubbles.

88

next time...

For gingered melon foam, scoop out the flesh
from 2 halved, deseeded Charentais melons,
then purée with 2 chopped spring onions and
150 g (5 oz) low-fat crème fraîche in a blender
or food processor. Add 150 ml (¼ pint) ginger
beer and blend until frothy. Pour into shallow
bowls or back into the melon shells to serve.

sour cherry soup

SERVES 6

300 ml (½ pint) white Riesling wine
450 ml (¾ pint) water
2 tablespoons caster sugar
1 cinnamon stick, halved
grated rind and juice of 1 lemon
475 g (15 oz) pack frozen pitted cherries
300 ml (½ pint) soured cream
ground cinnamon, to garnish

Pour the wine and measured water into a saucepan, add the sugar, cinnamon stick and lemon rind and juice and bring to the boil. Reduce the heat and simmer for 5 minutes.

Add the still-frozen cherries and simmer for 5 minutes. Discard the cinnamon stick, then ladle half the liquid and cherries into a blender or food processor. Add the soured cream and then purée, in batches if necessary, until smooth. Return the purée to the saucepan and mix well.

Pour the soup into a large bowl, cover and chill in the refrigerator at least 3 hours.

Ladle the chilled soup into shallow bowls so that the whole cherries can be seen and sprinkle with a little ground cinnamon. Serve with some cherries on stalks, if liked.

90

next time...

For peppered strawberry soup, add the wine, water, sugar and lemon rind and juice to the saucepan as in the previous recipe, but replace the cinnamon stick with ½ teaspoon crushed coloured peppercorns. Simmer for 5 minutes as before, then add 500 g (1 lb) fresh strawberries, hulled and sliced or halved depending on their size, instead of the cherries. Continue as before, sprinkling with a little extra of the crushed peppercorns instead of the ground cinnamon to garnish.

91

beef & noodle broth

SERVES 2

300 g (10 oz) rump or sirloin steak
2.5 cm (1 inch) piece of fresh root ginger, peeled
and grated
2 teaspoons soy sauce
50 g (2 oz) dried vermicelli rice noodles
600 ml (1 pint) beef stock (see page 9)
1 red chilli, deseeded and finely chopped
1 garlic clove, thinly sliced
2 teaspoons caster sugar
2 teaspoons vegetable oil
75 g (3 oz) sugar snap peas, halved lengthways
small handful of Thai basil, torn into pieces

Trim any fat from the beef. Mix the ginger with
1 teaspoon of the soy sauce and smooth over
both sides of the beef.

Cook the noodles according to the packet
instructions. Drain and rinse thoroughly in
cold water.

Pour the stock into a saucepan, add the chilli,
garlic and sugar and bring to a gentle simmer.
Cover and simmer gently for 5 minutes.

Meanwhile, heat the oil in a small, heavy-based
frying pan, add the beef and fry for 2 minutes
on each side. Transfer the beef to a chopping
board, cut it in half lengthways and then cut it
across into thin strips.

Add the noodles, sugar snap peas, basil and
remaining soy sauce to the broth and heat
gently for 1 minute. Stir in the beef strips and
serve immediately.

92

next time...

For minted chicken broth, make the broth as
in the previous recipe, replacing the steak
with 300 g (10 oz) skinless chicken breast
fillets and the beef stock with 600 ml (1 pint)
chicken stock (see page 9), frying the chicken
for 5–6 minutes on each side until thoroughly
cooked. Serve the broth garnished with some
torn mint leaves.

93

beery oxtail & butter bean soup

SERVES 6

1 tablespoon sunflower oil
500 g (1 lb) oxtail pieces
1 onion, finely chopped
2 carrots, diced
2 celery sticks, diced
200 g (7 oz) potato, diced
1 small bunch of mixed herbs
2 litres (3½ pints) beef stock (see page 9)
450 ml (¾ pint) strong ale
2 teaspoons English mustard
2 tablespoons Worcestershire sauce
1 tablespoon tomato purée
410 g (13½ oz) can butter beans, rinsed
    and drained
salt and pepper
chopped parsley, to garnish

Heat the oil in a large saucepan, add the oxtail pieces and fry until browned on one side. Turn the oxtail pieces over, add the onion and fry, stirring, until browned on all sides. Stir in the carrots, celery, potato and herbs and cook for a further 2–3 minutes, stirring frequently.

Pour in the stock and ale, then add the mustard, Worcestershire sauce, tomato purée and beans. Season well with salt and pepper and bring to the boil, stirring. Reduce the heat, half-cover and simmer gently for 4 hours.

Lift the oxtail and herbs out of the pan with a slotted spoon and put on to a plate. Discard the herbs and cut the meat off the bones, discarding any fat. Return the meat to the pan and reheat, then taste and adjust the seasoning if needed.

Ladle the soup into bowls, sprinkle with chopped parsley and serve with crusty bread.

94

next time...

For chillied oxtail & red bean soup, fry the oxtail and onion in the oil as in the previous recipe, then add and cook the vegetables for 2–3 minutes, omitting the bunch of mixed herbs, and stir in 2 garlic cloves, finely chopped, 2 bay leaves, 1 teaspoon hot chilli powder and 1 teaspoon eah crushed cumin and coriander seeds. Pour in the beef stock with a 400 g (13 oz) can chopped tomatoes, 1 tablespoon tomato purée and a rinsed and drained 410 g (13½ oz) can red kidney beans. Bring to the boil, then simmer and continue as before.

95

sweet potato & red pepper soup

SERVES 4

2 tablespoons vegetable oil
1 red onion, chopped
1 red pepper, cored, deseeded and chopped
550 g (1 lb 2 oz) sweet potatoes, chopped
½ teaspoon ground cumin
8 cherry tomatoes
1.2 litres (2 pints) vegetable stock (see page 10)
25 g (1 oz) creamed coconut, chopped
salt and pepper

TO GARNISH
natural yogurt
coriander sprigs

Heat the oil in a saucepan, add the onion and red pepper and fry for 3–4 minutes. Stir in the sweet potatoes, cumin and tomatoes and cook for a further 2–3 minutes.

Pour in the stock and bring to the boil, then reduce the heat and simmer for 12 minutes. Stir in the creamed coconut and cook for a further 2–3 minutes.

Leave the soup to cool slightly, then purée in the pan with a stick blender or in batches in a blender or food processor until smooth, returning to the pan. Reheat gently and season to taste with salt and pepper.

Ladle the soup into bowls and garnish each serving with a swirl of natural yogurt and a coriander sprig.

96

next time...

For sweet potato & parsnip soup, fry the onion in the oil as in the previous recipe, but omit the red pepper. Stir in 500 g (1 lb) sweet potatoes, diced, 200 g (7 oz) parsnip, diced, and 2 garlic cloves, finely chopped, with the cumin and tomatoes and cook for a further 2–3 minutes. Pour in the vegetable stock and then continue as before.

97

caribbean pepper pot soup

SERVES 6

2 tablespoons olive oil
1 onion, finely chopped
1 Scotch bonnet chilli, deseeded and finely
    chopped, or 2 hot red Thai chillies with seeds,
    chopped
2 red peppers, cored, deseeded and diced
2 garlic cloves, finely chopped
1 large carrot, diced
200 g (7 oz) potato, diced
1 bay leaf
1 thyme sprig
400 ml (14 fl oz) can full-fat coconut milk
600 ml (1 pint) beef stock (see page 9)
cayenne pepper, to taste
salt

TO GARNISH
200 g (7 oz) rump steak
2 teaspoons olive oil

Heat the oil in a large saucepan, add the
onion and fry gently for 5 minutes, stirring
frequently, until softened and just beginning
to turn golden. Stir in the chilli, red peppers,
garlic, carrot, potato and herbs and fry for
5 minutes, stirring.

Pour in the coconut milk and stock and season
to taste with salt and cayenne. Bring to the
boil, stirring, then reduce the heat, cover and
simmer for 30 minutes, or until the vegetables
are tender. Discard the herbs, then taste and
adjust the seasoning if needed.

Rub the steak with the oil and season lightly
with salt and cayenne. Heat a griddle pan or
frying pan over a high heat, and when hot, add
the steak and fry for 2–5 minutes on each side,
according to your liking. Remove the steak
from the pan and leave to rest for 5 minutes,
then slice thinly.

Ladle the soup into bowls, garnish with the
steak slices and serve with crusty bread.

98

next time...

For prawn & spinach pepper pot soup, make the
soup as in the previous recipe, replacing the
beef stock with 600 ml (1 pint) fish stock. After
simmering for 30 minutes, stir in 200 g (7 oz)
raw peeled prawns, defrosted, rinsed with cold
water and drained if frozen, and 125 g (4 oz)
spinach leaves. Simmer for 3–4 minutes until
the prawns turn pink and are cooked through
and the spinach is just wilted, then serve the
soup immediately.

99

london particular

SERVES 6

300 g (10 oz) dried green split peas, soaked
   in cold water overnight
25 g (1 oz) butter
4 rindless smoked streaky bacon rashers,
   diced, plus 4 grilled and diced
   to garnish
1 onion, roughly chopped
1 carrot, diced
2 celery sticks, diced
1.5 litres (2½ pints) ham or chicken stock
   (see page 9)
salt and pepper
handful of parsley, chopped, to garnish

Drain the soaked split peas in a colander, rinse
under cold running water and drain again.

Melt the butter in a large saucepan, add the raw
diced bacon and onion and fry for 5 minutes,
stirring occasionally, until the onion is softened.
Add the carrot and celery and fry for 5 minutes,
stirring, until golden.

Add the split peas and stock and bring to the
boil, stirring. Boil rapidly for 10 minutes, then
reduce the heat, cover and simmer for 1 hour,
or until the peas are tender.

Leave to cool slightly, then purée half the soup,
in batches if necessary, in a blender or food
processor until smooth. Return the purée to the
pan and reheat, then season to taste with salt
and pepper.

Ladle the soup into bowls and sprinkle the
chopped parsley and diced grilled bacon over
the top to garnish.

100

next time...

For mixed pea broth, soak 300 g (10 oz) dried
soup mix (a blend of yellow and green split
peas, pearl barley and red lentils) in cold water
overnight. Make the soup as in the previous
recipe, replacing the soaked green split peas
with the drained soaked soup mix. Serve topped
with 4 slices of bread cut from a white bread roll,
toasted and spread with 25 g (1 oz) butter mixed
with 2 teaspoons anchovy relish or 3 drained
canned anchovies, finely chopped.

101

callaloo

SERVES 6

3 tablespoons groundnut oil
1 large onion, finely chopped
4 spring onions, finely chopped
2 garlic cloves, crushed
1 red chilli, deseeded and finely chopped
1 teaspoon ground turmeric
1 thyme sprig, crumbled
250 g (8 oz) okra, conical stalk end discarded
    and thinly sliced
500 g (1 lb) callaloo or spinach leaves, tough
    stems discarded and roughly chopped
900 ml (1½ pints) vegetable or chicken stock
    (see pages 10 and 9)
a few saffron threads
425 ml (14 fl oz) full-fat coconut milk
250 g (8 oz) fresh or canned crab meat
juice of ½ lime
dash of hot pepper sauce
salt and pepper

Heat the oil in a large saucepan, add the onion,
spring onions and garlic and fry gently for 5
minutes, or until softened, stirring frequently.
Add the chilli, turmeric and thyme and stir over
a low heat for 1–2 minutes.

Stir in the okra, then add the callaloo or spinach
leaves. Turn up the heat and cook, stirring,
until the leaves start to wilt. Reduce the heat
and add the stock and saffron. Bring to the boil,
then reduce the heat, cover and simmer for
20 minutes.

Add the coconut milk and crab meat and stir
well. Heat gently for 4–5 minutes and then
season to taste with salt and pepper. Just before
serving the soup, stir in the lime juice and hot
pepper sauce.

102

oven-baked vegetable
soup

SERVES 4

1 onion, roughly chopped
2 garlic cloves, chopped
2 large carrots, thinly sliced
1 leek, thickly sliced
1 large parsnip, diced
175 g (6 oz) swede, diced
4 tablespoons olive oil
2 teaspoons clear honey
4 thyme sprigs
4 rosemary sprigs
2 bay leaves
4 ripe tomatoes, quartered
1.2 litres (2 pints) vegetable stock (see page 10)
salt and pepper

Toss the onion, garlic, carrots, leek, parsnip
and swede with the oil and honey in a bowl,
then put into a roasting tin and add all the
herbs. Roast in a preheated oven, 200°C (400°F),
Gas Mark 6, for about 50 minutes–1 hour, or
until all the vegetables are golden and tender,
adding the tomatoes halfway through. Remove
from the oven and reduce the oven temperature
to 190°C (375°F), Gas Mark 5.

Remove and discard the herbs, then transfer
the roasted vegetables to a blender or food
processor. Add half the stock and purée until
smooth, then blend in the remaining stock.

Pour the soup into a casserole dish and season
to taste with salt and pepper. Cover and bake
for 20 minutes, or until heated through.

Serve in soup bowls with slices of buttered toast.

103

pork & beetroot goulash soup

SERVES 4

2 tablespoons olive oil
450 g (14½ oz) boneless lean pork, diced
2 onions, sliced
1 teaspoon hot smoked paprika
1 teaspoon caraway seeds
750 g (1½ lb) piece of smoked bacon knuckle
3 bay leaves
1.2 litres (2 pints) water
300 g (10 oz) raw beetroot, peeled and diced
300 g (10 oz) red cabbage, finely sliced
3 tablespoons tomato purée

Heat the oil in a large saucepan, add the pork and fry until browned all over. Add the onions, paprika and caraway and fry for 5 minutes, or until the onions are browned.

Add the piece of bacon knuckle, the bay leaves and measured water. Bring to the boil, then reduce the heat to its lowest setting, cover and simmer very gently for 2 hours, or until the bacon knuckle is very tender and the meat falls easily from the bone.

Lift the knuckle out with a slotted spoon on to a plate and leave until cool enough to handle. Pull the meat from the bone and shred it back into the pan, discarding the skin.

Add the beetroot, cabbage and tomato purée to the pan, re-cover and simmer for 15 minutes, or until the beetroot and cabbage are tender. Taste and adjust the seasoning if needed.

Ladle the soup into bowls and serve with rye bread, if liked.

104

next time...

For pork & beetroot chilli soup, brown the pork in the oil as in the previous recipe, then mix in the onions, replacing the hot smoked paprika and caraway seeds with 1 teaspoon chilli powder and ½ teaspoon each ground cumin and allspice. Fry for 5 minutes, stirring frequently. Add the bacon knuckle and water, omitting the bay leaves, and bring to the boil, then cover and simmer very gently for 1½ hours. Take the meat off the knuckle bone and cut into small pieces, then return to pan with the diced beetroot as before, along with a rinsed and drained 400 g (14 oz) can red kidney beans, 25 g (1 oz) dark chocolate and 2 tablespoons tomato purée. Re-cover and simmer for 15 minutes, or until the beetroot is tender. Ladle the soup into bowls and top with tortilla chips and spoonfuls of guacamole.

105
chicken mulligatawny
soup

SERVES 6

1 tablespoon sunflower oil
1 onion, finely chopped
1 carrot, diced
1 dessert apple, peeled, cored and diced
2 garlic cloves, finely chopped
250 g (8 oz) tomatoes, skinned if liked and
    roughly chopped
4 teaspoons medium curry paste
50 g (2 oz) sultanas
125 g (4 oz) dried red lentils, rinsed and drained
1.5 litres (2½ pints) chicken stock (see page 9)
125 g (4 oz) leftover cooked chicken, cut into
    shreds
salt and pepper
coriander sprigs, to garnish

Heat the oil in a saucepan, add the onion
and carrot and fry for 5 minutes, stirring
frequently, until softened and just turning
golden around the edges. Stir in the apple,
garlic, tomatoes and curry paste and cook for
2 minutes.

Add the sultanas, lentils and stock, season to
taste with salt and pepper and bring to the boil.
Reduce the heat, cover and simmer for 1 hour
until the lentils are soft.

Mash the soup to make a coarse purée. Add the
cooked chicken and heat thoroughly, then taste
and adjust the seasoning if needed.

Ladle the soup into bowls and garnish with
coriander sprigs. Serve with poppadums or
warm naan bread.

106
next time...

For citrus carrot mulligatawny soup, fry
1 onion, finely chopped, and 500 g (1 lb) carrots,
diced, in 2 tablespoons sunflower oil in a
saucepan for 5 minutes. Omitting the apple,
garlic, tomatoes, curry paste and sultanas,
stir in the red lentils as in the previous recipe,
along with the grated rind and juice of 1 orange
and ½ lemon. Replace the chicken stock with
1.5 litres (2½ pints) vegetable stock (see page
10), then continue cooking the soup as before.
Leave the soup to cool slightly, then purée
in the pan with a stick blender or in batches
in a blender or food processor until smooth,
returning to the pan. Reheat, then taste and
adjust the seasoning. Serve with croûtons (see
page 13).

107

tomato & bread soup

SERVES 4

1 kg (2 lb) really ripe vine tomatoes, skinned, deseeded and chopped
300 ml (½ pint) vegetable stock (see page 10)
6 tablespoons extra virgin olive oil
2 garlic cloves, crushed
1 teaspoon sugar
2 tablespoons chopped basil, plus extra leaves to garnish
100 g (3½ oz) ciabatta bread
1 tablespoon balsamic vinegar
salt and pepper

Put the tomatoes into a saucepan with the stock, 2 tablespoons of the oil, the garlic, sugar and chopped basil. Bring to the boil slowly, then reduce the heat, cover and simmer gently for 30 minutes.

Crumble the bread into the soup and stir over a low heat until it has thickened. Stir in the vinegar and the remaining oil and season to taste with salt and pepper. Serve immediately, or leave to cool to room temperature if preferred. Garnish with basil leaves.

108

next time...

For tomato & bread soup with roasted peppers, halve, core and deseed 1 red and 1 orange pepper. Arrange skin-side up in a foil-lined grill pan, brush with 1 tablespoon olive oil and cook under a hot grill for 10 minutes until the skins are blackened and the peppers are softened. Wrap the foil around the peppers, then leave them to cool for 10 minutes. Peel the skins off the peppers and slice. Add to a saucepan with 1.5 kg (3 lb) skinned and deseeded tomatoes and the stock, oil, garlic, sugar and basil as in the recipe above. Bring to the boil slowly, then continue as above.

109

butter bean & tomato soup

SERVES 4

3 tablespoons olive oil
1 onion, finely chopped
2 celery sticks, thinly sliced
2 garlic cloves, thinly sliced
2 x 400 g (13 oz) cans butter beans, rinsed and drained
4 tablespoons tomato purée
900 ml (1½ pints) vegetable stock (see page 10)
1 tablespoon chopped thyme
salt and pepper
Parmesan cheese shavings, to garnish

Heat the oil in a saucepan, add the onion and fry for 3 minutes until softened. Add the celery and garlic and fry for 2 minutes.

Stir in the beans, tomato purée, stock, thyme and a little salt and pepper. Bring to the boil, then reduce the heat, cover and simmer gently for 15 minutes. Sprinkle with Parmesan shavings and serve with bread.

110

next time...

For spiced carrot, lentil & tomato soup, heat 2 tablespoons olive oil in a saucepan and fry 1 onion, chopped, 2 garlic cloves, crushed, and 375 g (12 oz) carrots, chopped, for 10 minutes. Instead of butter beans, add a rinsed and drained 400 g (13 oz) can green lentils, 2 teaspoons ground coriander, 1 teaspoon ground cumin and 1 tablespoon chopped thyme and fry for 1 minute. Stir in 1 litre (1¾ pints) stock, a 400 g (13 oz) can chopped tomatoes and 2 teaspoons lemon juice and bring to the boil. Reduce the heat, cover and simmer gently for 20 minutes. Purée in the pan with a stick blender or in batches in a blender or food processor until smooth, then reheat to serve.

111

white bean soup with toasted garlic & chilli oil

SERVES 6

250 g (8 oz) dried white beans, such as haricot or cannellini, soaked in cold water overnight
vegetable or chicken stock (see pages 10 and 9), or cold water, to cover
handful of sage leaves
150 ml (¼ pint) olive oil
4 garlic cloves, 2 finely chopped, 2 thinly sliced
2 tablespoons chopped sage or rosemary
large pinch of chilli flakes
salt and pepper
roughly chopped parsley, to garnish

Drain the beans and put them into a flameproof casserole dish. Cover with stock or water to a depth of 5 cm (2 inches) above the beans and push the sage leaves in among the beans. Bring to the boil, then cover tightly and bake in a preheated oven, 160°C (325°F), Gas Mark 3, for 40 minutes–1 hour until the beans are tender, depending on their freshness. Leave them in their cooking liquid.

Put half the beans, the cooked sage leaves and all the liquid into a blender or food processor and purée until smooth. Return the purée to the soup. If the soup is thicker than liked, add extra water or stock to thin it.

Heat half the oil in a frying pan, add the chopped garlic and fry gently, stirring frequently, until soft and golden. Add the chopped sage or rosemary and fry, stirring, for 30 seconds. Stir the mixture into the soup and reheat until boiling, then reduce the heat and simmer gently for 10 minutes. Season well with salt and pepper. Pour into a tureen or ladle into soup bowls.

Heat the remaining oil in the frying pan, add the sliced garlic and fry gently until golden (don't let it become too dark, or it will be bitter), then stir in the chilli flakes. Dip the base of the pan into cold water to stop the garlic cooking, then spoon the garlic and oil over the soup. Sprinkle with chopped parsley to garnish and serve immediately.

112

next time...

For white bean & rocket soup, cook the beans in the stock or water with the sage leaves as in the previous recipe. Then purée half the beans, the cooked sage and all the liquid with 40 g (1½ oz) rocket leaves until smooth. Mix with the remaining beans and continue as before.

113

squash, kale & mixed bean soup

SERVES 6

1 tablespoon olive oil
1 onion, finely chopped
2 garlic cloves, finely chopped
1 teaspoon smoked paprika
500 g (1 lb) butternut squash, sliced, deseeded, peeled and diced
2 small carrots, diced
500 g (1 lb) tomatoes, skinned if liked and roughly chopped
410 g (13½ oz) can mixed beans, drained
900 ml (1½ pints) vegetable or chicken stock (see pages 10 and 9)
150 g (5 oz) full-fat crème fraîche
100 g (3½ oz) kale, torn into bite-sized pieces
salt and pepper

Heat the oil in a saucepan, add the onion and fry gently for 5 minutes, stirring frequently. Stir in the garlic and smoked paprika and cook briefly, then add the squash, carrots, tomatoes and beans.

Pour over the stock, season to taste with salt and pepper and bring to the boil, stirring. Reduce the heat, cover and simmer for 25 minutes until the vegetables are tender.

Stir the crème fraîche into the soup, then add the kale, pressing it just beneath the surface of the stock. Re-cover and cook for 5 minutes until the kale has just wilted.

Ladle the soup into bowls and serve with warm garlic bread.

114

next time...

For cheesy squash, pepper & mixed bean soup, fry the onion in the oil, then add the garlic, smoked paprika, squash, tomatoes and beans as in the previous recipe, replacing the carrots with 1 red pepper, cored, deseeded and diced. Pour over the stock, add 65 g (2½ oz) Parmesan rinds and season to taste with salt and pepper. Bring to the boil, then reduce heat, cover and simmer for 25 minutes. Stir in the crème fraîche but omit the kale. Discard the Parmesan rinds, ladle the soup into bowls and top with freshly grated Parmesan cheese.

115

mackerel & cider
vichyssoise

SERVES 3–4

50 g (2 oz) butter
625 g (1¼ lb) leeks, chopped, white and green
  parts kept separate
625 g (1¼ lb) new potatoes, diced
600 ml (1 pint) strong cider
600 ml (1 pint) fish stock (see page 10)
2 teaspoons Dijon mustard
300 g (10 oz) smoked mackerel fillets
5 tablespoons chopped chives, plus extra sprigs
  to garnish
plenty of freshly ground nutmeg
200 g (7 oz) crème fraîche
salt and pepper

Melt the butter in a large saucepan, add
the white leek parts and half the green leek
parts and gently fry for 5 minutes, stirring
occasionally. Add the potatoes, then stir in the
cider, stock and mustard and bring almost to
the boil. Reduce the heat and simmer gently for
20 minutes until the potatoes are soft but still
holding their shape.

Flake the smoked mackerel into small pieces,
discarding any skin and stray bones. Add to
the pan with the chopped chives, nutmeg and
remaining green leek parts. Simmer gently for
5 minutes.

Stir in half the crème fraîche and season to
taste with salt and pepper. Spoon into bowls,
top with the remaining crème fraîche and
garnish with chive sprigs.

116

next time...

For trout & white wine vichyssoise, make the
soup as in the previous recipe, replacing the
cider with 300 ml (½ pint) dry white wine and
using 900 ml (1½ pints) fish stock. Then replace
the mackerel with 500 g (1 lb) skinless rainbow
trout fillets and flake and cook as before.
Replace the crème fraîche with 150 ml (¼ pint)
single cream.

117

butternut squash
& rosemary soup

SERVES 4

1 butternut squash
2 tablespoons olive oil
a few rosemary sprigs, plus extra to garnish
150 g (5 oz) dried red lentils, rinsed and drained
1 onion, finely chopped
900 ml (1½ pints) vegetable stock (see page 10)
salt and pepper

Cut the squash in half, then use a spoon to scoop out the seeds and fibrous flesh and discard. Peel and cut the squash into small chunks. Put into a roasting tin, sprinkle over the oil and rosemary and season well with salt and pepper. Roast in a preheated oven, 200°C (400°F), Gas Mark 6, for 45 minutes.

Meanwhile, put the lentils in a saucepan, cover with water, bring to the boil and boil rapidly for 10 minutes. Drain and transfer the lentils to a clean saucepan with the onion and stock, bring to a simmer and cook for 5 minutes. Season to taste with salt and pepper.

Remove the squash from the oven, mash the flesh with a fork and add to the soup. Bring to the boil, then cover, reduce the heat and simmer for 25 minutes.

Ladle the soup into bowls and garnish with extra rosemary before serving.

118

next time...

For Indian spiced butternut squash soup, roast the squash, and cook and drain the lentils as in the previous recipe. Heat 1 tablespoon sunflower oil in a saucepan, add 1 onion, chopped, and fry for 5 minutes until softened. Stir in 2 teaspoons mild curry paste and a 3.5 cm (1½ inch) piece of fresh root ginger, peeled and finely chopped. Add the lentils and 900 ml (1½ pints) vegetable stock, bring to a simmer and cook for 5 minutes. Mash the roasted squash, add to the soup and finish cooking as before. Serve the soup garnished with torn coriander leaves.

119

fragrant tofu & noodle soup

SERVES 2

125 g (4 oz) firm tofu, diced
1 tablespoon sesame oil
75 g (3 oz) dried thin rice noodles
600 ml (1 pint) vegetable stock (see page 10)
2.5 cm (1 inch) piece of fresh root ginger, peeled
    and thickly sliced
1 large garlic clove, thickly sliced
3 dried kaffir lime leaves, torn in half
2 lemon grass stalks, halved and lightly bruised
handful of spinach or pak choi leaves
50 g (2 oz) bean sprouts
1-2 red chillies, deseeded and finely sliced
2 tablespoons coriander leaves
1 tablespoon Thai fish sauce

TO SERVE
chilli sauce
lime wedges

Put the tofu on a plate lined with kitchen paper and leave to stand for 10 minutes to drain.

Heat the oil in a wok until hot, add the tofu and fry for 2-3 minutes until golden brown, stirring frequently.

Meanwhile, soak the noodles in boiling water for 2 minutes, then drain.

Pour the stock into a large saucepan. Add the ginger, garlic, lime leaves and lemon grass and bring to the boil. Reduce the heat, add the tofu, noodles, spinach or pak choi, bean sprouts and chilli and heat through. Add the coriander and fish sauce, then pour into deep bowls. Serve with chilli sauce and lime wedges so that diners can season the soup to taste.

120

next time...

For tofu & satay soup, fry the tofu and soak and drain the noodles as in the previous recipe. Add the ginger and garlic to the stock, omitting the lime leaves and lemon grass, then stir in 2 tablespoons crunchy peanut butter and 1 tablespoon soy sauce. Simmer for 3 minutes, then add the tofu, noodles, spinach or pak choi, bean sprouts and chilli and heat through. Sprinkle with coriander leaves and serve with lime wedges.

121

kale soup with garlic croûtons

SERVES 8–10

50 g (2 oz) butter
1 onion, chopped
2 carrots, sliced
500 g (1 lb) kale, thick stems discarded, plus
    2 kale leaves, finely shredded, to garnish
1.2 litres (2 pints) water
600 ml (1 pint) vegetable stock (see page 10)
1 tablespoon lemon juice
300 g (10 oz) potatoes, sliced
pinch of grated nutmeg
salt and pepper

GARLIC CROÛTONS
6–8 tablespoons olive oil
3 garlic cloves, sliced
6–8 slices of white or brown bread, crusts
    removed, cut into 1 cm (½ inch) cubes

Melt the butter in a large saucepan, add the onion and fry for 5 minutes until softened and just beginning to turn golden. Add the carrots and kale in batches and cook for 2 minutes, stirring constantly.

Add the measured water, stock, lemon juice, potatoes and nutmeg, and season to taste with salt and pepper. Bring to the boil, stirring occasionally, then reduce the heat, cover and simmer for 35 minutes, or until all the vegetables are soft. Purée in batches in a blender or food processor, adding extra water if it is too thick. Return to the pan.

Heat the oil for the croûtons in a large frying pan, add the garlic and cook over a medium heat for 1 minute. Add the bread cubes and fry, turning frequently, until evenly golden brown. Remove the croûtons with a slotted spoon and drain on kitchen paper. Discard the garlic, then add the finely shredded kale to the pan and fry, stirring constantly, until crispy.

Taste the soup and adjust the seasoning if needed, then reheat without boiling. Serve in soup bowls with the croûtons and crispy kale.

122

next time...

For spiced kale soup with garlic & chilli croûtons, fry the onion and add the carrots and kale in batches as in the previous recipe, then stir in 1 teaspoon smoked paprika and 2 garlic cloves, chopped, and cook for 2 minutes, stirring constantly. Continue making the soup as before, but add ¼ teaspoon chilli flakes to the oil when frying the croûtons.

123

bloody mary soup

SERVES 6

1 tablespoon olive oil, plus extra to serve
1 onion, chopped
1 red pepper, cored, deseeded and diced
2 celery sticks, sliced, plus 6 small celery sticks
    with leaves to garnish
500 g (1 lb) plum tomatoes, chopped
900 ml (1½ pints) vegetable stock (see page 10)
2 teaspoons caster sugar
4 teaspoons Worcestershire sauce
4 teaspoons tomato purée
4 tablespoons vodka
a few drops of Tabasco sauce
salt and pepper

Heat the oil in a saucepan, add the onion and
fry for 5 minutes until softened. Stir in the red
pepper, celery and tomatoes and cook for
5 minutes, stirring occasionally. Add the stock,
sugar, Worcestershire sauce, tomato purée and
a little salt and pepper and bring to the boil,
then reduce the heat, cover and simmer for
15 minutes.

Leave the soup to cool slightly, then purée in
batches in a blender or food processor until
smooth. Pass the purée through a fine sieve into
a large bowl if you want an extra-smooth soup.
Stir in the vodka and Tabasco and taste and
adjust the seasoning if needed. Cover and chill
in the refrigerator for at least 3 hours.

Ladle the soup into small bowls or glasses and
add the small celery sticks with leaves, drizzle
with a little extra olive oil and sprinkle with a
little extra pepper to garnish.

124

next time...

For Virgin Mary & pesto soup, make the soup
as in the previous recipe, replacing the tomato
purée with 4 teaspoons sun-dried tomato paste,
then purée with 1 tablespoon pesto. Chill as
before and serve with a little extra pesto added
to each bowl, garnished with a few tiny basil
leaves.

125

beer broth with mini meatballs

SERVES 6

25 g (1 oz) butter
1 onion, chopped
200 g (7 oz) potato, diced
125 g (4 oz) swede or parsnip, diced
1 carrot, diced
2 tomatoes, skinned and roughly chopped
½ lemon, sliced
900 ml (1½ pints) beef stock (see page 9)
450 ml (¾ pint) can lager
¼ teaspoon ground cinnamon
¼ teaspoon grated nutmeg
100 g (3½ oz) green cabbage, finely shredded
salt and pepper

MEATBALLS
250 g (8 oz) extra-lean minced beef
40 g (1½ oz) long-grain white rice
3 tablespoons chopped parsley, plus extra
    to garnish (optional)
¼ teaspoon grated nutmeg

Melt the butter in a large saucepan, add the onion and fry gently for 5 minutes until just turning golden around the edges. Stir in the root vegetables, tomatoes and lemon slices.

Pour in the stock and lager, then add the spices and season well with salt and pepper. Bring to the boil, stirring, then reduce the heat, cover and simmer for 45 minutes.

Meanwhile, mix all the meatball ingredients together in a bowl. Divide the mixture into 18 equal-sized portions and shape into small balls with wetted hands. Cover and chill in the refrigerator until needed.

Add the meatballs to the soup and bring the soup back to the boil, then reduce the heat, cover and simmer for 10 minutes. Add the cabbage, re-cover and simmer for a further 10 minutes until tender and the meatballs are cooked through. Taste and adjust the seasoning if needed. Ladle into bowls and sprinkle with a little chopped parsley to garnish, if liked.

126

next time...

For beer broth with suet dumplings, gently fry 500 g (1 lb) onions, thinly sliced, in the butter for 20 minutes until very soft. Sprinkle with 2 teaspoons brown sugar and fry for a further 10 minutes, stirring frequently, until it becomes caramelized. Add the lemon slices, stock, lager and spices as in the previous recipe, omitting the root vegetables and tomatoes. Bring to the boil, then cover and simmer for 20 minutes. Mix 100 g (3½ oz) self-raising flour with 50 g (2 oz) vegetable suet, 2 tablespoons chopped parsley and salt and pepper in a bowl. Stir in 4 tablespoons water, then shape into small balls. Add to the simmering soup, re-cover and cook for 10 minutes until light and fluffy, then ladle into bowls and serve immediately.

127

cheesy butternut squash soup

SERVES 6

2 tablespoons olive oil
1 onion, roughly chopped
1 butternut squash, about 750 g (1½ lb), halved,
    deseeded, peeled and cut into chunks
1–2 garlic cloves, finely chopped
2 large sage sprigs
1 litre (1¾ pints) vegetable and chicken stock
    (see pages 10 and 9)
65 g (2½ oz) Parmesan cheese rinds
salt and pepper

TO FINISH
vegetable oil, for deep-frying
1 small bunch of sage
grated Parmesan cheese

Heat the oil in a saucepan, add the onion and fry
for 5 minutes until softened and just beginning
to turn golden. Add the squash, garlic and sage
and fry for 5 minutes, stirring.

Pour in the stock, add the Parmesan rinds and
season well with salt and pepper. Bring to the
boil, then reduce the heat, cover and simmer for
45 minutes until the squash is tender.

Remove and discard the sage and Parmesan
rinds. Leave the soup to cool slightly, then purée
in the pan with a stick blender or in batches
in a blender or food processor until smooth,
returning to the pan. Reheat, adding extra stock
if needed, then taste and adjust the seasoning.

Fill a small saucepan halfway with oil and heat
until a cube of day-old bread sizzles the moment
it is added. Tear the sage leaves from the stems,
add to the hot oil and fry for 1–2 minutes until
crisp. Remove with a slotted spoon and drain on
kitchen paper.

Ladle the soup into bowls and top with some
of the crispy sage and a sprinkling of grated
Parmesan, serving the remaining leaves and
extra Parmesan in small bowls for diners to add
their own as desired.

128

next time...

For Halloween pumpkin soup, fry the onion in
the oil as in the previous recipe. Add a 1.5 kg
(3 lb) pumpkin, quartered, deseeded, peeled
and cut into cubes, to the onion and fry for
5 minutes. Stir in 1 teaspoon each ground
cumin, coriander and ginger instead of the
garlic and sage, then pour in the stock. Bring to
the boil, then cover and simmer for 30 minutes.
Purée and reheat the soup as before to serve,
omitting the crispy sage and grated Parmesan.

129

russian borscht

SERVES 6

25 g (1 oz) butter
1 tablespoon sunflower oil
1 onion, finely chopped
375 g (12 oz) raw beetroot, peeled and diced
2 carrots, diced
2 celery sticks, diced
150 g (5 oz) red cabbage, cored and chopped
300 g (10 oz) potatoes, diced
2 garlic cloves, finely chopped
1.5 litres (2½ pints) beef stock (see page 9)
1 tablespoon tomato purée
6 tablespoons red wine vinegar
1 tablespoon brown sugar
2 bay leaves

TO FINISH
200 ml (7 fl oz) soured cream
1 small bunch of dill, fronds torn

Melt the butter with the oil in a saucepan, add the onion and fry for 5 minutes until softened. Add the beetroot, carrots, celery, red cabbage, potatoes and garlic and fry for 5 minutes, stirring frequently.

Stir in the stock, tomato purée, vinegar and sugar. Add the bay leaves and season well with salt and pepper. Bring to the boil, then reduce the heat, cover and simmer for 45 minutes until the vegetables are tender. Remove and discard the bay leaves, then taste and adjust the seasoning if needed.

Ladle into bowls and top with spoonfuls of the soured cream, torn dill fronds and a grinding of pepper. Serve with rye bread.

130

next time...

For vegetarian borscht with pinched dumplings, soak 40 g (1½ oz) dried mushrooms in 300 ml (½ pint) boiling water for 15 minutes. Make the soup as in the previous recipe, replacing the beef stock with 1.2 litres (2 pints) vegetable stock (see page 10) and adding the soaked mushrooms and their liquid. For the dumplings, mix 125 g (4 oz) plain flour, ¼ teaspoon caraway seeds and salt and pepper together in a bowl, then stir in 2 beaten eggs and enough water to form a smooth dough. Shape into a log, pinch off pieces and add to the simmering soup. Re-cover and cook for 10 minutes until spongy, before serving without the soured cream and dill.

131

spinach bouillabaisse

SERVES 6

2 tablespoons olive oil
1 onion, finely chopped
1 fennel bulb, trimmed and any green feathery
    fronds reserved, cored and diced
400 g (13 oz) potatoes, diced
4 garlic cloves, finely chopped
3 large pinches of saffron threads
1.8 litres (3 pints) vegetable or chicken stock
    (see pages 10 and 9)
150 ml (¼ pint) dry white wine
125 g (4 oz) baby spinach leaves
6 eggs
salt and pepper

Heat the oil in a large saucepan (or shallow sauté pan if possible), add the onion and fry for 5 minutes until just beginning to soften. Add in the diced fennel, potatoes and garlic and fry for a further 5 minutes, stirring.

Mix in the saffron, stock and wine, then season to taste with salt and pepper and bring to the boil. Reduce the heat, cover and simmer for 15 minutes, or until the potatoes are tender, stirring occasionally.

Add the spinach, tearing the larger leaves into pieces, and simmer for 2–3 minutes until just beginning to wilt. Taste and adjust the seasoning if needed. Lift most of the vegetables out with a slotted spoon and divide among shallow serving bowls.

Add the eggs one at a time to the remaining hot stock, leaving a little space between them, and simmer gently for 3–4 minutes until the whites are just set and the yolks are cooked to your liking.

Lift the poached eggs out of the soup carefully with a slotted spoon and place on top of the vegetables in the soup bowls. Ladle the stock around the eggs and top with any reserved, snipped green fennel fronds and a grinding of pepper. Serve with toasted olive ciabatta bread.

132

next time...

For creamy spinach & fennel soup, make the soup as in the previous recipe but using 1.2 litres (2 pints) stock with the white wine. Once the spinach has just wilted, leave the soup to cool slightly, then purée in the pan with a stick blender or in batches in a blender or food processor, returning to the pan. Reheat, omit the eggs and serve topped with spoonfuls of crème fraîche and some fennel or dill fronds.

133

crab bisque

SERVES 6

25 g (1 oz) butter
1 onion, roughly chopped
2 tablespoons brandy
40 g (1½ oz) long-grain white rice
300 ml (½ pint) fish stock (see page 10)
150 g (5 oz) prepared crab on the shell, plus
    1 crab to garnish (optional)
2 canned anchovy fillets, drained and chopped
½ teaspoon mild paprika, plus extra to garnish
cayenne pepper, to taste
200 ml (7 fl oz) milk
150 ml (¼ pint) double cream
salt

Melt the butter in a saucepan, add the onion and fry gently for 5 minutes until softened. Add the brandy, and when bubbling, flame with a long match and quickly stand back. As soon as the flames have subsided, stir in the rice and then pour in the stock.

Scoop the dark and white crab meat out of the shell into the pan and then mix in the anchovies and paprika. Season with a little salt and cayenne pepper and bring to the boil. Reduce the heat, cover and simmer for 20 minutes.

Leave the soup to cool slightly, then purée in the pan with a stick blender or in batches in a blender or food processor, returning to the pan. Stir in the milk and cream. Bring just to the boil, being careful not to overheat, then reduce the heat to a simmer, stirring until the soup is hot all the way through. Taste and adjust the seasoning if needed.

Pour the soup into teacups. Pick out the crab meat from the extra crab (if using) and flake into pieces. Serve in a separate bowl for diners to sprinkle over their soup and garnish with a little extra paprika.

134

next time...

For crab & salmon chowder, fry the onion in butter as in the previous recipe, then stir in 200 g (7 oz) potato, diced, and fry for 5 minutes. Add the brandy and flame as before. Mix in 600 ml (1 pint) fish stock along with the dark and white crab meat, anchovies and paprika as before and bring to the boil, then cover and simmer for 15 minutes. Add 300 g (10 oz) salmon fillet, cut into 2 thick slices, re-cover and simmer for 10 minutes. Lift the salmon out with a slotted spoon and break into flakes, discarding the skin and any stray bones. Return the salmon to the soup and stir in 200 ml (7 fl oz) milk and 150 ml (¼ pint) double cream. Reheat gently before serving.

135

apple & celery soup

SERVES 6

25 g (1 oz) butter
1 onion, roughly chopped
1 baking potato, about 250 g (8 oz), diced
1 cooking apple, about 250 g (8 oz), quartered,
    cored, peeled and diced
1 head of celery, base trimmed
750 ml (1¼ pints) vegetable and chicken stock
    (see pages 10 and 9)
300 ml (½ pint) milk
salt and pepper

STILTON & WALNUT CREAM
50 g (2 oz) Stilton, rinded and diced
25 g (1 oz) walnut pieces, chopped
6 tablespoons full-fat crème fraîche
2 tablespoons chopped chives or green parts of
    2 spring onions, chopped

Melt the butter in a saucepan, add the onion and
fry for 5 minutes until just beginning to soften.
Stir in the potato and apple, cover and fry gently
for 10 minutes, stirring occasionally.

Thickly slice the celery sticks, add with the leaves
to the onion mixture and cook for 2–3 minutes,
stirring. Pour over the stock, season to taste with
salt and pepper and bring to the boil. Reduce the
heat, cover and simmer for 15 minutes until the
celery is soft but still a pale green.

Leave the soup to cool slightly, then purée
in the pan with a stick blender or in batches
in a blender or food processor until smooth,
returning to the pan. Add the milk and reheat.
Taste and adjust the seasoning if needed.

Stir half the Stilton and half the walnuts into
the crème fraîche in a small bowl, then mix in
the chives or spring onion and a little salt and
pepper. Ladle the soup into shallow bowls, then
spoon the crème fraîche mixture into the centre.
Sprinkle with the remaining cheese and nuts and
add a grinding of pepper.

136

next time...

For apple & parsnip soup, fry the onion in the
butter as in the previous recipe and then the
apple along with 625 g (1¼ lb) parsnips, diced,
omitting the potato. Stir in 1½ teaspoons
crushed cumin seeds and ½ teaspoon ground
turmeric, then mix in 900 ml (1½ pints) chicken
or vegetable stock and season to taste with salt
and pepper. Bring to the boil, then reduce the
heat, cover and then simmer for 45 minutes.
Purée and reheat with the milk, then make
the Stilton and crème fraîche cream as before,
but adding ½ teaspoon finely chopped red
chilli instead of the walnuts. Sprinkle with the
remaining cheese before serving.

137

split pea & parsnip
soup

SERVES 6

250 g (8 oz) dried yellow split peas, soaked in
    cold water overnight
300 g (10 oz) parsnips, cut into chunks
1 onion, roughly chopped
1.5 litres (2½ pints) vegetable and chicken stock
    (see pages 10 and 9)
salt and pepper

CORIANDER BUTTER
1 teaspoon cumin seeds, roughly crushed
1 teaspoon coriander seeds, roughly crushed
2 garlic cloves, finely chopped
75 g (3 oz) butter, softened
1 small bunch of coriander

Drain the soaked split peas in a colander, rinse
under cold running water and drain again.
Put them into a saucepan with the parsnips,
onion and stock. Bring to the boil and boil for
10 minutes. Reduce the heat, cover and simmer
for 1 hour, or until the split peas are soft.

Meanwhile, add the cumin and coriander seeds
and garlic for the butter to a small saucepan
and dry-fry over a medium heat until lightly
toasted. Mix into the butter with the coriander
leaves and a little salt and pepper. Roll the
butter up in clingfilm or foil into a log and chill
in the refrigerator until firm.

Roughly mash the soup or leave the soup to
cool slightly, then purée in the pan with a
stick blender or in batches in a blender or food
processor until smooth, returning to the pan.
Reheat, then stir in half the coriander butter
until melted. Add a little extra stock if needed
and season to taste with salt and pepper.

Ladle the soup into bowls and top each serving
with a slice of the remaining coriander butter.
Serve with toasted pitta breads.

138

next time...

For split pea & carrot soup with chilli butter,
make the soup as in the previous recipe,
replacing the parsnips with 300 g (10 oz)
carrots, diced. Meanwhile, make a chilli butter
by mixing 75 g (3 oz) butter with the grated rind
and juice of 1 lime, 2 spring onions, chopped,
and ½–1 large mild red chilli to taste, finely
chopped. Purée the soup and reheat, adding
half the chilli butter, then serve topped with the
remaining butter cut into slices as before.

139

lettuce, pea
& tarragon soup

SERVES 4

25 g (1 oz) butter
8 spring onions, sliced
750 g (1½ lb) frozen peas
1 tablespoon chopped tarragon leaves
1 Cos (Romaine) lettuce, finely shredded
1 litre (1¾ pints) hot vegetable stock (see
    page 10)
2 tablespoons double cream
salt and pepper
tarragon sprigs, to garnish (optional)

Melt the butter in a large saucepan, add the spring onions and fry for 2 minutes, stirring. Stir in the peas, half the tarragon and the lettuce and cook for 1 minute.

Pour in the stock and bring to the boil, then reduce the heat, cover and simmer for about 5 minutes, or until the vegetables are tender.

Leave the soup to cool slightly, then purée in a blender or food processor with the remaining tarragon until smooth. Season to taste with salt and pepper.

Pour the soup into bowls, swirl a litte of the cream into each bowl and add a grinding of pepper. Garnish with tarragon sprigs, if liked.

140

next time...

For **broccoli, green bean & lettuce soup**, fry the spring onions in the butter as in the previous recipe. Then mix in 500 g (1 lb) frozen broccoli and 250 g (8 oz) frozen sliced green beans with half the tarragon and the lettuce and continue making the soup as before.

141

roasted tomato soup

SERVES 4

1 kg (2 lb) ripe tomatoes, halved
4 garlic cloves, unpeeled
2 tablespoons olive oil
1 onion, chopped
1 carrot, chopped
1 celery stick, sliced
1 red pepper, cored, deseeded and chopped
700 ml (1 pint 3 fl oz) hot vegetable stock
  (see page 10)
4 tablespoons grated Parmesan cheese,
  for sprinkling
salt and pepper

Put the tomato halves and garlic cloves into a roasting tin. Sprinkle with 1 tablespoon of the olive oil and some pepper and roast in a preheated oven, 200°C (400°F), Gas Mark 6, for 20 minutes.

After 10 minutes, heat the remaining oil in a saucepan, add the onion, carrot, celery and red pepper and gently fry for 10 minutes.

Remove the roasting tin from the oven and leave the contents to cool slightly, then squeeze the garlic flesh from its skins into the saucepan. Stir in the roasted tomatoes and all their juices with the stock.

Purée the soup in the pan with a stick blender, or in batches in a blender or food processor until smooth, returning to the pan. Reheat and season to taste with salt and pepper. Ladle into bowls and sprinkle with the grated Parmesan.

142

next time...

For quick tomato soup, heat 2 tablespoons olive oil in a saucepan, add 1 onion, 1 carrot, 1 celery stick and 700 g (1½ lb) chopped tomatoes all chopped, and fry for 5 minutes. Pour in a 400 g (13 oz) can chopped tomatoes and 900 ml (1½ pints) hot vegetable stock. Add 1 tablespoon sundried tomato purée and simmer for 10 minutes, then add a small handful of basil leaves and leave to cool slightly. Purée in the pan with a stick blender, or in batches in a blender or food processor until smooth, returning to the pan. Reheat and season to taste with salt and pepper, then serve with an extra drizzle of olive oil.

143

basque fish soup

SERVES 6

2 tablespoons olive oil
1 onion, finely chopped
½ green pepper, cored, deseeded and diced
½ red pepper, cored, deseeded and diced
1 courgette, diced
2 garlic cloves, finely chopped
250 g (8 oz) potatoes, cut into chunks
½ teaspoon smoked paprika
150 ml (¼ pint) red wine
1 litre (1¾ pints) fish stock (see page 10)
400 g (13 oz) can chopped tomatoes
1 tablespoon tomato purée
2 whole mackerel, gutted and rinsed with cold
    water inside and out
cayenne pepper, to taste
salt

Heat the oil in a large saucepan, add the onion
and fry gently for 5 minutes until softened.
Add the peppers, courgette, garlic and potatoes
and fry for 5 minutes, stirring. Mix in the
paprika and cook for 1 minute.

Pour in the wine, stock, tomatoes, tomato
purée and salt and cayenne to taste. Bring to
the boil, stirring, then add the whole mackerel.
Reduce the heat, cover and simmer gently for
20 minutes until the fish flakes easily when
pressed with a knife.

Lift the fish out with a slotted spoon and put
on to a plate. Simmer the soup, uncovered, for
a further 15 minutes. Peel the skin off the fish,
then lift the flesh away from the backbone.
Flake into pieces, checking carefully for any
remaining bones.

Return the mackerel flakes to the soup and
reheat. Ladle into shallow bowls and serve
with lemon wedges and crusty bread.

144

next time...

For Portuguese fish soup, make the soup as
in the previous recipe, replacing the smoked
paprika with 2 bay leaves. Simmer for
20 minutes without the fish, then add 500 g
(1 lb) mixed tuna, cod or hake steaks and
250 g (8 oz) live mussels, scrubbed and
debearded and any cracked or open shells
discarded, instead of the mackerel. Cover and
simmer for 10 minutes, or until the mussels
have opened, then lift out both the mussels
and the fish steaks with a slotted spoon.
Flake the fish into pieces, discarding the skin
and any stray bones. Take the mussels out
of their shells, discarding any mussels that
remain closed. Return the fish and mussels
to the hot soup and serve sprinkled with
chopped coriander.

145

broccoli & cheese soup

serves 6

1 kg (2 lb) broccoli
50 g (2 oz) butter
1 onion, chopped
1 large potato, quartered
1.5 litres (2½ pints) vegetable stock (see
    page 10)
125 ml (4 fl oz) single cream
1 tablespoon lemon juice
1 teaspoon Worcestershire sauce
a few drops of Tabasco sauce, or to taste
125 g (4 oz) mature Cheddar cheese, grated
salt and pepper
watercress sprigs, to garnish

Cut off the broccoli stems, discarding any
tough parts, peel them and cut them into
2.5 cm (1 inch) pieces. Break the florets into
very small pieces and set them aside.

Melt the butter in a large saucepan and stir
in the onion and broccoli stems, then cover
and cook over a medium heat for 5 minutes,
stirring frequently.

Add the broccoli florets, potato and stock and
bring to the boil. Reduce the heat, half-cover
and simmer for 5 minutes. Season to taste
with salt and pepper and simmer for a further
20 minutes, or until all the vegetables are tender.

Leave the soup to cool slightly, then purée in
batches in a blender or food processor until
smooth. Transfer to a clean saucepan, add the
cream, lemon juice, Worcestershire sauce and
Tabasco and simmer gently for 3–5 minutes.
Don't allow the soup to boil, or it will curdle.
Just before serving, stir in the grated Cheddar.
Serve garnished with watercress sprigs.

146

next time...

For courgette soup with feta cheese, dice
1 kg (2 lb) courgettes and fry in the butter
with the onion instead of the broccoli as in the
previous recipe. Continue making the soup
as before, adding the potato and stock and
simmering until tender. Purée the soup with
the flesh scooped from 1 ripe avocado, halved
and stoned, then add the cream, lemon juice,
Worcestershire sauce and Tabasco as before
and gently heat through. Ladle into bowls and
top with 100 g (3½ oz) feta cheese, crumbled,
and some chopped mint.

147

cheat's bouillabaisse

SERVES 6

2 tablespoons olive oil
1 large onion, finely chopped
1 leek, thinly sliced
2 garlic cloves, finely chopped
500 g (1 lb) plum tomatoes, skinned and
    roughly chopped
2 large pinches of saffron threads, soaked in
    1 tablespoon boiling water for 10 minutes
150 ml (¼ pint) dry white wine
600 ml (1 pint) fish stock (see page 10)
2–3 thyme sprigs, leaves torn from the stems
500 g (1 lb) firm white fish fillets, such as
    monkfish, hake, haddock or cod, skinned
    and cubed
400 g (13 oz) frozen mixed seafood, defrosted,
    rinsed with cold water and drained
salt and pepper
½ small French bread, sliced and toasted

ROUILLE
3 roasted red peppers from a jar, drained
2–3 garlic cloves, peeled
1 teaspoon ready-prepared finely chopped red
    chilli (from a jar)
1 slice of white bread, torn into pieces
large pinch of saffron threads, soaked in
    1 tablespoon of boiling water for 10 minutes
3 tablespoons olive oil

Heat the oil in a large saucepan, add the onion
and leek and fry gently for 5 minutes, stirring
occasionally, until softened.

Add the garlic and tomatoes to the pan and fry
for 2–3 minutes, then mix in the saffron and
its soaking water, wine, stock and thyme, and
season to taste with salt and pepper. Cover and
simmer for 10 minutes.

Add the white fish, re-cover and simmer
gently for 3 minutes. Add the mixed seafood,
re-cover and simmer gently for a further
5 minutes until all the fish is just cooked.
Meanwhile, purée all the ingredients for the

rouille in a blender or food processor until
smooth. Spoon into a small bowl.

Ladle the bouillabaisse into bowls and serve
with the toasted bread topped with spoonfuls
of the rouille.

148

next time...

**For chunky chorizo, mushroom & seafood
soup**, fry the onion and leek in the oil as in the
previous recipe. Add 100 g (3½ oz) chorizo,
diced, and fry for 3 minutes, then stir in the
garlic and tomatoes along with 200 g (7 oz)
mushrooms, sliced, and fry for 3 minutes,
stirring. Mix in the saffron and its soaking
water, wine and thyme as before, replacing
the fish stock with 600 ml (1 pint) vegetable
stock (see page 10). Season to taste with salt
and pepper, cover and simmer for 10 minutes,
then add the frozen mixed seafood as before,
omitting the white fish, re-cover and simmer
gently for 5 minutes. Ladle the soup into bowls
and top with the toasted bread and spoonfuls of
the rouille as before.

149

pumpkin, orange & star anise soup

SERVES 6

25 g (1 oz) butter
1 onion, roughly chopped
1 small pumpkin, about 1.5 kg (3 lb), quartered,
   deseeded, peeled and diced
2 small oranges, rind removed with a zester
   and juice squeezed
1 litre (1¾ pints) vegetable or chicken stock (see
   pages 10 and 9)
3 whole star anise , plus 3 to garnish
salt and pepper
crushed black peppercorns, to garnish
   (optional)

SPICED ORANGE & CHILLI BUTTER
75 g (3 oz) butter
grated rind of 1 orange
1 large mild red chilli, deseeded and finely
   chopped
pinch each of ground turmeric and cloves

Melt the butter in a large saucepan, add the onion and fry gently for 5 minutes until softened. Add the pumpkin, toss in the butter and fry for 5 minutes, stirring.

Stir in the orange rind and juice, stock and star anise, season to taste with salt and pepper and bring to the boil. Reduce the heat, cover and simmer for 30 minutes until the pumpkin is soft, stirring occasionally.

Meanwhile, beat all the ingredients for the spiced orange and chilli butter together in a small bowl. Roll up the butter in clingfilm or foil into a log and chill in the refrigerator until firm and ready to serve.

Lift the star anise out with a slotted spoon and reserve for garnishing. Leave the soup to cool slightly, then purée in the pan with a stick blender or in batches in a blender or food processor until smooth, returning to the pan. Reheat the soup, then taste and adjust the seasoning if needed.

Ladle the soup into bowls and garnish each serving with a star anise, a slice of the spiced orange and chilli butter, and crushed black peppercorns, if liked. Serve with warm sesame bread rolls.

150

next time...

For chunky pumpkin, orange & chickpea soup, fry the onion and then the pumpkin in the butter as in the previous recipe. Mix in a drained 400 g (13 oz) can chickpeas with the orange rind and juice, stock and star anise, and season to taste with salt and pepper. Bring to the boil, then cover and simmer for 25 minutes. Ladle into bowls and top each serving with a slice of the spiced orange and chilli butter and a few toasted flaked almonds.

151

spinach soup
with haddock

SERVES 6

25 g (1 oz) butter
1 onion, roughly chopped
1 baking potato, about 250 g (8 oz), diced
1 litre (1¾ pints) vegetable or chicken stock
    (see pages 10 and 9)
¼ teaspoon grated nutmeg
225 g (7½ oz) baby spinach leaves
300 ml (½ pint) milk
400 g (13 oz) smoked haddock fillet, cut
    in two
9 quails' eggs
2 egg yolks
150 ml (¼ pint) double cream
salt and pepper

Melt the butter in a saucepan, add the onion and
fry gently for 5 minutes until softened. Stir in
the potato, cover and cook for 10 minutes,
stirring occasionally. Pour in the stock, add the
nutmeg and season to taste with salt and pepper.
Bring to the boil, then reduce the heat, cover and
simmer for 20 minutes until the potato is soft.
Reserve a few spinach leaves for garnishing and
add the rest to the pan. Re-cover and cook for
5 minutes until just wilted.

Leave the soup to cool slightly, then purée
in the saucepan with a stick blender or in
batches in a blender or food processor until
smooth, returning to the pan. Stir in the milk.
Set aside.

Steam the haddock for 8–10 minutes until
it flakes when pressed with a knife. Put the
quails' eggs into a small saucepan of cold water
and bring to the boil, then reduce the heat and
simmer for 2–3 minutes. Drain, rinse in cold
water, shell and cut in half.

Mix the 2 hen egg yolks with the cream.
Stir into the soup and bring just to the boil,
still stirring. Taste and adjust the seasoning if
needed. Flake the fish, discarding the skin and

any stray bones, and mound in the base
of shallow bowls. Top with the quails' egg
halves. Ladle the soup around the fish and
eggs, and garnish with the spinach leaves
and pepper.

152

next time...

For cream of nettle soup, make the soup as
in the previous recipe, replacing the spinach
with 200 g (7 oz) young nettle tops (pick using
rubber gloves so that you don't get stung and
rinse the leaves well in cold water). Purée the
soup, then finish with the milk, egg yolks and
cream as before. Omitting the quails' eggs,
serve garnished with diced smoked ham.

153

chestnut soup
with truffle oil

SERVES 6

500 g (1 lb) fresh chestnuts
50 g (2 oz) butter
1 onion, finely chopped
10 smoked streaky bacon rashers
200 g (7 oz) potato, diced
4 tablespoons brandy, plus a little extra to serve
900 ml (1½ pints) pheasant or beef stock (see
    page 9)
1 thyme sprig
large pinch of ground cinnamon
large pinch of grated nutmeg
salt and pepper
truffle oil, to garnish (optional)

Cut a cross in the top of each chestnut, add to a saucepan of boiling water and cook for 15 minutes. Drain and rinse with cold water so that they are cool enough to handle, remove the skins with a small sharp knife and roughly chop.

Melt the butter in a saucepan, add the onion and fry gently for 5 minutes until just beginning to turn golden around the edges. Dice 4 of the bacon rashers and add to the pan along with the potato and chestnuts. Fry gently for 5 minutes, stirring occasionally.

Add the brandy, and when bubbling, flame with a long match and quickly stand back. As soon as the flames have subsided, pour in the stock. Add the thyme and spices, season to taste with salt and pepper and bring to the boil. Reduce the heat, cover and simmer for 45 minutes.

Discard the thyme sprig and leave the soup to cool slightly, then purée half, in batches if necessary, in a blender or food processor until smooth. Return to the pan and reheat, then taste and adjust the seasoning if needed. Wrap each remaining rasher of bacon around a skewer and cook under a hot grill until crisp. Ladle the soup into cups and top with the bacon skewers. Drizzle with a little truffle oil, if liked, and a little extra brandy.

154

next time...

For walnut & celeriac soup, fry the onion in the butter, then add the diced bacon as in the previous recipe, replacing the potato and chestnuts with 375 g (12 oz) celeriac, peeled and diced, and 200 g (7 oz) walnut pieces. Fry gently for 5 minutes. Omitting the brandy, stir in the stock, thyme and spices and continue cooking the soup as before. Leave the soup to cool slightly, then purée all of it in the pan with a stick blender or in batches in a blender or food processor, returning to the pan. Add a little extra stock if needed, then reheat and serve with croûtons (see page 13).

155

clam, potato & bean soup

SERVES 6

2 tablespoons olive oil
125 g (4 oz) piece of unsmoked pancetta, diced
1 onion, chopped
375 g (12 oz) potatoes, diced
1 leek, sliced
2 garlic cloves, crushed
1 tablespoon chopped rosemary
2 bay leaves
400 g (13 oz) can cannellini beans, drained
900 ml (1½ pints) vegetable stock (see page 10)
1 kg (2 lb) live small clams or mussels, scrubbed
  and debearded, any cracked or open shells
  discarded
salt and pepper

GARLIC & PARSLEY OIL
150 ml (¼ pint) extra virgin olive oil
2 large garlic cloves, sliced
¼ teaspoon salt
1 tablespoon chopped parsley

Heat the oil in a large saucepan, add the pancetta and fry for 5 minutes until golden. Remove with a slotted spoon and set aside. Add the onion, potatoes, leek, crushed garlic, rosemary and bay leaves to the pan and fry for 10 minutes until softened. Stir in the beans and stock and bring to the boil, then reduce the heat and simmer gently for 20 minutes until the vegetables are tender.

Meanwhile, make the garlic and parsley oil. Heat the oil with the sliced garlic and salt in a small saucepan and simmer gently for 3 minutes. Leave to cool, then stir in the parsley.

Leave the soup to cool slightly, then purée half, in batches if necessary, in a blender or food processor until really smooth. Return to the pan and season to taste with salt and pepper. Stir in the clams or mussels and the pancetta. Cover and simmer gently for 5 minutes until the clams or mussels have opened, discarding any that remain closed. Spoon into bowls and drizzle with the garlic and parsley oil.

156

next time...

For clam, tomato & bean soup, fry 125 g (4 oz) chorizo, diced, instead of the pancetta in the oil as in the previous recipe, then remove and set aside. Fry the onion, potatoes, leek, garlic and herbs as before, then add 4 large tomatoes, skinned, if liked, and diced, with the beans and stock. Bring to the boil, then simmer for 20 minutes. Purée half the soup, then return to the pan, add the shellfish and the fried chorizo and cook as before. Drizzle with the garlic and parsley oil to serve.

157

157

gingered cauliflower soup

SERVES 6

25 g (1 oz) butter
1 tablespoon sunflower oil
1 onion, roughly chopped
1 cauliflower, cut into florets, woody core
   discarded, about 500 g (1 lb) when prepared
3.5 cm (1½ inch) piece of fresh root ginger,
   peeled and finely chopped
900 ml (1½ pints) vegetable or chicken stock
   (see pages 10 and 9)
300 ml (½ pint) milk
150 ml (¼ pint) double cream
salt and pepper

SOY-GLAZED SEEDS
1 tablespoon sunflower oil
2 tablespoons sesame seeds
2 tablespoons sunflower seeds
2 tablespoons pumpkin seeds
1 tablespoon soy sauce

Melt the butter with the oil in a large saucepan, add the onion and fry for 5 minutes until softened but not browned. Stir in the cauliflower florets and ginger, then pour in the stock and season to taste with salt and pepper. Bring to the boil, then reduce the heat, cover and simmer for 15 minutes until the cauliflower is just tender.

Meanwhile, heat the oil for the soy-glazed seeds in a frying pan, add the seeds and cook for 2–3 minutes, stirring, until lightly browned. Add the soy sauce, then quickly cover until the seeds have stopped popping. Set aside until ready to serve.

Leave the soup to cool slightly, then purée in the pan with a stick blender or in batches in a blender or food processor, returning to the pan. Stir in the milk and half the cream and bring just to the boil, then taste and adjust the seasoning if needed.

Ladle the soup into shallow bowls, swirl in the remaining cream and sprinkle with some of the seeds, serving the rest in a small bowl.

158

next time...

For creamy cauliflower & cashew soup, melt the butter with the oil and add the onion as in the previous recipe along with 50 g (2 oz) raw, unsalted cashew nuts. Fry until the onion is softened and the nuts are very lightly coloured. Mix in the cauliflower florets and stock as before, then season to taste with salt and pepper and a little grated nutmeg. Bring to the boil, then cover and simmer for 15 minutes. Meanwhile, fry 50 g (2 oz) raw, unsalted cashew nuts in 15 g (½ oz) butter in a frying pan until pale golden, then add 1 tablespoon honey and cook for a further 1–2 minutes, stirring, until golden and caramelized. Purée the soup and finish with the milk and cream as before, then ladle into bowls and top with the caramelized cashew nuts.

159

crab soup

SERVES 4-6

1 litre (1¾ pints) chicken stock (see page 9)
2.5 cm (1 inch) piece of fresh root ginger, peeled
   and very finely chopped
2 ripe tomatoes, skinned, deseeded and very
   finely chopped
½ small red or green chilli, deseeded and very
   finely chopped
2 tablespoons rice wine or dry sherry
1 tablespoon rice wine vinegar, white wine
   vinegar or cider vinegar
½ teaspoon sugar
1 tablespoon cornflour
about 150 g (5 oz) white crab meat, defrosted
   and drained thoroughly if frozen
salt and pepper
2 spring onions, finely sliced lengthways,
   to garnish

Pour the stock into a large saucepan and stir in
the ginger, tomatoes, chilli, rice wine or sherry,
vinegar and sugar. Bring to the boil, then
reduce the heat, cover and simmer for about
10 minutes.

Blend the cornflour with a little cold water in
a bowl to make a smooth paste, then pour
into the soup and stir to mix. Simmer for
1-2 minutes, stirring, or until the soup thickens.

Add the crab meat to the soup and stir gently
to mix in, then heat through for 2-3 minutes.
Season to taste with salt and pepper.

Serve the soup piping hot in warmed soup
bowls, sprinkled with the sliced spring onions.

160

spinach & broccoli soup

SERVES 4

50 g (2 oz) butter
2 tablespoons olive oil
1 onion, diced
1 garlic clove, finely chopped
2 potatoes, diced
250 g (8 oz) broccoli, chopped
300 g (10 oz) spinach leaves, chopped
900 ml (1½ pints) vegetable or chicken stock
   (see pages 10 and 9)
125 g (4 oz) Gorgonzola cheese, crumbled into
   small pieces
juice of ½ lemon
½ teaspoon grated nutmeg
salt and pepper
75 g (3 oz) toasted pine nuts, to garnish

Melt the butter with the oil in a saucepan, add
the onion and garlic and fry for 3 minutes,
stirring frequently. Add the potatoes, broccoli,
spinach and stock and bring to the boil, then
reduce the heat and simmer for 15 minutes.

Add the Gorgonzola to the soup with the lemon
juice and nutmeg, and season to taste with
salt and pepper. For a smooth consistency,
leave the soup to cool slightly, then purée in
the pan with a stick blender or in batches in a
blender or food processor, returning to the pan
and reheating. Alternatively, it can be left with
chunky pieces according to taste.

Spoon the soup into soup bowls and garnish
with the toasted pine nuts. Serve with warm
crusty bread.

161

roasted pepper soup
with black pepper cream

SERVES 4

6 large red or yellow peppers
3 tablespoons olive oil
4 leeks, white and pale green parts only, thinly
   sliced
750 ml (1¼ pints) vegetable or chicken stock
   (see pages 10 and 9)
2 teaspoons black peppercorns
75 g (3 oz) mascarpone cheese
75 ml (3 fl oz) milk
salt and pepper

Put the peppers into a large roasting tin and
roast in a preheated oven, 240°C (475°F), Gas
Mark 9, for 20–30 minutes, turning halfway
through, until they begin to char. Transfer the
roasted peppers to a plastic bag, close it tightly
and leave to steam for 10 minutes.

Peel the skins off the peppers, then pull out
the stalks – the seeds should come with them.
Halve the peppers, scrape out any remaining
seeds and roughly chop the flesh.

Heat the oil in a large saucepan, add the
leeks and fry gently for 10 minutes, stirring
occasionally, until soft but not browned. Add the
peppers, stock and a little salt and pepper. Bring
to the boil, then reduce the heat and simmer for
20 minutes.

Finely grind the black peppercorns using a
spice grinder or pestle and mortar. Beat the
mascarpone with the milk and ground pepper
in a small bowl. Season to taste with salt, then
cover and chill in the refrigerator until needed.

Leave the soup to cool slightly, then purée in
batches in a blender or food processor. Pass the
purée through a fine sieve back into the rinsed-
out pan. Reheat, then taste and adjust the
seasoning if needed. Serve the soup in warmed
bowls with dollops of the black pepper cream
and slices of toasted crusty bread.

162

next time...

For roasted ratatouille soup, put 2 large red
peppers and 1 orange pepper, halved, cored and
deseeded, into a roasting tin skin-side up with
1 small aubergine, cut into cubes, 2 courgettes,
sliced, and 1 red onion, cut into wedges.
Sprinkle with 2 garlic cloves, chopped, and
3 tablespoons olive oil. Roast as in the previous
recipe. Skin the peppers, then add all the
roasted vegetables and any pan juices to a large
saucepan with the stock and salt and pepper as
before, adding 1 tablespoon tomato purée and
omitting the leek. Cook, purée and reheat as
before, then serve topped with the black pepper
cream or with a drizzle of olive oil.

163

chicken & tarragon
soup with puff pastry

SERVES 6

6 chicken thighs
1 carrot, sliced
2 celery sticks, sliced
200 g (7 oz) leeks, thinly sliced, white and green
    parts kept separate
900 ml (1½ pints) chicken stock (see page 9)
200 ml (7 fl oz) white wine
50 g (2 oz) butter
25 g (1 oz) plain flour
grated rind of ½ orange
2 teaspoons Dijon mustard
1 tablespoon chopped tarragon
425 g (14 oz) pack frozen ready-rolled puff
    pastry, defrosted
1 egg, beaten, to glaze
salt and pepper

Put the chicken thighs into a large saucepan with the carrot, celery and white leek parts. Add the stock, wine and some salt and pepper. Bring to the boil, then reduce the heat, cover and simmer gently for 1 hour until the chicken is very tender.

Strain the stock through a sieve into a measuring jug. Discard the vegetables, then transfer the chicken to a chopping board. Take the chicken meat off the bones and cut it into small pieces, discarding the skin. If the stock measures more than 900 ml (1½ pints), return to the pan and boil rapidly to reduce.

Melt the butter in a smaller saucepan, add the green leek parts and fry for 2–3 minutes until softened. Stir in the flour and cook briefly, then gradually mix in the strained stock, bring to the boil and cook, stirring, until thickened slightly. Stir in the orange rind, mustard and tarragon. Taste and adjust the seasoning if needed. Divide the chicken among 6 x 300 ml (½ pint) ovenproof dishes so that the soup three-quarter fills the dishes (any more and they will overflow during baking).

Unroll the pastry, cut 6 circles slightly larger than the tops of the dishes, then 6 long strips about 1 cm (½ inch) wide from the trimmings. Brush the dish rims with a little beaten egg, stick the pastry strips around the rims, then brush these with egg before sticking the pastry lids in place. Flute the edges of the pastry with a small knife, then slash the lids lightly. Brush with egg, sprinkle with a little salt and bake in a preheated oven, 200°C (400°F), Gas Mark 6, for 20–25 minutes until golden and the soup is bubbling underneath. Stand the dishes on small plates and serve immediately.

164

next time...

For cod & tarragon soup with puff pastry, add 625 g (1¼ lb) cod loin to a saucepan with 1 carrot, 2 celery sticks and the white parts of 200 g (7 oz) leeks, all sliced. Add 150 ml (¼ pint) dry white wine and 750 ml (1¼ pints) vegetable stock (see page 10). Simmer for 10 minutes. Lift the fish out and flake. Strain the stock and continue as in the previous recipe.

165

chicken & coconut milk soup

SERVES 4

300 ml (½ pint) chicken stock (see page 9)
3 dried kaffir lime leaves, torn
½ lemon grass stalk, diagonally sliced
2.5 cm (1 inch) piece of fresh root galangal or
   ginger, peeled and finely sliced
100 ml (3½ fl oz) full-fat coconut milk
4 tablespoons Thai fish sauce
1 teaspoon palm sugar or light muscovado
   sugar
3 tablespoons lime juice
125 g (4 oz) skinless chicken breast fillets, cut
   into bite-sized pieces
2 tablespoons chilli oil or 2 small chillies, finely
   sliced (optional)

Pour the stock into a saucepan and bring to
a simmer, then stir in the lime leaves, lemon
grass and galangal or ginger. As the stock is
simmering, add the coconut milk, fish sauce,
sugar and lime juice and stir well.

Add the chicken and simmer for 5 minutes.

Just before serving, add the chilli oil or chillies,
if liked, and stir again. Serve the soup in bowls.

166

prawn & lemon grass soup

SERVES 4

375 g (12 oz) raw prawns in their shells
3 lemon grass stalks, cut into 2.5 cm (1 inch)
   pieces
1.2 litres (2 pints) water
475 g (15 oz) can straw mushrooms, drained
1 tomato, quartered and deseeded
6 dried kaffir lime leaves
1 spring onion, chopped
185 g (6½ oz) bean sprouts
juice of 3 limes
2 small red chillies, finely sliced
4 tablespoons Vietnamese or Thai fish sauce
salt and pepper
coriander leaves, to garnish

Peel and devein the prawns, reserving the
shells. Cut off the white part of each lemon
grass stalk, reserving the tops. Flatten the
lemon grass stalks with a cleaver or pestle.

Heat the measured water in a saucepan and
add the prawn shells and the lemon grass tops.
Bring the water slowly to the boil, then strain
through a sieve and return to the pan. Add the
flattened lemon grass, straw mushrooms,
tomato and lime leaves. Bring the liquid back
to the boil, then reduce the heat and simmer for
3–4 minutes.

Add the prawns, and when they have turned
pink, add the spring onion, bean sprouts, lime
juice, chillies and fish sauce. Season to taste
with salt and pepper and stir well.

Serve in bowls, garnished with coriander leaves.

167

green lentil & bacon
soup

SERVES 6–8

25 g (1 oz) butter
125 g (4 oz) rindless smoked lean bacon, finely
  chopped
1 garlic clove, finely chopped
1 onion, finely chopped
425 g (14 oz) dried green lentils, rinsed and
  drained
1 celery stick, sliced
1 large carrot, diced
1 parsley sprig
1 thyme sprig or ¼ teaspoon dried thyme
1 bay leaf
1.2 litres (2 pints) chicken stock (see page 9)
900 ml (1½ pints) water
1 lemon slice
salt and pepper

Melt the butter in a large saucepan, add the
bacon, garlic and onion and fry over a medium
to high heat for 5 minutes, stirring.

Reduce the heat and stir in the lentils, celery,
carrot and herbs. Pour in the stock and the
measured water. Bring to the boil, skimming
off the scum as it rises to the surface with a
slotted spoon. Add the lemon slice. Reduce the
heat, cover and simmer for 55 minutes–1 hour,
stirring occasionally.

If the soup is too thick, stir in a little more
water. Carefully remove and discard the herbs
and lemon slice, then season to taste with salt
and pepper.

Pour 600 ml (1 pint) of the soup into a
measuring jug and purée in a blender or food
processor until smooth. Return the purée to the
pan, stir well and reheat for 5 minutes. Serve the
soup in warmed soup bowls.

168

next time...

For green lentil, chorizo & kale soup, heat
2 tablespoons olive oil in a large saucepan,
add 125 g (4 oz) chorizo, diced, 2 garlic cloves,
finely chopped, and 1 onion, chopped, and fry
for a few minutes, stirring frequently, until
the onion is just turning golden. Stir in the
lentils, celery, carrot and herbs as in the
previous recipe, then pour in the stock and
water and continue making the soup as before.
After returning the purée to the pan, stir 100 g
(3½ oz) kale, shredded, into the soup and
simmer for 5 minutes until wilted, then ladle
into warmed bowls and serve.

169

vegetable broth with wontons

SERVES 6

WONTONS

125 g (4 oz) minced pork
½ teaspoon cornflour
1 teaspoon sesame oil
2 tablespoons soy sauce
1 small garlic clove, finely chopped
43 g (1¾ oz) can dark crab meat
1 egg, separated, yolk and white lightly beaten
18 x 9 cm (3¾ inch) square wonton wrappers

BROTH

1.2 litres (2 pints) chicken stock (see page 9)
1 bunch of asparagus, trimmed and thickly
    sliced
75 g (3 oz) mangetout, sliced
4 spring onions, thinly sliced
4 teaspoons fish sauce
4 tablespoons dry sherry
1 small bunch of coriander, two-thirds roughly
    chopped, the remaining sprigs to garnish

Mix together all the wonton ingredients except
the egg white and wrappers in a bowl. Cover and
chill in the refrigerator for 30 minutes.

Place 1 heaped teaspoonful of the pork mixture
in the centre of each wrapper, brush the edges
with a little egg white, then bring the edges up
and over the filling and twist together to make
mini parcels. Keep the wrappers covered with
a damp cloth to prevent them from drying out
before you fill them.

Put all the broth ingredients into a large
saucepan and bring to the boil. Add the
wontons, reduce the heat and simmer for
5 minutes until the filling is cooked through.

Ladle the broth and wontons into bowls,
3 wontons per serving, garnish with the
coriander sprigs and serve immediately.

170

next time...

For vegetable broth with chillied tuna, make
the broth as in the previous recipe, omitting
the wontons. Rub a 200 g (7 oz) thick-cut
tuna steak with a mixture of 1 teaspoon each
sesame and sunflower oil, 1 red chilli, deseeded
and finely chopped, and 1 garlic clove, finely
chopped. Heat a frying pan until hot, add the
tuna and dry-fry for 1½ minutes on each side
until browned on the outside but still pink in
the centre. Thinly slice and divide among
soup bowls. Ladle the broth around the tuna
and serve immediately, otherwise the soup will
overcook the tuna.

171

bean & sun-dried tomato soup

SERVES 4

3 tablespoons extra virgin olive oil
1 onion, finely chopped
2 celery sticks, thinly sliced
2 garlic cloves, thinly sliced
2 x 425 g (14 oz) cans cannellini beans, rinsed
    and drained
4 tablespoons sun-dried tomato paste
900 ml (1½ pints) vegetable stock (see page 10)
1 tablespoon chopped rosemary leaves
salt and pepper
Parmesan cheese shavings, to garnish

Heat the oil in a saucepan, add the onion and
fry for 3 minutes until softened. Add the celery
and garlic and fry for 2 minutes.

Stir in the beans, sun-dried tomato paste,
stock, rosemary and a little salt and pepper.
Bring to the boil, then reduce the heat, cover
and simmer gently for 15 minutes.

Ladle the soup into warmed soup bowls,
sprinkle with Parmesan shavings and serve.

172

next time...

For chickpea, tomato & rosemary soup, fry
the onion in the oil, then the celery and garlic
as in the previous recipe. Stir in 2 x 425 g
(14 oz) cans chickpeas, rinsed and drained,
3 tablespoons tomato purée instead of the sun-
dried tomato paste and 2 teaspoons harissa
paste, along with the stock and 1 tablespoon
chopped rosemary leaves. Cook and then serve
garnished with Parmesan shavings as before.

173

parsnip & fennel soup

SERVES 4–6

50 g (2 oz) butter
500 g (1 lb) parsnips, cut into 5 mm (¼ inch) dice
500 g (1 lb) fennel bulb, trimmed, cored and cut into 5 mm (¼ inch)
1 onion, chopped
3 tablespoons cornflour
1.2 litres (2 pints) hot vegetable or chicken stock (see pages 10 and 9)
150 ml (¼ pint) double cream
salt and pepper

Melt the butter in a large saucepan, add the parsnips, fennel and onion and cook over a medium heat for 15 minutes, or until the vegetables are soft, stirring.

Mix the cornflour with 150 ml (¼ pint) of the hot stock in a bowl until thick and smooth. Stir the cornflour mixture into the vegetables, then pour in the remaining hot stock, stirring the soup constantly.

Bring to the boil, then reduce the heat, half-cover and simmer for 20 minutes, stirring frequently. Season to taste with salt and pepper, stir in the cream and heat through without boiling.

Pour the soup into bowls and serve immediately.

174

mushroom soup with crispy bacon

SERVES 4–6

50 g (2 oz) butter
1 onion, finely chopped
1 garlic clove, finely chopped
375 g (12 oz) mushrooms, thinly sliced
2 tablespoons plain flour
600 ml (1 pint) chicken stock (see page 9)
150 ml (¼ pint) milk
1 tablespoon Manzanilla sherry (optional)
150 ml (¼ pint) double cream
4 rindless bacon rashers, cooked until crisp and broken into small pieces
salt and pepper
chervil sprigs, to garnish (optional)

Melt the butter in a large saucepan, add the onion, garlic and mushrooms and fry for a few minutes, stirring frequently, until soft and beginning to colour. Sprinkle over the flour and stir to combine. Gradually pour in the stock and milk, stirring well to blend. Bring to the boil, stirring constantly, then reduce the heat and simmer for 15–20 minutes.

Season the soup to taste with salt and pepper, then stir in the sherry (if using) and half the cream. Reheat the soup gently without boiling, then pour into bowls.

Whip the remaining cream until it is just holding its shape, then spoon a little on top of each serving of soup. Sprinkle with the bacon pieces and garnish with chervil sprigs, if liked.

175

hungarian chorba

SERVES 6

1 tablespoon sunflower oil
500 g (1 lb) stewing lamb on the bone
1 onion, finely chopped
1 carrot, roughly chopped
150 g (5 oz) swede, roughly chopped
2 teaspoons smoked paprika
50 g (2 oz) long-grain white rice
1 small bunch of dill, plus extra fronds, torn,
    to garnish
1.5 litres (2½ pints) lamb stock (see page 9)
4–6 tablespoons red wine vinegar
2 tablespoons brown sugar
2 eggs
salt and pepper

Heat the oil in a large saucepan, add the lamb
and brown on one side. Turn over, add the
onion, carrot and swede and cook until the
lamb is browned on the other side.

Sprinkle over the paprika and cook briefly, then
stir in the rice, dill and stock. Add the vinegar
and sugar, and season well with salt and pepper.
Bring to the boil, stirring, then reduce the heat,
cover and simmer for 2½ hours until the lamb
is very tender.

Lift the lamb out of the pan with a slotted
spoon and put on to a chopping board. Take the
meat off the bones and cut into small pieces,
discarding the fat. Return the meat to the pan.

Beat the eggs together in a bowl, then gradually
pour in a ladleful of the hot soup, whisking
constantly. Pour the egg mixture into the pan
and heat gently, stirring, until the soup has
thickened slightly, but don't allow it to boil, or
the eggs will scramble. Taste and adjust the
seasoning, adding more vinegar if needed.

Ladle the soup into bowls, garnish with torn
dill fronds and serve with pumpernickel bread.

176

next time...

For chicken & kohlrabi chorba, replace the
lamb with 6 chicken thighs and brown in the
oil as in the previous recipe. Add the onion and
carrot with 150 g (5 oz) kohlrabi, peeled and
diced, instead of the swede. Continue making
the soup as before, but simmer for 1½ hours.

177

corn & chicken chowder

SERVES 4–6

25 g (1 oz) butter
1 large onion, chopped
1 small red pepper, cored, deseeded and diced
625 g (1¼ lb) potatoes, diced
25 g (1 oz) plain flour
750 ml (1¼ pints) chicken stock (see page 9)
175 g (6 oz) drained canned or frozen sweetcorn
250 g (8 oz) cooked chicken, chopped
450 ml (¾ pint) milk
3 tablespoons chopped parsley, plus extra
    to garnish
salt and pepper
a few red chillies, sliced, to garnish

Melt the butter in a large saucepan, add
the onion, red pepper and potatoes and
fry over a medium heat for 5 minutes,
stirring occasionally.

Sprinkle in the flour and cook over a gentle
heat for 1 minute. Gradually stir in the stock
and bring to the boil, stirring. Reduce the heat,
cover and simmer for 10 minutes.

Stir in the sweetcorn, chicken, milk and
parsley, and season to taste with salt and
pepper. Re-cover and simmer gently for a
further 10 minutes, or until the potatoes are
just tender. Taste and adjust the seasoning
if needed.

Serve the chowder garnished with the sliced
chillies and extra chopped parsley.

178

next time...

For gammon & corn chowder, fry the onion,
red pepper and potatoes in the butter, then
add the flour and cook gently for 1 minute as
in the previous recipe. Stir in the stock and
bring to the boil, then simmer for 10 minutes.
Meanwhile, cook a 250 g (8 oz) smoked
gammon steak under a hot grill for 10 minutes,
turning halfway through. Trim off the fat and
dice the gammon. Stir into the soup with the
sweetcorn, milk and parsley, and finish cooking
as before.

179

oriental mussel soup

SERVES 4

1 tablespoon sunflower oil
3 spring onions, sliced
½ red pepper, cored, deseeded and diced
1 garlic clove, finely chopped
2.5 cm (1 inch) piece of fresh root ginger, peeled and grated
3 teaspoons ready-made red Thai curry paste
400 ml (14 fl oz) can full-fat coconut milk
450 ml (¾ pint) fish or vegetable stock (see page 10)
2 teaspoons Thai fish sauce
grated rind of 1 lime, plus extra zested strands to garnish
1 small bunch of coriander
500 g (1 lb) live mussels, scrubbed and debearded, any cracked or open mussels discarded

Heat the oil in a large, shallow saucepan, add the spring onions, red pepper, garlic and ginger and fry for 2 minutes. Stir in the curry paste and cook for 1 minute, then mix in the coconut milk, stock, fish sauce and lime rind. Bring to the boil, then reduce the heat and simmer for 5 minutes.

Snip half the coriander into the soup using scissors. Add the mussels, then cover and simmer for 8–10 minutes, or until the mussels have opened.

Lift the mussels out of the soup with a slotted spoon and put on to a large plate, discarding any that remain closed, then reserve half the opened mussels in their shells for garnishing. Take the remaining mussels out of their shells and stir them back into the soup.

Ladle the soup into bowls, top with the reserved mussels in shells and garnish with the remaining coriander, snipped, and a little zested lime rind. Serve with warm crusty bread for dunking into the soup.

180

next time...

For saffron mussel soup, heat 1 tablespoon olive oil in a large saucepan, add 3 spring onions, sliced, 2 garlic cloves, finely chopped, ½–1 large mild red chilli, according to taste, deseeded and finely chopped, ½ red pepper and ½ yellow or orange pepper, cored, deseeded and diced, and fry for a few minutes until softened. Add 3 large pinches of saffron threads, 150 ml (¼ pint) dry white wine and 750 ml (1¼ pints) fish or vegetable stock. Season to taste with salt and pepper and bring to the boil, then simmer for 5 minutes. Add and cook the mussels as in the previous recipe, taking all the mussels out of their shells and returning them to the soup. Ladle the soup into shallow bowls and garnish with snipped flat leaf parsley.

181

seafood gumbo

SERVES 6

1 tablespoon sunflower oil
1 onion, finely chopped
1 small carrot, diced
1 celery stick, diced
½ red pepper, cored, deseeded and diced
425 g (14 oz) tomatoes, skinned if liked and
    roughly chopped
1 large thyme sprig, plus extra leaves to garnish
    (optional)
¼ teaspoon chilli flakes
2 teaspoons tomato purée
1 litre (1¾ pints) vegetable or fish stock (see
    page 10)
40 g (1½ oz) long-grain white rice
400 g (13 oz) pack frozen mixed seafood,
    defrosted, rinsed with cold water and
    drained
43 g (1¾ oz) can dressed crab
75 g (3 oz) okra, conical stalk end discarded
    and sliced
salt and pepper

Heat the oil in a saucepan, add the onion and
fry gently for 5 minutes, stirring frequently,
until softened and just beginning to brown.
Stir in the carrot, celery and red pepper and fry
for a few minutes, stirring.

Mix in the tomatoes, thyme, chilli flakes and
tomato purée, then pour in the stock. Stir in the
rice, season to taste with salt and pepper and
bring to the boil. Reduce the heat, cover and
simmer for 20 minutes, stirring occasionally.

Halve any very large mussels in the seafood
mix, then stir into the soup with the remaining
seafood, the crab and okra. Cover and simmer
for 5 minutes, then taste and adjust the
seasoning if needed.

Ladle the gumbo into bowls and sprinkle with a
few thyme leaves to garnish, if liked. Serve with
crusty bread.

182

next time...

For chicken & ham gumbo, fry the onion in
the oil as in the previous recipe, along with 6
skinless chicken thigh fillets, diced. Continue
making the soup as before, replacing the mixed
seafood, crab and okra with 50 g (2 oz) cooked
ham, diced, and 75 g (3 oz) green beans, sliced.
Finishing cooking and serve as before.

183

cheat's curried vegetable soup

SERVES 6

2 tablespoons sunflower oil
1 onion, finely chopped
2 garlic cloves, finely chopped
4 teaspoons ready-made mild curry paste
2.5 cm (1 inch) piece of fresh root ginger, peeled, grated
2 small baking potatoes, diced
2 carrots, diced
1 small cauliflower, woody core discarded, florets cut into small pieces
75 g (3 oz) dried red lentils, rinsed and drained
1.5 litres (2½ pints) vegetable or chicken stock (see pages 10 and 9)
400 g (13 oz) can chopped tomatoes
200 g (7 oz) spinach leaves, any large leaves torn into pieces
salt and pepper

Heat the oil in a large saucepan, add the onion and fry for 5 minutes, stirring frequently, until softened. Stir in the garlic, curry paste and ginger and cook for 1 minute. Mix in the potatoes, carrots, cauliflower and lentils.

Pour in the stock and tomatoes, season to taste with salt and pepper and bring to the boil. Reduce the heat, cover and simmer for 30 minutes, or until the lentils are tender.

Add the spinach to the soup and cook for 2 minutes until just wilted. Taste and adjust the seasoning if needed.

Ladle the soup into shallow bowls and serve with warmed naan breads.

184

next time...

For curried aubergine soup, fry the onion in the oil as in the previous recipe along with 2 aubergines, diced, until the aubergines are lightly browned. Stir in the garlic, curry paste and ginger and cook for 1 minute. Then add the potatoes, carrots, lentils, stock and tomatoes, omitting the cauliflower, and after cooking as before, leave the soup to cool slightly, then purée in the pan with a stick blender or in batches in a blender or food processor until smooth, returning to the pan. Reheat, omitting the spinach, and check the seasoning. Ladle the soup into bowls, add a swirl of natural yogurt to each serving and sprinkle with chopped coriander, then serve with poppadums.

185

mushroom & madeira
soup

SERVES 6

50 g (2 oz) butter
1 tablespoon olive oil
1 onion, chopped
400 g (13 oz) cup mushrooms, sliced
2 large flat mushrooms, sliced
2 garlic cloves, finely chopped
125 ml (4 fl oz) Madeira or medium sherry
900 ml (1½ pints) vegetable and chicken stock
    (see pages 10 and 9)
40 g (1½ oz) long-grain white rice
2 thyme sprigs, plus extra leaves to garnish
450 ml (¾ pint) milk
150 ml (¼ pint) double cream
salt and pepper

TO GARNISH
25 g (1 oz) butter
250 g (8 oz) exotic mushrooms, any large sliced

Melt the butter with the oil in a large saucepan, add the onion and fry gently for 5 minutes, stirring frequently, until just turning golden around the edges. Add the cup and flat mushrooms and garlic and fry over a high heat for 2–3 minutes, stirring, until golden.

Stir in the Madeira or sherry, stock, rice and thyme sprigs, then season to taste with salt and pepper and bring to the boil. Reduce the heat, cover and simmer for 30 minutes.

Discard the thyme and let the soup cool slightly, then purée in the pan with a stick blender or in batches in a blender or food processor until smooth. Return to the pan and stir in the milk and cream. Reheat gently without boiling, then taste and adjust the seasoning if needed.

Melt the butter for the garnish in a frying pan, add the exotic mushrooms and fry over a high heat for 2 minutes, stirring, until golden.

Ladle the soup into shallow soup bowls, gently spoon the fried exotic mushrooms into the centre and garnish with a few thyme leaves.

186

next time...

For **mushroom & miso soup**, fry 1 onion, chopped, in 2 tablespoons sunflower oil in a large saucepan for a few minutes until softened. Add the mushrooms and garlic and fry as in the previous recipe. Stir in 4 tablespoons rice wine and 2 tablespoons miso paste, then add 900 ml (1½ pints) vegetable stock and the rice as before. Bring to the boil, then cover and simmer for 30 minutes. Purée the soup as before, then mix in 600 ml (1 pint) unsweetened almond milk and reheat gently. Ladle the soup into bowls and top with toasted flaked almonds.

187

five-spice duck soup
with pak choi

SERVES 4

1.2 litres (2 pints) duck stock (see page 9)
grated rind and juice of 1 orange
4 tablespoons medium sherry
¼ teaspoon Chinese five-spice powder
5 cm (2 inch) piece of fresh root ginger, peeled
    and thinly sliced
1 tablespoon soy sauce
2 tablespoons Chinese plum sauce
125–175 g (4–6 oz) leftover cooked duck,
    stripped from the carcass before the stock
    was made, shredded
½ bunch of spring onions, thinly sliced
2 heads of pak choi, thickly sliced
salt and pepper (optional)

Pour the stock into a saucepan, then add the
orange rind and juice, sherry, spice powder and
ginger. Stir in the soy sauce and plum sauce,
then bring to the boil, stirring. Reduce the heat,
cover and simmer gently for 15 minutes.

Add the duck, spring onions and pak choi and
simmer for 5 minutes. Taste and add a little
salt and pepper if needed, then ladle the soup
into bowls.

188

next time...

For herbed duck broth with noodles, soak 50 g
(2 oz) dried fine egg noodles in boiling water for
5 minutes, then drain. Heat the duck stock as
in the previous recipe, then replace the orange
rind and juice with the grated rind and juice of
½ lemon and add with the spice powder and
ginger, omitting the sherry. Stir in soy sauce,
omitting the plum sauce, and bring to the boil,
then cover and simmer gently for 15 minutes.
Add 3 tablespoons each chopped flat leaf
parsley and mint, then add the leftover cooked
shredded duck as before, season to taste with
salt and pepper and simmer for 5 minutes.
Divide the noodles among bowls and ladle the
hot broth over the top.

189

steamboat soup

SERVES 4–6

125 ml (4 fl oz) vegetable oil
10 garlic cloves, thinly sliced
1 tablespoon tamarind pulp
150 ml (¼ pint) boiling water
1.2 litres (2 pints) water
2 tablespoons Thai fish sauce
1 teaspoon caster sugar
1 small pineapple, peeled, cored and cut into
　chunks
175 g (6 oz) tomatoes, quartered
8 spring onions, finely sliced
250 g (8 oz) raw peeled tiger prawns
3 squid, cleaned and cut into thick rings
250 g (8 oz) skinless rainbow trout fillets, cut
　into pieces

TO GARNISH
handful of coriander leaves
handful of basil leaves
2 large red chillies, diagonally sliced

Heat the oil in a small saucepan, and when it
is hot, deep-fry the garlic, a few slices at a time,
until golden brown. Remove the garlic with a
slotted spoon and drain on kitchen paper.

Put the tamarind pulp into a heatproof bowl with
the measured boiling water and set aside for
20 minutes to soften and dissolve. Strain the
liquid through a sieve, discarding the pods and
tamarind stones, and put into a saucepan with
the remaining measured water, fish sauce,
sugar, pineapple, tomatoes and spring onions.
Slowly bring to the boil.

If using a traditional steamboat cooker, pour
the flavoured stock into the hot pan containing
smoking coals and add the tiger prawns,
squid rings and pieces of fish. Simmer gently
for 6–8 minutes. Alternatively, pour the hot
stock into a large, heavy-based saucepan, add
the seafood and fish and simmer gently for
6–8 minutes, or until cooked and tender.

Serve while the fish is still cooking, topped with
the herbs, chilli slices and the deep-fried garlic.

190

next time...

For chicken & bamboo shoot steamboat soup,
fry the garlic and make the broth as in the
previous recipe. Add 500 g (1 lb) skinless
chicken breast fillets, thinly sliced, and a
drained 200 g (7 oz) can bamboo shoot slices
instead of the prawns, squid and trout. Bring to
the boil, then reduce the heat and simmer for
12–15 minutes until the chicken is thoroughly
cooked. Ladle into bowls and top with the
coriander and basil leaves, chilli slices and
deep-fried garlic as before.

191

roasted tomato & chilli soup with black olive cream

SERVES 4–6

1.5 kg (3 lb) ripe tomatoes, preferably plum
6 tablespoons olive oil
1½ teaspoons sea salt
1 tablespoon caster sugar
1 large red chilli
3–4 shallots or 1 onion, chopped
1 garlic clove, crushed
600 ml (1 pint) water
2–4 tablespoons lime juice
salt and pepper

OLIVE CREAM
50 g (2 oz) pitted black olives
50 g (2 oz) crème fraîche

Cut the tomatoes in half lengthways and, holding each half over a bowl, scoop out the seeds with a teaspoon. Reserve the tomato seeds and any juice.

Lightly grease a baking sheet with a little of the oil and lay the tomatoes on it, cut-side up. Sprinkle them with about 4 tablespoons of the remaining oil, the sea salt and sugar. Add the chilli and roast in a preheated oven, 180°C (350°F), Gas Mark 4, for 45–50 minutes, removing the chilli after 20 minutes when it is well charred and blistered. Leave to cool, then skin, deseed and chop it roughly.

Meanwhile, chop the olives for the olive cream very finely, fold them into the crème fraîche and season to taste with salt and pepper.

Heat the remaining oil in a saucepan over a medium heat, add the shallots or onion and cook for 6–8 minutes, or until lightly golden and softened, stirring occasionally. Add the garlic and cook for 2 minutes, stirring.

Add the roasted tomatoes with any liquid from the baking sheet, the reserved tomato seeds and juice, the roasted chilli and the measured water. Bring the soup to the boil, then reduce the heat and simmer for 10–12 minutes.

Leave the soup to cool slightly, then purée in batches in a blender or food processor. Pass the purée through a sieve back into the pan. Reheat, then season to taste with salt and pepper and the lime juice.

Ladle the soup into bowls and top with spoonfuls of the olive cream.

192

next time...

For roasted tomato & pumpkin soup, prepare 1 kg (2 lb) tomatoes as in the previous recipe, then put them on to the oiled baking sheet with 500 g (1 lb) deseeded, peeled and diced pumpkin (weight when prepared). Drizzle with the oil and roast, then continue making the soup as before.

193

lentil, pancetta & scallop soup

SERVES 4

50 g (2 oz) dried Puy lentils, rinsed and drained
1 tablespoon olive oil
1 small leek, diced
75 g (3 oz) pancetta, diced
1 garlic clove, finely chopped
4 tablespoons Pernod
600 ml (1 pint) fish stock (see page 10)
grated rind of ½ lemon
150 ml (¼ pint) double cream
1 small bunch of parsley, chopped
25 g (1 oz) butter
200 g (7 oz) pack frozen baby scallops, defrosted,
   rinsed with cold water and well drained
salt and pepper

Bring a saucepan of water to the boil, add the lentils and simmer for 20 minutes until just tender. Drain into a sieve, rinse under cold running water and drain again, then set aside. Wash and dry the pan.

Heat the oil in the cleaned pan, add the leek, pancetta and garlic and fry for 5 minutes, stirring, until the pancetta is just beginning to turn golden. Add the Pernod, and when bubbling, flame with a long match and quickly stand well back. As soon as the flames subside, pour in the stock. Add the lemon rind and a little salt and pepper and bring to the boil, then reduce the heat and simmer for 10 minutes.

Stir in the cooked lentils, cream and parsley, gently heat through, then taste and adjust the seasoning if needed.

Meanwhile, melt the butter in a frying pan, add the scallops and fry over a medium–high heat for 3–4 minutes, turning halfway through, until golden and just cooked through.

Ladle the soup into shallow bowls and spoon the scallops into a small mound in the centre.

194

next time...

For creamy pancetta & mussel soup, make the soup as in the previous recipe. When the stock has simmered for 10 minutes, add 500 g (1 lb) live mussels, scrubbed and debearded and any cracked or open mussels discarded. Cover and simmer for 8–10 minutes, or until the mussels have opened. Discard any that remain closed, then spoon into bowls. Stir the cream and parsley into the soup and reheat gently as before, then ladle over the mussels.

195

chorizo, fennel & potato soup

SERVES 8–10

3 tablespoons olive oil
1 onion, chopped
400 g (13 oz) fennel bulb, trimmed, cored and
  chopped
150 g (5 oz) chorizo, diced
500 g (1 lb) floury potatoes, cut into small dice
1 litre (1¾ pints) chicken or ham stock (see
  page 9)
3 tablespoons finely chopped coriander
3 tablespoons crème fraîche
salt and pepper

Heat the oil in a large saucepan, add the onion
and fennel and fry gently for about 10 minutes,
stirring occasionally, until very soft and
beginning to brown.

Add the chorizo, potatoes and stock and bring
to the boil. Reduce the heat, cover and simmer
gently for 20 minutes, or until the potatoes are
very tender.

Leave the soup to cool slightly, then purée in
the pan with a stick blender or in batches in a
blender or food processor until fairly smooth,
returning to the pan. Stir in the coriander and
crème fraîche and heat through gently, then
season to taste with salt and pepper. Serve in
small cups.

196

next time...

For **chorizo, celery & potato soup**, fry the onion
in the oil as in the recipe above, replacing the
fennel with 400 g (13 oz) celery sticks, chopped.
Continue making the soup as before but
without puréeing, stirring the coriander and
crème fraîche through just before serving.

197

summer vegetable soup

SERVES 4

1 teaspoon olive oil
1 leek, finely sliced
1 large potato, chopped
900 ml (1½ pints) vegetable stock (see page 10)
450 g (14½ oz) mixed summer vegetables,
  such as peas, asparagus, broad beans and
  courgettes
2 tablespoons chopped mint
2 tablespoons low-fat crème fraîche
salt and pepper

Heat the oil in a saucepan, add the leek and fry
for 3–4 minutes until softened.

Add the potato and stock, bring to a simmer
and cook for 10 minutes. Stir in all the
remaining vegetables and the mint and bring
to the boil, then reduce the heat and simmer for
10 minutes.

Leave the soup to cool slightly, then purée
in the pan with a stick blender or in batches
in a blender or food processor until smooth,
returning to the pan. Stir in the crème fraîche
and heat through gently, then season to taste
with salt and pepper and serve.

198

next time...

For **chunky summer vegetable soup with mixed
herb gremolata**, make the soup as in the recipe
above but without puréeing. Meanwhile, for
the gremolata, mix together 2 tablespoons each
chopped basil and flat leaf parsley, the grated
rind of 1 lemon and 1 small garlic clove, finely
chopped. Ladle the soup into bowls and serve
topped with 2 tablespoons crème fraîche and
the gremolata.

199

lentil, mustard & chickpea
soup

SERVES 4

½ teaspoon coconut oil or olive oil
¼ teaspoon mustard seeds
½ teaspoon ground cumin
½ teaspoon ground turmeric
1 small onion, diced
1.5 cm (¾ inch) piece of fresh root
   ginger, peeled and finely chopped
1 garlic clove, finely chopped
100 g (3½ oz) dried red lentils, rinsed
   and drained
250 g (8 oz) rinsed and drained
   canned chickpeas
900 ml (1½ pints) hot vegetable stock
   (see page 10)
50 g (2 oz) baby spinach leaves
salt and pepper

Heat the oil in a saucepan and stir in the dry spices.
When the mustard seeds start to pop, add the onion,
ginger and garlic and fry gently for a few minutes,
stirring frequently, until the onion is softened.

Add the lentils and chickpeas and stir well to coat. Pour in
the stock and bring to the boil, then reduce the heat and
simmer for 14–16 minutes, or until the lentils are tender.

Stir in the spinach and cook briefly until wilted, then
season to taste with salt and pepper. Ladle the soup into
bowls and serve.

200

cauliflower & cumin
soup

SERVES 4

2 teaspoons sunflower oil
1 onion, chopped
1 garlic clove, crushed
2 teaspoons cumin seeds
1 cauliflower, cut into small florets, woody core
    discarded, about 500 g (1 lb) when prepared
1 large potato, chopped
450 ml (¾ pint) vegetable stock (see page 10)
450 ml (¾ pint) semi-skimmed milk
2 tablespoons low-fat crème fraîche
2 tablespoons chopped coriander leaves
salt and pepper

Heat the oil in a saucepan, add the onion, garlic
and cumin seeds and fry for 3–4 minutes,
stirring frequently. Stir in the cauliflower,
potato, stock and milk and bring to the boil.
Reduce the heat and simmer for 15 minutes.

Leave the soup to cool slightly, then purée
in the pan with a stick blender or in batches
in a blender or food processor until smooth,
returning to the pan. Stir through the crème
fraîche and coriander and reheat gently, then
season to taste with salt and pepper. Serve with
slices of crusty wholemeal bread.

201

next time...

For curried cauliflower soup, fry the onion
and garlic in the oil as in the recipe above,
omitting the cumin. Stir in 2 tablespoons mild
curry paste and cook for 1 minute, then add
the cauliflower, potato, stock and milk. Finish
making the soup as above, then serve with
some mini poppadums.

202

roast root vegetable
soup

SERVES 6

4 carrots, chopped
2 parsnips, chopped
olive oil, for spraying
1 leek, finely chopped
1.2 litres (2 pints) vegetable stock (see page 10)
2 teaspoons thyme leaves, plus extra sprigs
    to garnish
salt and pepper

Put the carrots and parsnips into a roasting tin,
spray lightly with olive oil and season to taste
with salt and pepper. Roast in a preheated oven,
200°C (400°F), Gas Mark 6, for 1 hour or until
the vegetables are very soft.

Meanwhile, put the leek into a large saucepan
with the stock and 1 teaspoon of the thyme.
Bring to a simmer, then cover and simmer
gently for 20 minutes.

Purée the roasted root vegetables in a blender
or food processor until smooth, adding a little
of the stock if necessary. Transfer to the stock
saucepan, season to taste with salt and pepper
and add the remaining thyme. Stir and simmer
for 5 minutes to reheat.

Ladle into bowls and serve garnished with
thyme sprigs.

203

next time...

For roast butternut squash soup, halve, deseed,
peel and thickly slice a 750 g (1 ½ lb) butternut
squash. Put into a roasting tin, spray lightly
with olive oil and season to taste with salt
and pepper. Roast in a preheated oven, 200°C
(400°F), Gas Mark 6, for 45 minutes. Use
instead of the roasted root vegetables in the
recipe above to make the soup.

204

venison, red wine & lentil soup

SERVES 6

6 venison sausages
1 tablespoon olive oil
1 onion, roughly chopped
2 garlic cloves, finely chopped
200 g (7 oz) potato, diced
1 carrot, diced
4 tomatoes, skinned if liked and roughly
  chopped
125 g (4 oz) dried green lentils, rinsed
  and drained
300 ml (½ pint) red wine
1.5 litres (2½ pints) beef or pheasant stock
  (see page 9)
2 tablespoons cranberry sauce
1 tablespoon tomato purée
1 teaspoon ground allspice
2 bay leaves
1 thyme sprig
salt and pepper

Cook the sausages under a hot grill for about 10 minutes, turning frequently, until evenly browned and just cooked.

Meanwhile, heat the oil in a large saucepan, add the onion and fry for 5 minutes, stirring occasionally, until softened and just beginning to brown. Add the garlic, potato and carrot and fry briefly, then mix in the tomatoes and lentils.

Pour in the wine and stock, then add the cranberry sauce, tomato purée, allspice and herbs. Season well with salt and pepper, then slice the sausages and add to the pan. Bring to the boil, stirring, then reduce the heat, cover and simmer gently for 1¼ hours. Taste and adjust the seasoning if needed.

Ladle the soup into bowls and serve with French bread croûtons (see page 13), rubbed with a little garlic and sprinkled with parsley.

205

next time...

For pheasant, bacon & black pudding soup, omitting the sausages, fry the onion in the oil as in the previous recipe with 150 g (5 oz) rindless smoked streaky bacon, diced. Then add 125 g (4 oz) black pudding, diced, and the leftover diced meat from a roast pheasant along with the garlic, potato and carrot and fry briefly, before adding the tomatoes and lentils as before. Continue making the soup as before, using pheasant stock.

206

red pepper & courgette
soup

SERVES 4

3 tablespoons olive oil
2 onions, finely chopped
1 garlic clove, crushed
3 red peppers, cored, deseeded and roughly
  chopped
2 courgettes, roughly chopped
900 ml (1½ pints) vegetable stock (see page 10)
salt and pepper

Heat 2 tablespoons of the oil in a large
saucepan, add the onions and fry gently for
5 minutes, or until softened and golden brown.
Stir in the garlic and fry gently for 1 minute.
Add the red peppers and half the courgettes
and fry for 5–8 minutes, or until softened.

Add the stock or water to the pan, season to
taste with salt and pepper and bring to the boil.
Reduce the heat, cover and simmer gently for
20 minutes until the vegetables are tender.

Leave to cool slightly, then purée the soup in
the pan with a stick blender or in batches in a
blender or food processor, returning to the pan.
Reheat, then taste and adjust the seasoning
if needed. Meanwhile, heat the remaining oil
in a frying pan and gently fry the remaining
courgette for 5 minutes. Serve the soup in bowls
topped with the fried courgette.

207

next time...

For red pepper & carrot soup, fry the onion
and then the garlic in the oil as in the recipe
above. Replace the courgettes with 2 carrots,
diced, and add with the peppers, then continue
making the soup as above. Purée and reheat,
then serve topped with spoonfuls of garlic and
herb soft cheese and some chopped chives.

208

summer green pea
soup

SERVES 4

15 g (1 oz) butter
1 bunch of spring onions, chopped
1.25 kg (2½ lb) fresh peas, shelled, or 500 g (1 lb)
  frozen peas
750 ml (1¼ pints) vegetable stock (see page 10)
2 tablespoons thick natural yogurt or
  single cream
whole nutmeg, for grating
chopped chives, to garnish

Melt the butter in a large saucepan, add the
spring onions and fry gently for a few minutes,
stirring frequently, until softened but not
browned. Add the peas and stock and bring to
the boil. Reduce the heat and simmer for up
to 15 minutes for fresh peas or 5 minutes for
frozen peas, or until tender. Don't overcook
fresh peas, or they will lose their flavour.

Leave to cool slightly, then purée the soup in
the pan with a stick blender or in batches in a
blender or food processor, returning to the pan.
Stir in the yogurt or cream and grate in a little
nutmeg. Reheat gently, if necessary, before
serving, garnished with chopped chives.

209

next time...

For minted pea & broad bean soup, fry the
spring onions in the butter as in the recipe
above, then add 625 g (1¼ lb) fresh peas and
625 g (1¼ lb) fresh broad beans, shelled, or
250 g (8 oz) frozen peas and 250 g (8 oz) frozen
broad beans, 2 mint sprigs and the stock. Cook
as above, then purée and reheat. Ladle the soup
into bowls and top with 4 tablespoons double
cream, swirled into the soup, and a few tiny
mint leaves.

210

seafood & corn chowder

SERVES 6

25 g (1 oz) butter
½ bunch of spring onions, sliced, white and
　green parts kept separate
200 g (7 oz) potato, diced
300 ml (½ pint) fish stock (see page 10)
1 large bay leaf
150 g (5 oz) smoked haddock fillet
150 g (5 oz) haddock or cod fillet
50 g (2 oz) frozen sweetcorn
200 g (7 oz) frozen seafood mix, defrosted,
　rinsed with cold water and drained
300 ml (½ pint) milk
150 ml (¼ pint) double cream
2 tablespoons chopped parsley
salt and pepper
6 large bread rolls, tops sliced off and centres
　hollowed out, to serve

Melt the butter in a saucepan, add the white
spring onion parts and the potato and toss
in the butter, then cover and fry gently for
10 minutes, stirring occasionally, until only
just beginning to colour.

Pour in the stock and add the bay leaf, then lay
the fish fillets on top and season with salt and
pepper. Bring to the boil, then reduce the heat,
cover and simmer gently for 20 minutes until
the potatoes are tender. Lift the fish out of the
soup with a slotted spoon and put on to a plate.
Flake into pieces, discarding the skin and any
stray bones.

Return the fish to the soup, add the remaining
green spring onion tops, sweetcorn, shellfish
and milk and bring back to the boil. Reduce the
heat, re-cover and simmer for 5 minutes until
the seafood is reheated. Remove and discard
the bay leaf. Pour in the cream, add the parsley
and taste and adjust the seasoning if needed,
then reheat. Ladle the soup into the hollowed-
out bread rolls. Scoop out the soup with a small
spoon, then eat the bread last when steeped in
all the fishy flavours.

211

next time...

For chicken & corn chowder, fry 6 small
skinless chicken thigh fillets, diced, with the
white spring onion parts in the butter as in
the previous recipe for 5 minutes until just
turning golden. Then add the diced potato,
cover and fry gently for 5 minutes. Pour in
300 ml (½ pint) chicken stock (see page 9), add
1 large bay leaf and season to taste with salt
and pepper. Bring to the boil, then cover and
simmer gently for 30 minutes. Add the green
spring onion tops, sweetcorn and milk as
before along with 50 g (2 oz) cooked ham, diced,
re-cover and simmer gently for 5 minutes, then
mix in the double cream and reheat as before.
Serve in the hollow-out bread rolls or bowls.

212

salmon & tarragon
sabayon

SERVES 6

400 g (13 oz) skinless salmon fillet, cut in two
4 tablespoons Noilly Prat
4 spring onions, thinly sliced, white and green
    parts kept separate
pared rind of 1 lemon
600 ml (1 pint) fish stock (see page 10)
4 egg yolks
1 tablespoon finely chopped tarragon, plus
    extra sprigs to garnish (optional)
1 teaspoon Dijon mustard
25 g (1 oz) butter, at room temperature
150 ml (¼ pint) double cream
salt and pepper

Put the salmon pieces into a saucepan with the Noilly Prat, white spring onion parts, lemon rind and stock. Season to taste with salt and pepper and bring to the boil. Reduce the heat, cover and simmer for 10 minutes until the fish is cooked and flakes easily when pressed with a knife.

Lift the fish out of the stock with a slotted spoon on to a plate and break into pieces, discarding any stray bones. Cover with foil to keep warm.

Whisk the egg yolks, chopped tarragon, mustard and butter together in a large bowl. Strain the hot stock through a sieve into a jug, then gradually pour it into the egg mixture, whisking constantly until smooth. Return to the saucepan, add the cream and remaining green spring onion tops, then whisk over a low heat for 4–5 minutes until the mixture is frothy and slightly thickened. Take care not to overheat the soup, or the eggs will curdle. Taste and adjust the seasoning if needed.

Divide the salmon among shallow bowls. Pour the hot frothy sabayon around the salmon, garnish with tarragon sprigs, if liked, and serve immediately.

213

next time...

For seafood sabayon, put 200 g (7 oz) cod loin and 200 g (7 oz) salmon fillet into a saucepan with the Noilly Pratt, white spring onion parts, lemon rind and stock as in the previous recipe. Season to taste with salt and pepper and bring to the boil, then cover and simmer for 10 minutes. Continue making the sabayon as before. Ladle into bowls, then divide the cod and salmon among the bowls and top with 100 g (3½ oz) white crab meat, defrosted and drained thoroughly if frozen.

214

red pepper & ginger soup

SERVES 4

3 red peppers, halved, cored and deseeded
1 red onion, quartered
2 garlic cloves, unpeeled
1 teaspoon olive oil
5 cm (2 inch) piece of fresh root ginger, peeled
    and grated
1 teaspoon ground cumin
1 teaspoon ground coriander
1 large potato, chopped
900 ml (1½ pints) vegetable stock (see page 10)
4 tablespoons fromage frais
salt and pepper

Put the red peppers skin-side up in a nonstick roasting tin with the onion and garlic cloves. Roast in a preheated oven, 200°C (400°F), Gas Mark 6, for 40 minutes, or until the peppers have blistered and the onion quarters and garlic cloves are soft. If the onion quarters start to brown too much, cover them with the pepper halves and continue roasting.

Meanwhile, heat the oil in a saucepan, add the ginger, cumin and coriander and cook gently for 5 minutes until the ginger is soft. Add the potato and stir well, then season to taste with salt and pepper. Pour in the stock and bring to a simmer, cover and cook gently for 30 minutes.

Transfer the roasted peppers to a plastic bag, close it tightly and leave to steam for 10 minutes. Add the roasted onion to the saucepan, and when cool enough, squeeze the garlic flesh from its skins into the pan. Peel the skins off the peppers and add all but one half to the soup. Simmer for 5 minutes.

Leave the soup to cool slightly, then purée in batches in a food processor or blender until smooth. Return to the saucepan, and thin with a little water and reheat if necessary.

Spoon the soup into bowls. Slice the remaining pepper half into strips and place on top of the soup with a spoonful of fromage frais.

215

next time...

For **red pepper & pesto soup**, roast the red peppers, onion and garlic cloves as in the previous recipe. Then heat the oil in a saucepan, add 2 teaspoons pesto along with the diced potato, omitting the fresh ginger and spices, and fry gently for 2–3 minutes. Continue making the soup as before.

216

scottish cullen skink

SERVES 6

25 g (1 oz) butter
1 onion, roughly chopped
500 g (1 lb) potatoes, diced
1 large Finnan haddock or 300 g (10 oz)
    smoked haddock fillet
1 bay leaf
900 ml (1½ pints) fish stock (see page 10)
150 ml (¼ pint) milk
6 tablespoons double cream
salt and pepper
chopped parsley, to garnish

Melt the butter in a saucepan, add the onion and fry gently for 5 minutes until softened, stirring occasionally. Stir in the potatoes, cover and cook gently for 5 minutes.

Lay the haddock on top, add the bay leaf and stock and season with salt and pepper. Bring to the boil, then reduce the heat, cover and simmer for 30 minutes, or until the potatoes are tender.

Remove and discard the bay leaf. Lift the fish out of the pan with a slotted spoon and put on to a plate. If using a Finnan haddock, loosen the bones with a small knife, then lift away the backbone and head. Break the fish into flakes, discarding the skin, and check for any remaining bones. If using haddock fillet, simply break the fish into flakes, discarding the skin and any stray bones. Return two-thirds of the fish to the pan.

Purée the soup in the pan with a stick blender or in batches in a blender or food processor until smooth, returning to the pan. Stir in the milk and cream. Bring just to the boil, then reduce the heat and simmer gently until thoroughly hot. Taste and adjust the seasoning if needed.

Ladle the soup into bowls, sprinkle with the reserved fish and garnish with chopped parsley. Serve with toasted barley bannocks or soda griddle scones.

217

next time...

For Scottish ham & haddie bree, fry the onion in the butter as in the previous recipe, then add 6 rindless smoked streaky bacon rashers, diced, with the potatoes and cook until they are just beginning to turn golden. Add the fish, bay leaf, stock and salt and pepper and cook as before. Lift the fish out of the soup, break into flakes, discarding any bones and skin, and return all of it to the soup. Then without puréeing, stir in the milk and cream and reheat as before. Serve as a chunky soup topped with chopped chives.

218

spicy coriander & lentil soup

SERVES 8

2 tablespoons vegetable oil
2 onions, chopped
2 garlic cloves, chopped
2 celery sticks, chopped
500 g (1 lb) dried red lentils, rinsed and drained
400 g (13 oz) can tomatoes, drained
1 red chilli, deseeded and chopped (optional)
1 teaspoon paprika
1 teaspoon harissa paste
1 teaspoon ground cumin
1.2 litres (2 pints) vegetable stock (see page 10)
salt and pepper
2 tablespoons chopped coriander, to garnish

Heat the oil in a large saucepan, add the onions, garlic and celery and fry gently for a few minutes until softened.

Add the lentils and tomatoes and mix well, then stir in the chilli (if using), paprika, harissa, cumin and stock, and season to taste with salt and pepper. Bring to a simmer, then cover and cook gently for 40–50 minutes until the lentils are soft, stirring occasionally and adding a little more stock or water if the soup gets too thick.

Serve the soup immediately in bowls, garnished with the chopped coriander.

219

next time...

For spicy coriander & white bean soup, fry the onions, garlic and celery in the oil as in the previous recipe. Rinse and drain 2 x 425 g (14 oz) cans haricot or cannellini beans, add to the pan with the chilli, flavourings and stock and simmer for 40–50 minutes as before. Then roughly mash some of the beans to thicken the soup and stir in 4 tablespoons chopped flat leaf parsley and 2 tablespoons chopped coriander just before serving in bowls.

220

courgette & dill soup

SERVES 8

2 tablespoons sunflower or light olive oil
1 large onion, chopped
2 garlic cloves, crushed
1 kg (2 lb) courgettes, sliced
1.5 litres (2½) pints vegetable or chicken stock
  (see pages 10 and 9)
2–4 tablespoons finely chopped dill, plus extra
  fronds to garnish
salt and pepper
125 ml (4 fl oz) single cream, to garnish

Heat the oil in a saucepan, add the onion
and garlic and fry for a few minutes, stirring
frequently, until softened but not browned. Add
the courgettes, cover the pan with greaseproof
paper and cook over a low heat for 10 minutes
until the courgettes are soft.

Pour in 1.2 litres (2 pints) of the stock and bring
to a simmer, cover the pan with a lid and cook
gently for 10–15 minutes.

Leave to cool slightly, then strain the liquid
through a sieve into a bowl. Purée the
courgettes with a little of the stock in a blender
or food processor until smooth, then pour into
a clean saucepan. Add the strained courgette
stock and the remaining stock, along with
the chopped dill. Season to taste with salt and
pepper and bring to the boil.

Pour the soup into bowls, add a swirl of the
cream to each serving and garnish with
dill fronds.

221

next time...

For mixed squash & dill soup, heat
2 tablespoons sunflower oil in a saucepan,
add 1 onion, chopped, and 2 garlic cloves,
crushed, and fry for 5 minutes. Add 500 g (1 lb)
courgettes or marrow, diced or deseeded and
diced, and 500 g (1 lb) deseeded, peeled and
diced pumpkin or butternut squash (weight
when prepared), cover the pan with greaseproof
paper and cook over a low heat for 10 minutes.
Then add the stock and continue making the
soup as before.

222

mushroom hot & sour soup

SERVES 4–6

1.2 litres (2 pints) fish stock (see page 10)
1 lemon grass stalk, lightly bruised
3 dried kaffir lime leaves or 3 pieces of lime peel
2 Thai red chillies, halved and deseeded, plus
    extra, sliced, to garnish
2 tablespoons lime juice
1–2 tablespoons Thai fish sauce
50 g (2 oz) drained canned bamboo shoots
125 g (4 oz) oyster mushrooms
2 spring onions, finely sliced

Pour the stock into a saucepan and add the lemon grass, lime leaves or lime peel and chillies. Bring to a simmer and continue simmering for 10 minutes. Strain the liquid through a sieve into a clean saucepan. Reserve a little of the red chilli from the sieve and discard the remaining seasonings.

Add the lime juice and fish sauce to taste to the stock with the bamboo shoots, mushrooms and reserved chilli. Simmer for 5 minutes. Ladle the soup into bowls and sprinkle with the spring onions, then garnish with fresh red chilli slices.

223

next time...

For vegetarian tomato hot & sour soup, make the soup as in the recipe above, replacing the fish stock with 1.2 litres (2 pints) vegetable stock (see page 10), the fish sauce with 2 tablespoons light soy sauce and the mushrooms with 4 tomatoes, skinned, deseeded and chopped, and 1½ red peppers, cored, deseeded and diced.

224

chicken soup with lockshen

SERVES 6

2 litres (3½ pints) chicken stock (see page 9)
150–200 g (5–7 oz) cooked chicken, shredded
100 g (3½ oz) lockshen (dried vermicelli pasta)
salt and pepper
chopped parsley, to garnish (optional)

Bring the stock to the boil in a large saucepan, add the shredded chicken and heat thoroughly. Meanwhile, bring a separate saucepan of water to the boil, add the lockshen and simmer for 4–5 minutes until tender.

Drain the lockshen, divide it among bowls so that it makes a small nest in the base of each, then ladle the soup on top. Garnish with a little chopped parsley, if liked.

225

next time...

For chicken soup with kneidlach, to make the kneidlech, put 125 g (4 oz) medium matzo meal into a bowl with a pinch of ground ginger, a little salt and pepper and 1 beaten egg. Add 1 tablespoon melted schmalz (chicken fat, available from Kosher butchers) or dairy-free spread and mix in 5–6 tablespoons hot chicken stock or water to make a pliable dough. Divide into 20 portions, shape into small balls and put on to a plate. Cover and chill in the refrigerator for 1 hour. Add to a saucepan of simmering water and cook for 25 minutes until they rise to the surface of the water and are spongy. Meanwhile, make the soup as in the recipe above, omitting the lockshen, then ladle into bowls. Drain the kneidlach well, add to the soup and serve immediately.

226

fennel & lemon
soup

SERVES 4

50 ml (2 fl oz) olive oil
3 large spring onions, chopped
250 g (8 oz) fennel bulb, trimmed, cored and
    finely sliced
1 potato, diced
finely grated rind and juice of 1 lemon
900 ml (1½ pints) vegetable or chicken stock
    (see pages 10 and 9), plus extra if needed
salt and pepper

Heat the oil in a large saucepan, add the spring onions and fry for 5 minutes until softened. Stir in the fennel, potato and lemon rind and cook for 5 minutes, stirring frequently, until the fennel begins to soften.

Pour in the stock and bring to the boil, then reduce the heat, cover and simmer for about 15 minutes until the vegetables are tender.

Leave the soup to cool slightly, then purée in batches in a blender or food processor until smooth. Pass the purée through a fine sieve to remove any strings of fennel back into the rinsed-out saucepan. The soup should not be too thick, so add more stock if necessary. Taste and season well with salt and pepper and the lemon juice, then reheat gently.

Pour the soup into bowls and serve with slices of toasted crusty bread, or croûtons (see page 13).

227

next time...

For fennel & trout soup, soften the vegetables in the oil, add the stock and bring to the boil, then simmer as in the previous recipe, while steaming 2 rainbow trout fillets above the simmering soup in a covered steamer pan for 10 minutes, or until the fish flakes easily when pressed with a knife. Lift the trout out of the steamer, then break into flakes, discarding the skin and any stray bones. Spoon into the base of 4 shallow serving bowls and ladle the soup over the top.

228

green bean, miso & noodle soup

SERVES 2

3 tablespoons brown miso paste
1 litre (1¾ pints) vegetable stock (see page 10)
25 g (1 oz) fresh root ginger, peeled and grated
2 garlic cloves, thinly sliced
1 small hot red chilli, deseeded and thinly sliced
100 g (3½ oz) dried soba, wholemeal or plain noodles
1 bunch of spring onions, finely shredded
100 g (3½ oz) shelled fresh or frozen peas
250 g (8 oz) runner beans, shredded
3 tablespoons mirin
1 tablespoon sugar
1 tablespoon rice wine vinegar

Blend the miso paste with a dash of the stock in a saucepan to make a thick, smooth paste. Add a little more of the stock to thin the paste and then pour in the remainder. Add the ginger, garlic and chilli and bring almost to the boil.

Reduce the heat to a gentle simmer, stir in the noodles and cook for about 5 minutes, stirring, until they have softened into the stock.

Add all the remaining ingredients and stir well. Simmer gently for 1–2 minutes until the vegetables have softened slightly. Ladle into bowls and serve immediately.

229

carrot & ginger soup

SERVES 4

2 tablespoons olive oil
1 large onion, chopped
1–2 garlic cloves, crushed
1 tablespoon peeled and finely grated fresh root ginger
375 g (12 oz) carrots, sliced
900 ml (1½ pints) vegetable or chicken stock (see pages 10 and 9)
2 tablespoons lime or lemon juice
salt and pepper

TO GARNISH
soured cream
2 spring onions, finely chopped

Heat the oil in a saucepan, add the onion, garlic and ginger and fry for 5–6 minutes, or until softened. Add the carrots and stock and bring to the boil, then reduce the heat and simmer for 15–20 minutes, or until the carrots are tender.

Leave the soup to cool slightly, then purée in batches in a blender or food processor with the lime or lemon juice until smooth. Pass the purée through a fine sieve back into saucepan, season to taste and reheat.

Pour the soup into bowls and top each serving with a spoonful of soured cream and a sprinkle of the spring onions.

230

greek chicken
avgolomeno

SERVES 6

2 litres (3½ pints) chicken stock (see page 9)
125 g (4 oz) dried orzo, macaroni or other small
   pasta shapes
25 g (1 oz) butter
25 g (1 oz) plain flour
4 egg yolks
grated rind and juice of 1 lemon, plus extra rind
   to garnish (optional) and wedges to serve
salt and pepper

TO GARNISH (OPTIONAL)

125 g (4 oz) leftover cooked chicken, stripped
   from the carcass before the stock was made,
   finely shredded
oregano leaves, torn

Bring the stock to the boil in a large saucepan
and add the pasta, then reduce the heat and
simmer for 8–10 minutes until just tender.

Meanwhile, melt the butter in a small
saucepan and stir in the flour to make a paste.
Gradually mix in 2 ladlefuls of the hot stock
and bring to the boil, stirring, then remove the
pan from the heat.

Beat the egg yolks with the lemon rind and
some salt and pepper in a bowl, then slowly
stir in the lemon juice until smooth. Gradually
pour in the hot sauce from the small pan,
stirring constantly.

Once the pasta is ready, stir a further 2 ladlefuls
of hot stock into the lemon mixture, then pour
back into the large pan and mix well. (Don't be
tempted to add the eggs and lemon directly to
the pasta stock, or it may curdle.)

Ladle the soup into shallow bowls. Top with
the shredded chicken, some extra lemon rind
and torn oregano leaves, if liked. Serve with
lemon wedges.

231

next time...

For cod avgolomeno, bring 2 litres (3½ pints)
strained fish stock (see page 10) to the boil in
a large saucepan, add 125 g (4 oz) dried small
pasta shapes and 625 g (1¼ lb) skinless cod
fillet and simmer for 8–10 minutes until both
are tender. Lift the fish out with a slotted spoon
on to a plate and break into flakes, discarding
the skin and any stray bones, then return to the
pan. Make the sauce with the butter, flour and
some of the stock, then mix into the egg yolk
and lemon mixture as in the previous recipe.
Stir in the second batch of hot stock, before
mixing back into the large pan. Ladle the soup
into bowls and top with snipped chives or a
little snipped chervil.

232

italian tortellini
in brodo

SERVES 6

500 g (1 lb) tomatoes
1.5 litres (2½ pints) chicken stock (see page 9)
200 ml (7 fl oz) dry white wine
1 tablespoon sun-dried tomato paste
1 small bunch of basil, roughly torn into pieces
300 g (10 oz) pack spinach and ricotta tortellini
    or a filling of your choice
6 tablespoons freshly grated Parmesan cheese,
    plus extra for sprinkling
salt and pepper

Cut a cross in the base of each tomato, put into a bowl and cover with boiling water. Leave the tomatoes to soak for 1 minute, then drain, refresh in cold water and peel away the skins. Quarter the tomatoes, scoop out the seeds and dice the flesh.

Put the tomatoes into a large saucepan, add the stock, wine and tomato paste and season to taste with salt and pepper. Bring to the boil, then reduce the heat and simmer gently for 5 minutes.

Add half the basil and all the tortellini, bring back to the boil and cook for 3–4 minutes until the pasta is just tender. Stir in the Parmesan and taste and adjust the seasoning if needed.

Ladle the soup into bowls, sprinkle with a little extra grated Parmesan and garnish with the remaining basil leaves.

233

next time...

For gnocchi & pesto broth, combine the tomatoes, stock, wine and tomato paste in a large saucepan as in the previous recipe, then stir in 2 tablespoons pesto and season to taste with salt and pepper. Bring to the boil, then simmer gently for 5 minutes. Omit the basil and add 300 g (10 oz) chilled gnocchi instead of the tortellini and 125 g (4 oz) spinach leaves, shredded, then simmer for 5 minutes until the gnocchi rise to the surface and the spinach has wilted. Stir in the freshly grated Parmesan as before, check the seasoning and serve in bowls, sprinkled with extra grated Parmesan.

234

cajun red bean
soup

SERVES 6

2 tablespoons sunflower oil
1 large onion, chopped
1 red pepper, cored, deseeded and diced
1 carrot, diced
1 baking potato, diced
2–3 garlic cloves, chopped (optional)
2 teaspoons mixed Cajun spice
400 g (13 oz) can chopped tomatoes
1 tablespoon brown sugar
1 litre (1¾ pints) vegetable stock (see page 10)
425 g (14 oz) can red kidney beans, rinsed
    and drained
50 g (2 oz) okra, conical stalk end discarded
    and sliced
50 g (2 oz) green beans, thinly sliced
salt and pepper

Heat the oil in a large frying pan, add the onion and fry for 5 minutes until softened. Add the red pepper, carrot, potato and garlic (if using) and fry for 5 minutes. Stir in the Cajun spice, tomatoes, sugar, stock and plenty of salt and pepper and bring to the boil.

Stir in the kidney beans and bring to the boil, then reduce the heat, cover and simmer for 45 minutes until the vegetables are tender.

Add the okra and green beans, re-cover and simmer for 5 minutes until just cooked.

Ladle the soup into bowls and serve immediately with crusty bread.

235

next time...

For Hungarian paprika & red bean soup, make the soup as in the previous recipe, replacing the Cajun spice with 1 teaspoon paprika. Once the soup has simmered for 45 minutes, omit the green vegetables and leave to cool slightly, then purée the soup in the pan with a stick blender or in batches in a blender or food processor until smooth, returning to the pan. Reheat, then ladle the soup into bowls and serve topped with 2 tablespoons soured cream and a few caraway seeds.

236

vietnamese beef
pho

SERVES 6

1 teaspoon sunflower oil
1 teaspoon Szechuan peppercorns, roughly
   crushed
1 lemon grass stalk, sliced
1 cinnamon stick, broken into pieces
2 star anise
4 cm (1½ inch) piece of fresh root ginger, peeled
   and sliced
1 small bunch of coriander
1.5 litres (2½ pints) beef stock (see page 9)
1 tablespoon fish sauce
juice of 1 lime
100 g (3½ oz) dried fine rice noodles
250 g (8 oz) rump or flash-fry beef steak,
   trimmed of fat and thinly sliced
100 g (3½ oz) bean sprouts, rinsed and drained
4 spring onions, thinly sliced
1 large mild red chilli, thinly sliced

Heat the oil in a saucepan, add the Szechuan
peppercorns, lemon grass, cinnamon, star anise
and ginger and cook for 1 minute to release their
flavours. Cut the stems from the coriander and
add them to the pan with the stock. Bring to the
boil, stirring, then reduce the heat, cover and
simmer for 40 minutes.

Strain the broth through a sieve, discarding the
flavourings, and return to the pan. Stir in the
fish sauce and lime juice.

Cook the noodles in a separate saucepan
of boiling water according to the packet
instructions, then drain and divide among
bowls. Add the steak to the broth and simmer
for 1–2 minutes until cooked. Divide the bean
sprouts, spring onions and chilli among the
bowls, then ladle the hot broth on top and
sprinkle with the remaining coriander leaves,
torn into pieces.

237

next time...

For Vietnamese prawn soup, make the broth as
in the previous recipe, replacing the beef stock
with 1.5 litres (2½ pints) chicken or vegetable
stock (see pages 9–10) and the cinnamon
stick with 2 kaffir lime leaves. Add 200 g (7 oz)
raw peeled prawns and 150 g (5 oz) button
mushrooms, sliced, to the finished broth in
place of the steak and simmer for 4–5 minutes
until the prawns turn pink. Ladle the hot soup
over the bean sprouts, spring onions and chilli,
then sprinkle with the torn coriander as before.

238

iced green gazpacho

SERVES 4

2 celery sticks with their leaves
1 small green pepper, cored and deseeded
1 large cucumber, peeled
3 slices of stale white bread, crusts removed
1 green chilli, deseeded
4 garlic cloves
1 teaspoon clear honey
150 g (5 oz) walnuts, lightly toasted
200 g (7 oz) baby spinach leaves
50 g (2 oz) basil leaves
4 tablespoons cider vinegar
250 ml (8 fl oz) extra virgin olive oil, plus extra
   for drizzling
6 tablespoons natural yogurt
475 ml (16 fl oz) iced water
handful of ice cubes
salt and pepper

Roughly chop the celery, green pepper, cucumber, bread, chilli and garlic.

Put into a blender or food processor with the honey, walnuts, spinach, basil, vinegar, oil, yogurt, most of the iced water, the ice cubes and plenty of salt and pepper. Whizz until smooth, adding the remaining iced water if needed to achieve the desired consistency. Taste and adjust the seasoning if needed.

Pour the soup into chilled bowls, drizzle with extra virgin olive oil and serve with croûtons (see page 13).

239

next time...

For iced rocket & lettuce gazpacho, make the soup as in the previous recipe, replacing the walnuts and spinach with 100 g (3½ oz) toasted almonds, roughly chopped, 100 g (3½ oz) rocket leaves and 1 Little Gem lettuce, sliced, and omitting the cider vinegar. Once blended, stir in white wine vinegar to taste.

240

potato soup with parsley

SERVES 4

1.5 litres (2½ pints) beef stock (see page 9)
4 potatoes, coarsely grated
1 egg yolk
1 hard-boiled egg yolk, mashed
50 ml (2 fl oz) single cream
50 g (2 oz) Parmesan cheese, freshly grated
1 tablespoon finely chopped parsley
salt and pepper

Pour the stock into a saucepan and bring to the boil. Sprinkle the grated potatoes with salt and pepper to taste, then drop them into the stock and cook for 15 minutes, stirring occasionally.

Beat the fresh egg yolk in a soup tureen. Add the mashed hard-boiled egg yolk, cream, Parmesan and parsley and beat together.

Carefully pour 250 ml (8 fl oz) of the hot stock into the egg mixture, stirring constantly. Reheat the remaining stock and potatoes, then gradually add to the tureen, stirring constantly.

Sprinkle the soup with croûtons (see page 13) and ladle into bowls to serve.

241

scallop & broccoli
broth

SERVES 4

1.2 litres (2 pints) vegetable or chicken stock
(see pages 10 and 9)
25 g (1 oz) fresh root ginger, peeled and cut into
thin strips, peelings reserved
1 tablespoon soy sauce
3 spring onions, finely diagonally sliced
500 g (1 lb) broccoli, cut into small florets
1 small red chilli, deseeded and finely sliced
(optional)
12 large scallops, with roes
a few drops of Thai fish sauce, to taste
juice of ½ lime, or to taste
sesame oil, to garnish

Put the stock into a large saucepan with the
ginger peelings, bring to the boil and boil for
15 minutes. Set aside and leave to steep for a
further 15 minutes.

Strain the stock through a sieve into a clean
saucepan. Add the soy sauce, ginger strips,
spring onions, broccoli and chilli (if using) and
simmer for 5 minutes.

Add the scallops and simmer for 3 minutes, or
until they are just cooked through. Season to
taste with Thai fish sauce and lime juice.

Lift the scallops out with a slotted spoon and
put 3 in each bowl. Divide the broccoli among
the bowls and pour over the hot broth. Top each
serving with a few drops of sesame oil and
serve immediately.

242

next time...

For mixed seafood & broccoli broth, make the
broth as in the previous recipe, replacing the
scallops with a 200 g (7 oz) pack frozen mixed
seafood, defrosted, rinsed with cold water and
drained, to the broth. Simmer for 3–4 minutes
until piping hot, then ladle into bowls.

243

pork ball & tofu soup

SERVES 4

600 ml (1 pint) chicken stock (see page 10)
1 garlic clove, finely chopped, plus 4, halved
½ teaspoon pepper
8 coriander roots, plus coriander leaves to
garnish
200 g (7 oz) silken tofu, cut into 2.5 cm (1 inch)
slices
1 sheet of nori, torn into shreds
2 tablespoons light soy sauce

PORK BALLS
65 g (2½ oz) minced pork
1 tablespoon light soy sauce
½ teaspoon pepper

Put the stock into a saucepan with all the
garlic, pepper and coriander roots and bring
to a simmer.

Meanwhile, for the pork balls, mix the pork,
soy sauce and pepper together in a bowl, then
shape the mixture into small balls.

Drop the pork balls into the soup and simmer
gently for 6–7 minutes.

Add the tofu, laver and soy sauce and stir for
30 seconds, then serve the soup in bowls,
garnished with coriander leaves.

244

haddock & shellfish
soup

SERVES 4

500 g (1 lb) undyed smoked haddock fillet
25 g (1 oz) butter
1 large leek, chopped
2 teaspoons medium curry paste
1 litre (1¾ pints) fish stock (see page 10)
50 g (2 oz) creamed coconut, chopped
3 bay leaves
150 g (5 oz) French beans, cut into 1 cm (½ inch)
    lengths
3 small courgettes, chopped
250 g (8 oz) mixed seafood, defrosted if frozen,
    rinsed with cold water and drained
100 ml (3½ fl oz) single cream
4 tablespoons finely chopped parsley
salt and pepper

Cut the haddock into small pieces, discarding
the skin and any stray bones.

Melt the butter in a large saucepan, add
the leek and gently fry for 3 minutes until
softened. Stir in the curry paste, stock and
creamed coconut and bring almost to the boil.
Reduce the heat, cover and simmer gently for
10 minutes until the leek is soft.

Stir in the bay leaves, beans and courgettes
and cook for 2 minutes until the vegetables are
slightly softened. Add the smoked haddock and
mixed seafood, 3 tablespoons of the cream and
the parsley and cook very gently for 5 minutes
until the haddock flakes easily when pressed
with a knife.

Season to taste with salt and pepper and ladle
the soup into bowls. Serve swirled with the
remaining cream.

245

next time...

For smoked salmon & mangetout soup, make
the soup as in the previous recipe, replacing
the smoked haddock with 500 g (1 lb) lightly
smoked salmon and the French beans with
150 g (5 oz) mangetout, sliced.

246

courgette & mint soup

SERVES 4

50 g (2 oz) butter
1 small onion, chopped
1–2 garlic cloves, crushed
750 g (1½ lb) courgettes, diced
finely grated rind of 1 lemon
600 ml (1 pint) vegetable or chicken stock (see
    pages 10 and 9), or water
2–3 tablespoons chopped mint
2 egg yolks
100 ml (3½ fl oz) double cream
salt and pepper
single cream, to garnish

Melt the butter in a saucepan over a low
heat, add the onion and garlic and cook for
5–6 minutes, or until softened. Stir in the
courgettes and lemon rind and cook for a
further 5–10 minutes, or until tender. Add the
stock or water and mint and bring to the boil,
then reduce the heat and simmer for 5 minutes.

Leave the soup to cool slightly, then purée in
batches in a blender or food processor until
smooth. Pass through a fine sieve back into
the saucepan. Reheat to just below boiling point.
Mix the egg yolks and double cream together
in a small bowl and whisk in a ladleful of the
hot soup. Whisk the egg mixture back into the
pan and heat gently, stirring, but don't allow
the soup to boil, or it will curdle. Season to taste
with salt and pepper.

Serve the soup in bowls and drizzle with
single cream.

247

next time...

For courgette & broccoli soup, make the
soup as in the previous recipe, but using 500 g
(1 lb) courgettes, diced, along with 250 g (8 oz)
broccoli, sliced.

248

barley soup with pork & cabbage

SERVES 6

4 tablespoons olive oil
1 garlic clove, chopped
1 onion, chopped
1.2 litres (2 pints) beef stock (see page 9)
750 ml (1¼ pints) water
300 g (10 oz) boneless lean pork, cut into 1.5 cm
    (¾ inch) strips
2 carrots, chopped
300 g (10 oz) spring or Savoy cabbage, roughly
    chopped
125 g (4 oz) pearl barley
300 g (10 oz) potatoes, cut into 1 cm (½ inch) dice
salt and pepper

Heat the oil in a large saucepan, add the garlic
and onion and fry over a medium heat for a few
minutes, stirring occasionally, until softened.

Stir in the stock, measured water, pork, carrots,
cabbage and pearl barley. Bring to the boil,
then reduce the heat, cover and simmer for
20 minutes.

Add the potatoes and season to taste with salt
and pepper. If the soup is too thick, add a
little water, then re-cover and simmer for a
further 30 minutes, stirring occasionally.
Serve in bowls.

249

spicy lentil & carrot soup

SERVES 4

2 tablespoons sunflower oil
1 garlic clove, finely chopped
1 teaspoon peeled and grated fresh root ginger
1 red chilli, finely chopped
1 onion, finely chopped
1 tablespoon smoked paprika, plus extra
  to garnish
700 g (1½ lb) carrots, finely chopped
150 g (5 oz) dried red lentils, rinsed and drained
150 ml (¼ pint) single cream
1 litre (1¾ pints) hot vegetable stock (see
  page 10)
100 g (3½ oz) crème fraîche
small handful of chopped coriander leaves
salt and pepper

CARAMELIZED ONIONS
15 g (1oz) butter
1 tablespoon olive oil
1 onion, thinly sliced

Heat the sunflower oil in a heavy-based saucepan, add the garlic, ginger, chilli, onion and smoked paprika and cook over a medium-high heat, stirring, for 1–2 minutes. Add the carrots, lentils, cream and stock and bring to the boil, then reduce the heat and simmer for 15–20 minutes.

Meanwhile, for the caramelized onions, melt the butter with the olive oil in a frying pan, add the onion and fry gently for 12–15 minutes, or until caramelized and golden brown, stirring occasionally. Remove with a slotted spoon, drain on kitchen paper and keep warm.

Leave the soup to cool slightly, then purée in the pan with a stick blender or in batches in a blender or food processor until smooth, returning to the pan. Reheat, then season well with salt and pepper.

Ladle into bowls and top with a dollop of crème fraîche, the chopped coriander and caramelized onions. Sprinkle with a little smoked paprika.

250

next time...

For spicy lentil & parsnip soup, fry the garlic, ginger, chilli, onion and smoked paprika in the oil as in the previous recipe, then add 750 g (1½ lb) parsnips, diced, instead of the carrots and continue making the soup as before.

251

iced tomato & pepper
soup with salsa verde

SERVES 4–6

1 kg (2 lb) vine-ripened tomatoes, cored
2 large red peppers, cored, deseeded and
roughly chopped
2 garlic cloves, chopped
1 small red chilli, deseeded and finely chopped
600 ml (1 pint) tomato juice or passata
6 tablespoons olive oil
2 tablespoons balsamic vinegar
600 ml (1 pint) crushed ice
salt and pepper

SALSA VERDE
2 garlic cloves, finely chopped
4 anchovy fillets in oil, rinsed and chopped
3 tablespoons each chopped parsley, mint and
basil
2 tablespoons salted capers, rinsed and
chopped
150 ml (¼ pint) olive oil
2 tablespoons lemon juice

Cut a cross in the base of each tomato, put into
a heatproof bowl and cover with boiling water.
Leave the tomatoes to soak for 1 minute, then
drain, refresh in cold water and peel away the
skins. Halve the tomatoes around the middle
and gently squeeze out and discard the seeds.

Put the tomatoes into a blender or food
processor with the red peppers, garlic and chilli
and blend to a rough purée. Pour the purée into
a large bowl and stir in the tomato juice or
passata, oil and vinegar. Season to taste with
salt and pepper, then cover and chill in the
refrigerator overnight.

Pound the garlic for the salsa verde with
1 teaspoon salt until creamy using a pestle
and mortar. Tip it into a small bowl and stir
in the anchovies, herbs, capers, oil, lemon juice
and pepper to taste.

Stir the crushed ice into the chilled soup and
serve with the salsa verde.

252

next time...

For iced **Mediterranean soup**, skin, halve
and deseed 750 g (1½ lb) tomatoes as in the
previous recipe. Add to a blender or food
processor with 250 g (8 oz) courgettes, diced,
and the red peppers, garlic and chilli, and purée
as before. Serve with a drizzle of basil oil or a
spoonful of pesto.

253

mussel soup with saffron, basil & spinach

SERVES 4

pinch of saffron threads
125 ml (4 fl oz) boiling water
175 ml (6 fl oz) dry white wine
750 g (1½ lb) live mussels, scrubbed and
    debearded, any cracked or open mussels
    discarded
2 tablespoons olive oil
2 shallots, finely chopped
1 garlic clove, finely chopped
200 ml (7 fl oz) double cream
175 g (6 oz) baby spinach leaves
15 basil leaves, shredded

Put the saffron into a small heatproof bowl,
pour over the measured boiling water and leave
to infuse.

Pour the wine into a saucepan large enough to
accommodate all the mussels, bring to the boil
and add the mussels. Cover with a tight-fitting
lid and cook, shaking the pan frequently, for
2–3 minutes, or until the mussels have opened.

Tip the mussels into a larger colander over
a bowl. Take the mussels out of their shells,
discarding any mussels that remain closed.
Strain the mussel liquid through a muslin-
lined sieve and set aside.

Heat the oil in a saucepan, add the shallots
and garlic and cook gently for 5–6 minutes,
or until softened but not browned. Add the
strained mussel liquid, cream and saffron and
its soaking liquid and bring to the boil. Reduce
the heat and add the spinach, half the basil and
all the mussels. Simmer for 2 minutes, then
remove from the heat and stir in the remaining
basil leaves. Serve the soup in bowls.

254

next time...

For mussel soup with saffron, basil &
tomato, make the soup as in the previous
recipe, replacing the spinach with 250 g (8 oz)
tomatoes, skinned, deseeded and diced, and
1 red pepper, roasted, cored, deseeded and
chopped. Simmer for 2 minutes, then ladle the
soup into bowls and top with the remaining
shredded basil.

255

french onion soup

SERVES 4

25 g (1 oz) butter
2 tablespoons olive oil
500 g (1 lb) large onions, halved and thinly
  sliced
1 tablespoon caster sugar
3 tablespoons brandy
150 ml (¼ pint) red wine
1 litre (1¾ pints) beef stock (see page 9)
1 bay leaf
salt and pepper

CHEESY CROÛTES
4–8 slices French bread
1 garlic clove, halved
40 g (1½ oz) Gruyère cheese, grated

Melt the butter with the oil in a saucepan, add the onions and toss in the butter and oil, then fry very gently for 20 minutes until very soft and just beginning to turn golden around the edges, stirring occasionally.

Stir in the sugar and fry the onions for a further 20 minutes, stirring more frequently towards the end of cooking until the onions are caramelized to a rich dark brown. Add the brandy, and when bubbling, flame with a long match and quickly stand well back.

As soon as the flames subside, add the wine, stock and bay leaf, and season to taste with salt and pepper. Bring to the boil, then reduce the heat, cover and simmer for 20 minutes. Taste and adjust the seasoning if needed.

Toast the bread on both sides under a hot grill, then rub with the cut surface of the garlic. Sprinkle with the cheese, put back under the grill and cook until the cheese is bubbling. Ladle the soup into bowls and top with the cheesy croûtes.

256

next time...

For apple & onion soup, fry the onions as in the previous recipe and add 1 small cooking apple, peeled, cored and grated, along with the sugar. When the onions are caramelized, flame with 3 tablespoons Calvados or brandy, then add 150 ml (¼ pint) dry cider, 1 litre (1¾ pints) chicken stock (see page 9) and 2 thyme sprigs, and season to taste with salt and pepper. Bring to the boil, then simmer for 20 minutes. Serve the soup with the garlic-rubbed toasts topped with grilled Camembert slices and sprinkled with a little extra thyme.

257

thai prawn broth

SERVES 4

1.2 litres (2 pints) vegetable stock (see page 10)
2 teaspoons ready-made red Thai curry paste
4 dried kaffir lime leaves, torn into pieces
3–4 teaspoons Thai fish sauce
2 spring onions, sliced
150 g (5 oz) shiitake mushrooms, sliced
125 g (4 oz) dried soba noodles
½ red pepper, cored, deseeded and diced
125 g (4 oz) pak choi, thinly sliced
250 g (8 oz) frozen peeled prawns, defrosted,
    rinsed with cold water and drained
1 small bunch of coriander leaves, torn into
    pieces

Pour the stock into a saucepan, add the curry paste, lime leaves, fish sauce to taste, spring onions and mushrooms and bring to the boil, then reduce the heat and simmer for 5 minutes.

Bring a separate saucepan of water to the boil, add the noodles and cook for 3 minutes.

Add the remaining ingredients to the soup and simmer for 2 minutes until piping hot.

Drain the noodles, rinse with fresh hot water and spoon into the base of each serving bowl. Ladle over the hot broth and serve immediately with small bowls of Thai fish sauce and dark soy sauce for seasoning.

258

next time...

For Thai tamarind broth, pour the stock into a saucepan, add 2 teaspoons tamarind concentrate and ¼ teaspoon ground turmeric, then the curry paste and flavourings as in the recipe above. Bring to the boil, then simmer for 5 minutes. Finish making the broth as above, omitting the prawns.

259

fennel vichyssoise

SERVES 6

25 g (1 oz) butter
1 fennel bulb, about 200–250 g (7–8 oz), trimmed
    and green feathery fronds reserved, cored
    and roughly chopped
4 spring onions, thickly sliced
150 g (5 oz) potato, diced
450 ml (¾ pint) chicken stock (see page 9)
250 ml (8 fl oz) milk
150 ml (¼ pint) double cream
salt and pepper

Melt the butter in a saucepan, add the fennel, spring onions and potato and toss in the butter. Cover and cook gently for 10 minutes until softened but not browned, stirring occasionally.

Pour in the stock, season to taste with salt and pepper and bring to the boil. Reduce the heat, cover and simmer for 15 minutes, or until the vegetables are just tender.

Leave the soup to cool slightly, then purée in batches in a blender or food processor until smooth. Pass the purée through a fine sieve back into the saucepan, then press the coarser pieces of fennel through the sieve using the back of a ladle. Stir in the milk and cream, then taste and adjust the seasoning if needed. Cover and chill in the refrigerator for at least 3 hours.

Ladle the soup into small bowls half-filled with ice and garnish with the reserved snipped green fennel fronds.

260

next time...

For classic vichyssoise, fry 375g (12 oz) leeks, sliced, with the potato in the butter as in the recipe above. Continue as above, but add only half the cream to the soup, swirling in the rest in the bowls. Garnish with snipped chives.

261

guinea fowl & bean
soup

SERVES 4–6

250 g (8 oz) dried black-eyed beans, soaked in
  cold water overnight
1 kg (2 lb) oven-ready guinea fowl
1 onion, sliced
1 garlic cloves, crushed
1.5 litres (2½ pints) chicken stock (see page 9)
½ teaspoon ground cloves
50 g (2 oz) can anchovy fillets, drained and
  finely chopped
150 g (5 oz) wild mushrooms
3 tablespoons tomato purée
100 g (3½ oz) watercress, tough stems discarded
salt and pepper

Drain the beans and put into a large saucepan.
Cover with water and bring to the boil. Boil for
10 minutes, then drain through a colander.

Put the guinea fowl into the bean saucepan and
add the drained beans, onion, garlic, stock and
cloves. Bring just to the boil, then reduce the
heat to its lowest setting, cover and simmer
very gently for 1¼ hours until the guinea fowl
is very tender.

Lift the guinea fowl out on to a plate and leave
until cool enough to handle. Flake all the meat
from the bones, discarding the skin. Chop up
any large pieces of meat and return all the meat
to the pan.

Ladle a little of the stock into a small bowl with
the anchovies and mix together so that the
anchovies are blended with the stock.

Add the anchovy mixture, mushrooms and
tomato purée to the soup and season to taste
with salt and plenty of black pepper. Reheat
gently for a few minutes, then stir in the
watercress just before serving.

262

next time...

For chicken & haricot bean soup, make the
soup as in the previous recipe, replacing the
black-eyed beans with 250 g (8 oz) dried haricot
beans and the guinea fowl with 4 chicken
legs, flaking the cooked meat from the bones
and discarding the skin as before. Just before
serving the soup, stir in 100 g (3½ oz) rocket
leaves, chopped, instead of the watercress.

263

prawn bisque

SERVES 4

50 g (2 oz) butter
1 small carrot, finely chopped
½ small onion, finely chopped
½ celery stick, finely chopped
500 g (1 lb) raw prawns in their shells
250 ml (8 fl oz) dry white wine
2 tablespoons brandy
1.2 litres (2 pints) fish stock (see page 10)
1 bouquet garni
25 g (1 oz) long-grain white rice
100 ml (3½ fl oz) double cream
pinch of cayenne pepper
salt and pepper
4 tablespoons chopped parsley, to garnish

Melt the butter in a large, heavy-based
saucepan, add the carrot, onion and celery
and fry for 8–10 minutes, or until softened
and lightly golden, stirring occasionally.
Increase the heat, add the prawns and cook
for 3–4 minutes until they have turned pink
all over.

Add the wine and brandy and bring to the
boil, then reduce the heat and simmer for
3–4 minutes, or until the prawns are cooked.
Lift the prawns out with a slotted spoon and
leave until cool enough to handle, then peel
and devein the prawns, reserving the shells.
Chop the prawns and set aside.

Bring the liquid back to the boil and boil rapidly
for 2–3 minutes, or until reduced by one-third.
Add the reserved prawn shells with the stock,
bouquet garni and rice. Bring to the boil,
then reduce the heat and simmer gently for
15–20 minutes, or until the rice is tender.

Remove and discard the bouquet garni.
Leave the soup to cool slightly, then purée,
including the shells, in batches in a blender
or food processor with three-quarters of the
prawn meat. Pass the purée through a fine
sieve into a clean saucepan, pressing with
the back of a ladle to push through as much

liquid as possible. Add the cream and cayenne,
and season to taste with salt and pepper.

Bring the soup back to the boil, then reduce
the heat, add the reserved chopped prawns and
cook for 1–2 minutes, or until heated through.

Serve the bisque in warmed soup bowls,
sprinkled with the chopped parsley.

264

next time...

For prawn & tomato bisque, make the bisque
as in the previous recipe, adding 300 g (10 oz)
tomatoes, chopped (there is no need to skin
or deseed), and 1 tablespoon tomato purée to
the pan after the cooked prawns have been
removed. Bring the liquid back to the boil and
boil rapidy for 5-8 minutes, or until reduced
by one-third. Add the prawn shells and 900 ml
(1½ pints) fish stock, along with the bouquet
garni and rice, then finish making the bisque
as before.

265

beef, tamarind & sweet potato soup

SERVES 6

1 tablespoon sunflower oil
1 onion, finely chopped
250 g (8 oz) boneless lean stewing beef,
    cut into small dice
2 garlic cloves, finely chopped
2.5 cm (1 inch) piece of fresh root ginger,
    peeled and finely chopped
1 tablespoon plain flour
1 tablespoon tomato purée
1 tablespoon tamarind paste
1 tablespoon dark brown soft sugar
1 litre (1¾ pints) beef stock (see page 9)
½ teaspoon chilli flakes
¼ teaspoon ground allspice
500 g (1 lb) sweet potatoes, diced
50 g (2 oz) long-grain brown rice
salt and pepper

TO GARNISH
chopped spring onions
chopped coriander

Heat the oil in a large saucepan, add the onion and fry over a medium heat for 5 minutes, stirring frequently, until softened.

Stir in the beef, garlic and ginger and fry for 5 minutes, stirring frequently, until the beef is evenly browned.

Mix in the flour, tomato purée, tamarind paste and sugar, then add the stock, chilli flakes and allspice, and stir in the sweet potatoes. Bring to the boil and season with salt and pepper, then reduce the heat, cover and simmer for 1 hour, stirring occasionally.

Stir in the rice, re-cover and simmer for a further 30 minutes, or until both the rice and beef are tender. Taste and adjust the seasoning if needed.

Ladle the soup into bowls, sprinkle with chopped spring onions and coriander and serve with warm flatbreads.

266

mediterranean salmon
soup with rouille

SERVES 6

25 g (1 oz) butter
1 tablespoon olive oil
1 onion, finely chopped
1 carrot, finely diced
1 potato, no more than 200 g (7 oz), diced
1 garlic clove, finely chopped
1 teaspoon paprika, plus extra to garnish
2 large pinches of saffron threads
2 tomatoes, skinned and diced
1 tablespoon tomato purée
900 ml (1½ pints) fish stock (see page 10)
125 ml (4 fl oz) dry white wine
2 salmon steaks, about 200 g (7 oz) each
150 ml (¼ pint) milk
150 ml (¼ pint) single cream
salt and pepper

ROUILLE TOASTS

1 large mild red chilli, deseeded and chopped
1 garlic clove, finely chopped
3 tablespoons mayonnaise
1 small baguette, cut into 12 slices

Melt the butter with the oil in a large saucepan, add the onion and fry gently for 5 minutes, stirring occasionally, until softened. Add the carrot and potato and cook for 5 minutes.

Stir in the garlic, paprika, saffron and tomatoes and cook for 1 minute. Add the tomato purée, stock and wine. Lower the salmon steaks into the stock and season generously with salt and pepper. Bring the stock to the boil, then reduce the heat, cover and simmer for 10–12 minutes, or until the salmon flakes easily when pressed lightly with a knife.

Lift the salmon out of the pan with a slotted spoon on to a plate and flake it into pieces, discarding the skin and any stray bones. Reserve one-quarter of the salmon for garnishing, then return the rest to the pan and stir in the milk and cream.

Purée the soup in the pan with a stick blender or in batches in a blender or food processor until smooth, returning to the pan. Reheat gently without boiling, then taste and adjust the seasoning if needed.

Meanwhile, for the rouille toasts, purée the chilli, garlic and mayonnaise with a little salt and pepper in a blender or food processor until smooth. Toast the bread slices lightly on both sides and top with tiny spoonfuls of the rouille.

Ladle the soup into warmed bowls, sprinkle in the reserved salmon flakes and float the rouille toasts on top. Garnish with a sprinkle of paprika and serve immediately.

267

next time...

For chunky Mediterranean salmon soup with Puy lentils, cook 100 g (3½ oz) dried Puy lentils, rinsed and drained, in a saucepan of boiling water for 20–25 minutes. Drain, rinse under cold running water and drain again. Make the soup as in the previous recipe using 4 tomatoes, skinned and diced, instead of 2. Once the salmon is cooked, removed and flaked into pieces, check that the potato in the soup is fully soft, and if not, simmer the soup for a further 5–10 minutes before returning all the salmon to the pan. Stir in the cooked lentils with 150 ml (¼ pint) single cream, omitting the milk, and 3 tablespoons chopped flat leaf parsley. Taste and adjust the seasoning, then reheat gently without puréeing, leaving the soup chunky. Serve in bowls topped with the rouille toasts, if liked.

268

clam chowder

SERVES 6–8

48–60 live clams, scrubbed and any cracked
  or open clams discarded
40 g (1½ oz) butter
125 g (4 oz) smoked streaky bacon, rinded
  and diced
2 large onions, finely chopped
2 celery sticks, diced
1–2 leeks, sliced
2 tablespoons finely chopped parsley,
  plus extra to garnish
2 bay leaves
1 thyme sprig, leaves stripped from the stem
900 ml (1½ pints) water
4–5 medium potatoes, diced
pinch of grated nutmeg
2 tablespoons plain flour
1–2 teaspoons Worcestershire sauce
salt (if needed) and pepper

Put the clams on a baking sheet and bake in
a preheated oven, 200°C (400°F), Gas Mark 6,
for 2–3 minutes, or until they open slightly,
discarding any that remain firmly closed.
Open the shells over a bowl to catch all the
clam juice. Snip off and discard the black-tipped
necks (which resemble a tube),then roughly
chop the coral-coloured and pink flesh and leave
the softer body meat whole.

Melt 25 g (1 oz) of the butter in a large
saucepan, add the bacon and fry for about
5 minutes, or until the fat starts to run.
Stir in the onions, cover and cook gently for
10 minutes. Then add the celery, leeks, parsley,
bay leaves and thyme, re-cover and cook
for 5 minutes. Add the reserved clam juice,
measured water, potatoes, nutmeg and pepper
to taste, stir well, then taste and season with
salt if needed. Re-cover and simmer gently for
about 10 minutes, or until the potatoes are
almost tender.

Meanwhile, beat the remaining butter with the
flour in a small bowl to a smooth paste.

Add the clams to the pan and simmer very
gently for 3–4 minutes; don't boil the soup,
or the clams will be tough and rubbery. Add a
piece of the butter and flour paste to the pan,
stirring well until fully incorporated, then
stir in a little more and continue until all the
paste has been added. Cook for a further
3–4 minutes, stirring constantly, until the
soup thickens slightly.

Increase the heat briefly for 10 seconds, then
remove from the heat. Add the Worcestershire
sauce to taste, stir and serve immediately in
warmed soup bowls.

269

next time...

For clam, chorizo & fennel chowder, cook the
clams as in the previous recipe. Fry 100 g
(3½ oz) chorizo, diced, in the butter instead
of the bacon, then add the onions and cook
as before. Replace the celery with 1 fennel
bulb, trimmed, cored and chopped, and
continue making the chowder as before,
using 3–4 potatoes, diced.

270

jerusalem artichoke soup with artichoke crisps

SERVES 4

1 small lemon
625 g (1¼ lb) Jerusalem artichokes
50 g (2 oz) butter
1 onion, chopped
1 garlic clove, crushed
1 celery stick, chopped
1 lemon thyme sprig, leaves stripped from the
  stem
1 litre (1¾ pints) vegetable or chicken stock (see
  pages 10 and 9)
vegetable oil, for deep-frying
175 ml (6 fl oz) single cream or milk
3 tablespoons finely grated Parmesan cheese
salt and pepper

Finely grate the rind of the lemon and set aside. Squeeze the juice into a large bowl of cold water. Carefully peel the artichokes, reserve 2 whole and add to the lemon water. Chop the rest into 1.5 cm (¾ inch) pieces, dropping them into the lemon water as you prepare them to prevent discoloration.

Melt the butter in a large saucepan, add the onion, garlic, celery, thyme and lemon rind and cook gently for 6–8 minutes, or until softened but not browned. Drain the chopped artichokes and add to the pan with the stock. Season to taste with salt and pepper and bring to the boil. Reduce the heat and simmer for 15 minutes, or until the artichokes are tender.

Meanwhile, drain the 2 reserved whole artichokes, slice them thinly and dry well on kitchen paper. Heat the oil for deep-frying in a deep saucepan to 180–190°C (350–375°F), or until a cube of bread browns in 30 seconds. Add the artichoke slices in batches and fry until crisp and golden. Remove with a slotted spoon and drain well on kitchen paper.

Leave the soup to cool slightly, then purée in a blender or food processor until smooth. Pass the purée through a fine sieve back into the saucepan. Stir in the cream or milk, and a little water if the soup is too thick, and taste and adjust the seasoning if needed. Reheat gently, then stir in the Parmesan.

Serve the soup in bowls, sprinkled with the artichoke crisps.

271

next time...

For Jerusalem artichoke & spinach soup, make up the soup as in the previous recipe, adding 100 g (3½ oz) spinach leaves to the cooked vegetable, artichoke and stock mixture. Simmer for 3–5 minutes, or until the spinach has just wilted but is still bright green, then purée and finish making the soup as before. Serve topped with the artichoke crisps and garnished with a few flat leaf parsley leaves.

272

smoky carrot & sweet potato soup

SERVES 6

4 tablespoons olive oil
1 onion, chopped
375 g (12 oz) carrots, diced
375 g (12 oz) sweet potato, diced
2 garlic cloves, finely chopped
1 teaspoon ground cumin
¾ teaspoon hot smoked paprika
1 litre (1¾ pints) vegetable stock (see page 10)
100 g (3½ oz) feta cheese, crumbled
salt and pepper
chopped mint, to garnish

Heat 1 tablespoon of the oil in a saucepan, add the onion and fry over a medium heat for 5 minutes, stirring occasionally, until softened.

Stir in the carrots, sweet potato, garlic, cumin, ½ teaspoon of the paprika and the stock. Season with a little salt and pepper and bring to the boil. Reduce the heat, cover and simmer for 40 minutes.

Meanwhile, mix the remaining 3 tablespoons of oil and the remaining ¼ teaspoon paprika together in a small bowl and set aside for the paprika to infuse the oil.

Leave the soup to cool slightly, then purée in the pan with a stick blender or in batches in a blender or food processor until smooth, returning to the pan. Reheat, then taste and adjust the seasoning if needed.

Ladle the soup into bowls, then spoon over a drizzle of the paprika oil, sprinkle over the feta and garnish with chopped mint.

273

cream of pumpkin & apple soup

SERVES 4

2 tablespoons olive oil
1 onion, chopped
600 g (1 lb 3 oz) deseeded and peeled pumpkin,
    cut into chunks
1 Bramley apple, peeled, cored and chopped
2 tomatoes, skinned and chopped
900 ml (1½ pints) vegetable stock (see page 10)
100 ml (3½ fl oz) double cream
1 tablespoon finely chopped flat leaf parsley
salt and pepper

Heat the oil in a large saucepan, add the onion and fry for 3–4 minutes. Add the pumpkin and stir to coat with the onions, then stir in the apple and tomatoes.

Pour in the stock and bring to the boil. Reduce the heat, cover and simmer for 20 minutes, or until the pumpkin is tender.

Leave the soup to cool slightly, then pour in the cream. Purée in the pan with a stick blender or in batches in a food processor or blender until smooth, returning to the pan. Reheat gently, then season to taste with salt and pepper.

Ladle the soup into bowls, sprinkle with the parsley and serve immediately.

274

next time...

For cream of parsnip & spiced apple soup, fry the onion in the oil as in the recipe above, then stir in 600 g (1 lb 3 oz) parsnip, diced, instead of the pumpkin. Add the apple with 1 teaspoon ground turmeric, 1 teaspoon roughly crushed fennel seeds and a large pinch of chilli flakes, omitting the tomatoes. Pour in the stock and continue making the soup as before.

275

moroccan fish soup

SERVES 6–8

3 tablespoons olive oil
2 onions, chopped
2 celery sticks, sliced
4 garlic cloves, crushed
1 red chilli, deseeded and chopped
1 cinnamon stick
½ teaspoon ground cumin
½ teaspoon ground coriander
2 large potatoes, chopped
1.5 litres (2½ pints) fish stock (see page 10) or water
3 tablespoons lemon juice
2 kg (4 lb) mixed skinless fish fillets, cut into small pieces, and shellfish, such as raw prawns in their shells and live clams and/or mussels, scrubbed and any cracked or open shells discarded
4 well-flavoured tomatoes, skinned, deseeded if liked and chopped
1 large bunch of mixed dill, flat leaf parsley and coriander, chopped
salt and pepper

Heat the oil in a large saucepan, add the onion and celery and fry gently for about 10 minutes, stirring occasionally, until softened and transparent, adding the garlic and chilli towards the end. Add the spices and cook, stirring, for 1 minute, then add the potatoes and cook, stirring, for a further 2 minutes.

Add the stock or water and lemon juice and bring to a simmer, then simmer gently, uncovered, for about 20 minutes, or until the potatoes are tender.

Stir in the fish and shellfish, tomatoes and herbs, and season with salt and pepper. Simmer gently for a few minutes until the fish flakes easily when pressed with a knife, the prawns have turned pink and the clams and/or mussels have opened, discarding any that remain closed. Serve in bowls.

276

chicory soup

SERVES 4

75 g (3 oz) butter
1 onion, diced
2 heads of chicory, finely chopped
50 ml (2 fl oz) dry white wine
1 litre (1¾ pints) milk
250 ml (8 fl oz) vegetable or chicken stock (see pages 10 and 9)
2 tablespoons cornflour
2 tablespoons freshly grated Parmesan cheese
8 slices of stale bread, buttered
salt and pepper

Melt 50 g (2 oz) of the butter in a saucepan, add the onion and fry gently for a few minutes until golden. Add the chicory and fry gently for 10 minutes. Season to taste with salt and pepper. Pour in the wine and simmer briskly until evaporated. Add most of the milk and all the stock and bring slowly to the boil. Mix the cornflour with the remaining milk to a smooth paste, add to the pan and simmer, stirring constantly, until thickened. Simmer for a further 25 minutes, stirring occasionally.

Meanwhile, toast the buttered stale bread on a baking sheet in a preheated oven, 200°C (400°F), Gas Mark 6, for about 10 minutes, or until golden brown.

Whisk the Parmesan and the remaining butter, cut into pieces, into the soup. Put the toast into bowls and pour over the hot soup.

277

next time...

For chicory, celery & Stilton soup, make the soup as in the recipe above, but using 1 head of chicory with 4 celery sticks, finely chopped, and omitting the Parmesan. Put the toast into the bowls, ladle over the hot soup and sprinkle with 125 g (4 oz) Stilton cheese, crumbled.

278

lobster & sweetcorn chowder

SERVES 4

2 cooked lobsters, 750 g (1½ lb) each
50 g (2 oz) butter
1 onion, finely chopped, plus 1 small onion, chopped
1 carrot, finely chopped
1 celery stick, finely chopped
1 thyme sprig
1 parsley sprig
1 bay leaves
1 litre (1¾ pints) water
200 g (7 oz) can sweetcorn, drained
1 small garlic clove, crushed
50 g (2 oz) pancetta, cut into small strips
300 ml (½ pint) milk
300 ml (½ pint) single cream
1 kg (2 lb) potatoes, cut into 1.5 cm (¾ inch) dice
cayenne pepper, to taste
4 tomatoes, skinned, deseeded and chopped
salt and pepper

Cut the lobsters in half lengthways and remove and discard the greyish-green tomalley (the liver), the gills and the intestinal vein running along the back. Smash the claws and remove the meat, cut up the remaining meat and set aside. Put the shells into a plastic bag and smash into small pieces with a rolling pin.

Melt half the butter in a large saucepan, add the finely chopped onion, carrot and celery and fry gently for 8–10 minutes, or until softened, stirring frequently.

Add the herbs, measured water and pieces of lobster shell. Bring to the boil, then reduce the heat and simmer for 30 minutes. Leave to cool slightly, then strain through a fine sieve into a blender or food processor. Add two-thirds of the sweetcorn to the blender or food processor and purée until smooth.

Melt the remaining butter in a large flameproof casserole, add the remaining chopped onion

and the garlic and fry gently for 5 minutes, stirring frequently. Add the pancetta and fry until golden.

Add the puréed sweetcorn mixture, the milk, cream, potatoes and remaining sweetcorn. Bring to the boil, then reduce the heat and simmer for 10–15 minutes, or until the potatoes are tender.

Season to taste with cayenne, salt and pepper, then stir in the tomatoes and lobster meat. Heat through without boiling and serve in bowls.

279

next time...

For speedy crab & sweetcorn soup, melt 50 g (2 oz) butter in a saucepan, add 1 onion, 1 carrot, 1 celery stick and 1 garlic clove, all finely chopped, and fry gently 5 minutes. Add 50 g (2 oz) pancetta, diced, and fry until golden. Drain a 200 g (7 oz) can sweetcorn and purée two-thirds with 600 ml (1 pint) vegetable stock (see page 10), add to the pancetta mixture with the remaining sweetcorn, 1 kg (2 lb) potatoes, diced, 300 ml (½ pint) each milk and single cream, a pinch of dried mixed herbs and 1 bay leaf. Simmer for 10–15 minutes until the potatoes are tender. Stir in 100 g (3½ oz) chilled fresh brown crab meat and 100 g (3½ oz) chilled white crab meat with 4 tomatoes, skinned, deseeded and chopped, and heat through without boiling. Season to taste with salt and cayenne pepper and serve.

280

red pepper & spicy chicken soup

SERVES 4

3 red peppers, halved, cored and deseeded
1 red onion, quartered
2 garlic cloves, unpeeled
1 teaspoon olive oil
5 cm (2 inch) piece of fresh root ginger, peeled
    and grated
1 teaspoon ground cumin
1 teaspoon ground coriander
1 large potato, chopped
900 ml (1½ pints) chicken stock (see page 9)
2 teaspoons Chinese five-spice powder
150 g (5 oz) skinless chicken breast fillets
4 tablespoons fromage frais
salt and pepper

Put the red peppers skin-side up into a nonstick roasting tin with the onion and garlic cloves. Roast in a preheated oven, 200°C (400°F), Gas Mark 6, for 40 minutes, or until the peppers have blistered and the onion quarters and garlic are very soft. If the onion quarters start to brown too much, cover them with the pepper halves and continue roasting.

Meanwhile, heat the oil in a saucepan, add the ginger, cumin and coriander and cook gently for 5 minutes until softened, stirring frequently. Add the potato and stir well, season to taste with salt and pepper and pour in the stock. Bring to the boil, then reduce the heat, cover and simmer for 30 minutes.

Sprinkle the five-spice powder over the chicken and cook under a medium grill for 20 minutes, turning halfway through, or until thoroughly cooked. Cut the chicken into fine shreds and set aside.

Transfer the roasted peppers to a plastic bag, close it tightly and leave it to steam for 10 minutes. Add the roasted onion to the soup, and when cool enough, squeeze the garlic flesh from its skins into the pan. Peel the skins off

the peppers and add to the soup, then simmer for 5 minutes.

Leave the soup to cool slightly, then purée in the pan with a stick blender or in batches in a blender or food processor until smooth, returning to the pan. Thin with a little water, if necessary, to achieve the desired consistency. Stir the shredded chicken into the soup and simmer for 5 minutes.

Spoon the soup into bowls and top each serving with a spoonful of fromage frais.

281

next time...

For red pepper soup with tikka chicken, roast the peppers, onion and garlic as in the previous recipe. Meanwhile, rub 150 g (5 oz) skinless chicken breast fillets with 2 teaspoons tikka masala curry paste mixed with 2 tablespoons low-fat natural yogurt. Place in a foil-lined grill pan and cook under a medium grill for 20 minutes, turning halfway through, or until thoroughly cooked. Finish making the soup as before. Ladle into bowls, top with the shredded chicken and serve with mini poppadums.

282

cauliflower dahl

SERVES 6

2 tablespoons sunflower oil
1 large onion, finely chopped
1 large cauliflower, cut into small florets,
    woody core discarded, about 500 g (1 lb)
    when prepared
3 garlic cloves, finely chopped
2 teaspoons cumin seeds, finely crushed
2 teaspoons coriander seeds, finely crushed
2 teaspoons black mustard seeds
1 teaspoon ground turmeric
250 g (8 oz) dried red lentils, rinsed and drained
2 litres (3½ pints) vegetable stock (see page 10)
1 small bunch of coriander, chopped
salt and pepper

Heat the oil in a large frying pan, add the onion
and fry over a medium heat for 5 minutes,
stirring frequently, until softened. Add the
cauliflower and garlic and fry for 3 minutes,
stirring frequently.

Sprinkle the cumin, coriander and mustard
seeds over the cauliflower and cook for a
further 2–3 minutes until just beginning to
brown around the edges.

Push one-third of the cauliflower and all the
onion to one side of the pan, then scoop out
and transfer to a large saucepan, keeping the
remaining two-thirds of the cauliflower in the
frying pan.

Add the turmeric, lentils and stock to the
cauliflower and onion in the saucepan. Bring
to the boil and season to taste with salt and
pepper. Reduce the heat, cover and simmer for
30–40 minutes until the lentils are tender.

Reheat the cauliflower in the frying pan. Stir
the chopped coriander into the dahl, then taste
and adjust the seasoning if needed.

Ladle the dahl into bowls, top with the spiced
cauliflower and serve immediately.

283

next time

For mushroom & spinach dahl, fry the onion
in oil as in the previous recipe, then add 500 g
(1lb) closed cup mushrooms, quartered, in place
of the cauliflower with the garlic and fry for
3 minutes, stirring. Continue making the dahl
as before, reserving two-thirds of the spiced
mushrooms in the frying pan, then continue as
before, adding 100 g (3½ oz) baby leaf spinach to
the lentil mix for the last 3 minutes of cooking, or
until just wilted. Ladle the dahl into bowls and
top with the reserved spiced mushrooms.

284

mexican soup
with avocado salsa

SERVES 4

2 tablespoons sunflower oil
1 large onion, chopped
2 garlic cloves, crushed
2 teaspoons ground coriander
1 teaspoon ground cumin
1 red pepper, cored, deseeded and diced
3 red chillies, deseeded and sliced
425 g (14 oz) can red kidney beans, rinsed
   and drained
750 ml (1¼ pints) tomato juice
1–2 tablespoons chilli sauce
25 g (1 oz) tortilla chips, crushed
salt and pepper
coriander sprigs, to garnish

AVOCADO SALSA
1 small ripe avocado
4 spring onions, finely chopped
1 tablespoon lemon juice
1 tablespoon chopped coriander
salt and pepper

Heat the oil in a large saucepan, add the onion, garlic, spices, red pepper and two-thirds of the chillies and fry gently for 10 minutes, stirring frequently. Stir in the beans, tomato juice and chilli sauce. Bring to the boil, then reduce the heat, cover and simmer gently for 30 minutes.

Meanwhile, to make the avocado salsa, stone, peel and finely dice the avocado. Put into a bowl and mix it with the spring onions, lemon juice and chopped coriander. Season to taste with salt and pepper, cover tightly with clingfilm and set aside.

Leave the soup to cool slightly, then purée in batches in a blender or food processor with the crushed tortilla chips until smooth. Return the soup to the rinsed-out saucepan, season to taste with salt and pepper and heat through.

Serve immediately in bowls with the avocado salsa, garnished with the remaining chilli slices and coriander sprigs.

285

next time...

For Mexican prawn soup with avocado salsa, make the soup as in the previous recipe, then purée and return to the rinsed-out pan. Add 200 g (7 oz) cooked peeled prawns, defrosted, rinsed with cold water and drained if frozen. Bring the soup to the boil, then simmer for 4–5 minutes, stirring, until piping hot. Ladle into bowls and serve as before.

286

gruyère soup with bacon & potatoes

SERVES 6–8

2 tablespoons olive oil
3 rindless smoked bacon rashers, chopped
2 onions, finely chopped
600 ml (1 pint) chicken stock (see page 9)
900 ml (1½ pints) water
625 g (1¼ lb) potatoes, cut into 1 cm (½ inch) dice
4 tablespoons plain flour
50 g (2 oz) Gruyère cheese, grated
1 tablespoon medium dry sherry
1 teaspoon Worcestershire sauce
3 tablespoons finely chopped parsley
salt and pepper

Heat the oil in a large saucepan, add the bacon and onions and fry over a medium heat for a few minutes, stirring frequently,until the onions are pale golden.

Add the stock, 600 ml (1 pint) of the measured water and the potatoes. Bring to the boil, then reduce the heat, cover and simmer, for 15 minutes, or until the potatoes are just tender.

Whisk the flour with the remaining water in a small bowl until well blended, then stir the mixture into the soup. Simmer for 5 minutes, stirring frequently.

Leave the soup to cool slightly, then purée 300 ml (½ pint) with the cheese in a blender or food processor. Stir the purée back into the soup, then add the sherry and Worcestershire sauce. Season to taste with salt and pepper. Simmer for 3–5 minutes, then stir in the parsley just before serving in warmed soup bowls.

287

next time...

For Gruyère soup with bacon & cauliflower, fry the bacon and onions in the oil until pale golden as in the previous recipe, then add the stock and 600 ml (1 pint) of the measured water with 325 g (11 oz) potatoes, diced, and 300 g (10 oz) cauliflower florets. Simmer for 15 minutes, then finish making the soup as before.

288

wonton soup

SERVES 4

20 small square wonton wrappers
1.2 litres (2 pints) chicken stock (see page 9)
2 pink Asian shallots or 1 small onion, finely
 chopped
2.5 cm (1 inch) piece of fresh root ginger, peeled
 and finely sliced
1 teaspoon caster sugar
4 spring onions, finely sliced
½ tablespoon light soy sauce
1 teaspoon rice vinegar
handful of roughly chopped parsley
1 teaspoon sesame oil
salt and pepper
chilli oil, to serve

FILLING
125 g (4 oz) cooked white fish fillet or cooked
 peeled prawns
125 g (4 oz) white crab meat, defrosted if frozen
2 spring onions, finely chopped
2.5 cm (1 inch) piece of fresh root ginger, peeled
 and finely chopped
1 garlic clove, crushed

Chop the fish or prawns and crab meat for the
filling very finely with the spring onions, chopped
ginger and garlic or put all the ingredients in a
blender or food processor and blend to a paste.

Place 1 teaspoon of the mixture in the centre of
each wrapper, brush around the filling with a
little water and fold the wrapper over to make a
triangle. Keep the wrappers covered with a damp
cloth to prevent them from drying out before you
fill them.

Put the stock into a saucepan with the shallots
or small onion and sliced ginger and bring to the
boil. Reduce the heat and add the sugar and filled
wontons. Simmer gently for 5 minutes.

Add the spring onions, soy sauce, vinegar and
parsley, and season to taste with salt and pepper.
Just before serving, add the sesame oil. Serve the
soup in bowls accompanied by small dishes of
chilli oil.

289

next time...

For cheat's gyoza soup, make the broth as in
the previous recipe. Cook a pack of 20 frozen
vegetable or prawn gyoza in a microwave oven
according to the pack instructions or cook in
the broth for 3–4 minutes if preferred. Divide
the gyoza among bowls, then ladle over the hot
broth. Garnish with chopped coriander and
serve immediately.

290

no time to shop pea soup

SERVES 6

2 tablespoons olive oil
1 onion, finely chopped
2 tomatoes, diced
250 g (8 oz) potatoes, cut into small dice
1 carrot, cut into small dice
1 garlic clove, finely chopped
1 litre (1¾ pints) vegetable or chicken stock (see
    pages 10 and 9)
200 g (7 oz) frozen peas
150 g (5 oz) frozen chopped spinach
1 tablespoon pesto, plus extra for topping
freshly grated Parmesan or Cheddar cheese,
    for sprinkling
salt and pepper
a few basil leaves, to garnish (optional)

Heat the oil in a saucepan, add the onion and fry over a medium heat for 5 minutes, stirring occasionally, until softened. Stir in the tomatoes, potatoes, carrot and garlic, cover and cook gently for 5 minutes.

Pour in the stock and bring to the boil, then season to taste with salt and pepper. Reduce the heat, cover and simmer for 20 minutes until the potatoes are tender.

Add the peas, spinach and pesto and simmer for 5 minutes, stirring frequently, until the green vegetables are piping hot. Taste and adjust the seasoning if needed.

Ladle the hot soup into bowls. Top with extra pesto, sprinkle with grated cheese and garnish with the basil leaves, if liked.

291

next time...

For creamy pea & pesto soup, make the soup as in the previous recipe, but omit the spinach when adding the peas and pesto. After simmering for 5 minutes, leave the soup to cool slightly, then purée in the pan with a stick blender or in batches in a blender or food processor until smooth, returning to the pan. Reheat and taste and adjust the seasoning, then ladle into bowls and swirl in 150 ml (¼ pint) double cream. Garnish with tiny basil leaves, if liked.

292

Heat the oil in a saucepan, add the chicken and fry over a medium heat for 5 minutes, stirring occasionally, until evenly browned.

SERVES 6

Stir in the onion, garlic and aubergine and fry for 3 minutes, stirring, then add the peppers and jerk seasoning and cook for 2 minutes.

1 tablespoon sunflower oil
2 skinless chicken breast fillets, diced
1 onion, finely chopped
2 garlic cloves, finely chopped
150 g (5 oz) aubergine, diced
1 red pepper, cored, deseeded and diced
1 orange or yellow pepper, cored, deseeded and diced
2 teaspoons jerk seasoning (wet rub)
400 g (13 oz) can full-fat coconut milk
600 ml (1 pint) chicken stock (see page 9)
300 g (10 oz) sweet potato, diced
salt and pepper
chopped coriander, to garnish

Pour in the coconut milk and stock, then mix in the sweet potato and a little salt and pepper. Bring to the boil, then reduce the heat, cover and simmer for 30–40 minutes until the potato is tender and the chicken cooked through. Taste and adjust seasoning if needed.

Ladle the hot soup into bowls and sprinkle with chopped coriander.

293

malaysian laksa

SERVES 4

3 tablespoons groundnut oil
2 large onions, finely chopped
4 garlic cloves, crushed
3 red bird's eye chillies, finely chopped
75 g (3 oz) roasted peanuts, chopped, plus
    1–2 tablespoons chopped to garnish
1 tablespoon ground coriander
1 tablespoon ground cumin
2 teaspoons ground turmeric
1.2 litres (2 pints) full-fat coconut milk
1 teaspoon shrimp paste
1–2 tablespoons sugar, to taste
375 g (12 oz) cooked chicken, shredded
175 g (6 oz) bean sprouts
500 g (1 lb) fresh flat rice noodles
4 spring onions, chopped, plus 4, chopped,
    to garnish
3 tablespoons chopped coriander leaves
salt and pepper
1 large red chilli, finely sliced, to garnish

Heat the oil in a saucepan, add the onions and fry over a medium heat for about 10 minutes, stirring frequently, until golden brown. Add the garlic, chillies, peanuts and ground spices and cook for 2–3 minutes, stirring, or until the spices have cooked through and released a strong aroma.

Stir in the coconut milk and shrimp paste, cover and simmer for 15 minutes. Season to taste with salt and pepper and the sugar. Add the shredded chicken and the bean sprouts and simmer for 5 minutes.

Blanch the noodles in boiling water according to the packet instructions, then drain and divide among large bowls. Sprinkle with the spring onions and coriander. Ladle over the hot broth and serve immediately, with the extra spring onions and peanuts and sliced red chilli in separate bowls for garnishing.

294

next time...

For prawn laksa, make the flavoured coconut broth as in the previous recipe, replacing the shredded chicken with 200 g (7 oz) raw peeled prawns, defrosted, rinsed with cold water and drained if frozen, adding with the bean sprouts. Simmer for 5 minutes until all the prawns have turned pink. Finish making the laksa and serve as before.

295

hot & sour prawn noodle soup

SERVES 4

500 g (1 lb) raw large prawns in their shells, defrosted if frozen
1 tablespoon sunflower oil
2 spring onions, roughly chopped, plus 2, cut into thin strips, to garnish
2.5 cm (1 inch) piece of fresh root ginger, peeled and chopped
1 small red or green chilli, deseeded and finely chopped
2 dried kaffir lime leaves or rind from 1 lime, cut into strips
2 lemon grass stalks, bruised and chopped into 2.5 cm (1 inch) pieces, or 1 tablespoon dried chopped lemon grass, soaked in hot water for 30 minutes
1.2 litres (2 pints) chicken stock (see page 9)
2–4 tablespoons lime juice
75 g (3 oz) dried fine egg or rice noodles
125 g (4 oz) small oyster mushrooms
coriander sprigs, to garnish

Peel and devein the prawns, reserving the shells. Rinse the prawns and set aside.

Heat the oil in a large saucepan, add the chopped spring onions, ginger and chilli and fry gently for 5 minutes until softened but not browned, stirring occasionally. Add the reserved prawn shells and cook for 3 minutes.

Stir in the lime leaves or rind, lemon grass (if using dried lemon grass, add with its soaking liquid), stock and 2 tablespoons lime juice. Bring to the boil, then reduce the heat and simmer for 20 minutes.

Meanwhile, cook the noodles according to the packet instructions, drain and set aside.

Strain the stock through a fine sieve into a clean saucepan. Taste and add more lime juice if needed. Bring back to the boil, then reduce the heat, add the prawns and simmer for 2 minutes, or until they have turned pink.

Add the mushrooms and simmer for 1–2 minutes, or until just soft. Stir in the cooked noodles and heat through.

Serve in bowls, sprinkled with the spring onion strips and coriander sprigs.

296

next time...

For hot & sour mixed vegetable soup, fry the spring onions, ginger and chilli as in the previous recipe. Then instead of the prawns and their shells, add 250 g (8 oz) sliced chestnut mushrooms. Stir in the lime leaves or rind, lemon grass and lime juice as before, replacing the chicken stock with 1.2 litres (2 pints) vegetable stock (see page 10). Bring to the boil, then simmer for 5 minutes. Add 75 g (3 oz) each mangetout and baby corn cobs, both sliced, and 12 cherry tomatoes, halved, and simmer for 3 minutes. Remove and discard the lime leaves and lemon grass, then add the oyster mushrooms and simmer for 1–2 minutes as before. Finally, stir in the cooked noodles and reheat, then garnish the soup as before.

297

risi e bisi with frazzled prosciutto

SERVES 4

3 tablespoons olive oil
1 onion, chopped
1.2 litres (2 pints) chicken stock (see page 9)
200 g (7 oz) risotto rice
750 g (1½ lb) fresh young peas, shelled, or 250 g
   (8 oz) frozen peas, defrosted
large pinch of sugar
4 slices of prosciutto
2 tablespoons chopped flat leaf parsley
50 g (2 oz) Parmesan cheese, finely grated, plus
   extra for sprinkling
salt and pepper

Heat 2 tablespoons of the oil in a large
saucepan, add the onion and fry for
5–10 minutes, or until softened but not
browned, stirring frequently.

Add the stock and bring to the boil, then
reduce the heat and stir in the rice. (If using
fresh peas, add them now and simmer gently
for 5 minutes before adding the rice.) Season to
taste with salt and pepper and add the sugar.
Cover and simmer gently for 15–20 minutes,
or until the rice is just tender, stirring
occasionally. (If using frozen peas, add them
after 10–15 minutes of cooking.)

Cut each slice of prosciutto in half lengthways.
Heat the remaining oil in a large frying pan,
add the prosciutto and cook over a high heat for
10–15 seconds, or until crisp. Remove with a
slotted spoon and drain on kitchen paper.

Stir the parsley and Parmesan into the soup,
then ladle into bowls, top with 2 pieces of the
frazzled prosciutto and sprinkle with extra
Parmesan.

298

next time...

For risi e bisi with smoked salmon, make the
soup as in the previous recipe, omitting the
prosciutto. Ladle the finished soup into bowls,
then top just with 125 g (4 oz) thinly sliced
smoked salmon, cut into thin strips, and
parmesan.

299

la ribollita

SERVES 8

150 ml (¼ pint) olive oil, plus extra for drizzling
1 onion, finely chopped
1 carrot, chopped
1 celery stick, chopped
2 leeks, finely chopped
4 garlic cloves, finely chopped
1 small white cabbage, shredded
1 large potato, chopped
4 courgettes, chopped
200 g (7 oz) dried cannellini beans, soaked in
    cold water overnight, drained and rinsed
400 g (13 oz) passata
2 rosemary sprigs
2 thyme sprigs
2 sage sprigs
1 dried red chilli
2 litres (3½ pints) water
500 g (1 lb) cavolo nero (Tuscan black cabbage)
    or Savoy cabbage, finely shredded
6 thick slices of coarse crusty white bread
1 garlic clove, bruised
freshly grated Parmesan cheese, for sprinkling
salt and pepper

Heat half the oil in a large saucepan, add the onion, carrot and celery and fry gently for about 10 minutes, stirring frequently. Add the leeks and garlic and cook for 10 minutes. Stir in the white cabbage, potato and courgettes and cook for a further 10 minutes, stirring frequently.

Stir in the soaked beans, passata, herbs, chilli, salt to taste and plenty of black pepper. Pour over the measured water (the vegetables should be well covered) and bring to the boil, then reduce the heat, cover and simmer for at least 2 hours, or until the beans are very soft.

Transfer 2–3 ladlefuls of the soup to a bowl and mash it well, then return to the pan. Stir in the cavolo nero or Savoy cabbage and simmer for a further 15 minutes. Leave the soup to cool, then cover and refrigerate overnight.

The next day, slowly reheat the soup, season if necessary and stir in the remaining oil. Toast the bread and rub it with the bruised garlic.

Ladle the soup into bowls and drizzle with olive oil, then top with the toast and sprinkle with freshly grated Parmesan.

300

next time...

For chicken ribollita, make the soup as in the previous recipe, replacing the measured water with 2 litre (3½ pints) chicken stock (see page 9). When reheating the soup the next day, add 175 g (6 oz) cooked chicken, diced, and heat until piping hot. Serve in bowls topped with the garlic-rubbed toast.

301

goulash soup

SERVES 6–8

3 tablespoons vegetable oil
750 g (1½ lb) boneless lean beef, cut into 2.5 cm
    (1 inch) strips
2 onions, chopped
2 celery sticks, sliced
2 garlic cloves, crushed
3 tablespoons paprika
1 tablespoon caraway seeds
1.2 litres (2 pints) beef stock (see page 9)
600 ml (1 pint) water
¼ teaspoon dried thyme
2 bay leaves
¼ teaspoon Tabasco sauce, or to taste
3 tablespoons tomato purée
250 g (8 oz) potatoes, cut into 1 cm (½ inch) dice
3 carrots, cut into 1 cm (½ inch) dice
6–8 teaspoons soured cream, to garnish
    (optional)

Heat the oil in a large saucepan, add the beef
in batches and fry over a medium heat until
browned on both sides, removing each browned
batch with a slotted spoon and draining on
kitchen paper. Add the onions and celery with
the garlic to the pan and fry for a few minutes,
stirring frequently, until transparent.

Remove the pan from the heat and stir in
the paprika, caraway seeds, stock and the
measured water. Add the thyme, bay leaves,
Tabasco and tomato purée and stir well, then
return the browned beef to the pan. Bring to
the boil, then reduce the heat, half-cover and
simmer for 30 minutes. Add the potatoes
and carrots, cover and simmer for a further
30 minutes, or until the potatoes are tender.

Remove and discard the bay leaves, then serve
the soup immediately in bowls, garnishing
each serving with a teaspoon of soured cream,
if liked.

302

next time...

For goulash soup with frankfurters, omit the
beef and fry the onions, garlic and celery,
then add the paprika, caraway, stock, water,
herbs, Tabasco and tomato purée as in the
previous recipe. Bring to the boil, then simmer
for 15 minutes. Add a 350 g (11½ oz) pack
chilled frankfurters, thickly sliced, with the
potatoes and carrots, then cover and simmer
for a further 30 minutes before serving.

303

spanish chickpea soup

SERVES 8-10

150 g (5 oz) dried chickpeas, soaked in cold
    water for 48 hours or 12 hours if covered with
    boiling water
1 small boneless smoked bacon hock joint,
    about 500–750 g (1–1½ lb)
1 onion, studded with 4 cloves
2 garlic cloves, crushed
1 bay leaf
1 thyme sprig or ¼ teaspoon dried thyme
1 marjoram sprig or ½ teaspoon dried
    marjoram
1 parsley sprig
1.8 litres (3 pints) water
1.8 litres (3 pints) hot chicken stock (see page 9)
300–375 g (10–12 oz) potatoes, cut into 1 cm
    (½ inch) dice
300 g (10 oz) Savoy cabbage, shredded
salt and pepper

Drain the chickpeas in a colander, rinse under cold running water and drain again.

Put the bacon joint into a deep saucepan and cover with cold water. Bring the water briefly to the boil, then drain.

Return the bacon joint to the rinsed-out pan. Add the soaked chickpeas, clove-studded onion, garlic, herbs and measured water. Bring to the boil, then reduce the heat, half-cover and simmer for 1½ hours. Remove and discard the onion and herbs. Lift the hock out, put it on to a chopping board and cut it into small pieces. Set the hock pieces aside.

Add the stock, potatoes and cabbage to the pan, cover and simmer for a further 30 minutes. Stir in the hock pieces and simmer for another 10 minutes. Season to taste with salt and pepper. Serve the soup in warmed soup bowls.

304

next time...

For Spanish chickpea soup with paprika oil, make the soup as in the previous recipe. While the hock joint, chickpeas and flavourings are simmering together, warm 4 tablespoons olive oil in a small saucepan with 1 teaspoon hot smoked paprika and 2 garlic cloves, finely chopped, for a few minutes. Remove the pan from the heat and leave to infuse. Ladle the finished soup into bowls and drizzle with the paprika oil.

305

slow-cooked oxtail & red onion with herb croûtons

SERVES 6

500 g (1 lb) oxtail pieces
1 tablespoon sunflower oil (if needed)
2 red onions, halved and thinly sliced
1 tablespoon soft light brown sugar
1.2 litre (2 pints) beef stock (see page 9)
1 teaspoon English mustard
1 tablespoon tomato purée
2 tablespoons sherry vinegar
1 large bay leaf
40 g (1½ oz) pearl barley
200 g (7 oz) carrots, diced
150 g (5 oz) parsnip, diced
175 g (6 oz) swede, diced
salt and pepper

HERB CROÛTONS
3 tablespoons olive oil
150 g (5 oz) rustic bread, cut into rough cubes
1 tablespoon dried parsley
¼ teaspoon dried mixed herbs

Heat a saucepan, add the oxtail and dry-fry over a low heat for 5 minutes until the fat begins to run. Add the oil, if needed, then add the onions and fry for 5 minutes, stirring the onions and turning the oxtail, until they are just beginning to colour.

Sprinkle the sugar over the onions and fry over a medium heat for 10 minutes, stirring, until the onions and are a deep golden and the oxtail is evenly browned.

Add the stock, mustard, tomato purée, vinegar, bay leaf and pearl barley, and season with salt and pepper. Bring to the boil, then reduce the heat, cover and simmer for 1½ hours.

Stir in the carrots, parsnip and swede and simmer for a further 1 hour until tender.

Lift the oxtail out of the pan with a slotted spoon and put on to a chopping board. Remove the meat from the bones and cut into small pieces, discarding any fatty pieces. Return the meat to the pan.

Heat the oil for the croûtons in a frying pan, add the bread cubes and toss in the oil, then sprinkle with the herbs. Fry over a medium heat, stirring frequently, until golden.

Ladle the hot soup into bowls, removing and discarding the bay leaf, and sprinkle with the herb croûtons.

306

cockle & bacon
chowder

SERVES 6

1 tablespoon sunflower oil
6 rindless smoked steaky bacon rashers, diced
1 onion, finely chopped
25 g (1 oz) butter
500 g (1 lb) potatoes, diced
2 garlic cloves, finely chopped
2 tablespoons plain flour
900 ml (1½ pints) vegetable or chicken stock
    (see pages 10 and 9)
pinch of grated nutmeg
150 g (5 oz) frozen sweetcorn
100 g (3½ oz) baby spinach leaves
175 g (6 oz) ready-prepared cockles, defrosted,
    rinsed with cold water and drained if frozen,
    or 2 x 155 g (5 oz) jars cockles, drained
250 ml (8 fl oz) milk
125 ml (4 fl oz) double cream
salt and pepper

Heat the oil in a saucepan, add the bacon and
onion and fry over a medium heat for 5 minutes,
stirring frequently, until pale golden. Add the
butter, and stir until melted, then mix in the
potatoes and garlic and fry gently for 5 minutes,
stirring constantly.

Sprinkle over the flour and stir to evenly mix.
Pour over the stock, season with the nutmeg
and salt and pepper to taste and bring to the
boil. Reduce the heat, cover and simmer for
20 minutes, or until potatoes are tender.

Stir in the sweetcorn, spinach, cockles and
milk and simmer for 5 minutes until piping
hot, then stir in the cream. Taste and adjust the
seasoning if needed, then ladle into bowls.

307

tomato & almond soup

SERVES 4

1 kg (2 lb) really ripe vine tomatoes, skinned,
    deseeded and chopped
300 ml (½ pint) vegetable stock (see page 10)
190 ml (⅓ pint) extra virgin olive oil
2 garlic cloves, crushed
1 teaspoon sugar
15 g (½ oz) basil leaves
100 g (3½ oz) day-old bread without crusts
100 g (3½ oz) toasted ground almonds
1 tablespoon balsamic vinegar
salt and pepper

Put the tomatoes into a saucepan with the
stock, 2 tablespoons of the oil, the garlic and
sugar and bring gradually to the boil. Reduce
the heat and simmer for 15 minutes.

Meanwhile, purée the basil leaves with the
remaining oil and a pinch of salt in a blender or
food processor until really smooth.

Tear the bread into pieces and divide among
serving bowls. Stir the toasted ground almonds
and vinegar into the soup. Ladle over the bread
and served drizzled with the basil oil.

308

next time...

For **tomato & cannellini bean soup**, make the
soup as in the previous recipe, adding a rinsed
and drained 400 g (14 oz) can cannellini beans
along with the tomatoes. Stir the toasted
ground almonds into the cooked soup with
the balsamic vinegar, then ladle into bowls
(omitting the bread) and drizzle with the basil
oil as before.

309

tangy carrot & orange soup

SERVES 6

2 tablespoons olive oil
1 onion, roughly chopped
750 g (1½ lb) carrots, diced
1 teaspoon fennel seeds, crushed
1 litre (1¾ pints) vegetable stock (see page 10)
grated zest and juice of 1 large orange
salt and pepper

Heat the oil in a saucepan, add the onion and fry over a medium heat for 5 minutes until softened, stirring occasionally. Stir in the carrots and crushed fennel seeds, cover and cook gently for 5 minutes.

Pour in stock and bring to the boil. Season to taste with salt and pepper, then reduce the heat, cover and simmer gently for 40 minutes until the carrots are tender.

Lift 3 large spoonfuls of carrots out of the soup with a slotted spoon and reserve for garnishing. Leave the soup to cool slightly, then purée in the pan with a stick blender or in batches in a blender or food processor until smooth, returning to the pan. Add the orange juice and reheat, then taste and adjust the seasoning if needed.

Ladle the soup into bowls, then sprinkle with the orange zest and reserved carrots, cutting the carrot pieces into smaller dice if necessary. Serve immediately.

310

next time...

For spiced carrot soup, fry the onion in the oil, then stir in carrots and crushed fennel seeds as in the previous recipe, adding 2 whole star anise, a pinch of chilli flakes and a 2 cm (¾ inch) piece of fresh root ginger, peeled and finely chopped. Cover and cook gently for 5 minutes, then continue making the soup as before, removing and discarding the star anise before puréeing. Finish the soup and garnish as before.

311

smooth spinach & kale
soup with brie toasts

SERVES 6

25 g (1 oz) butter
1 tablespoon olive oil
1 onion, chopped
2 garlic cloves, finely chopped
350 g (12 oz) potatoes, diced
1 teaspoon ground cumin
900 ml (1½ pints) vegetable stock (see page 10)
75 g (3 oz) baby spinach leaves
75 g (3 oz) kale, shredded
125 ml (4 fl oz) double cream
salt and pepper

BRIE TOASTS
2 oval-shaped rolls, each cut into 3 long slices
150 g (5 oz) brie, cut into 6 long thin slices
2 tablespoons pistachio nuts, roughly chopped
2 teaspoons clear honey

Melt the butter with the oil in a saucepan, add the onion and fry over a medium heat for 5 minutes until softened. Mix in the garlic, potatoes and cumin and fry for 5 minutes, stirring occasionally.

Pour in the stock, season with a little salt and pepper and bring to the boil. Reduce the heat, cover and simmer for 20 minutes. Add the spinach and kale and simmer for 5 minutes.

Leave the soup to cool slightly, then purée in the pan with a stick blender or in batches in a blender or food processor until smooth, returning to the pan. Stir in the cream and reheat gently.

Toast the bread slices on both sides, then top each with a slice of brie, a few pistachio nuts and a drizzle of honey. Cook under a hot grill for a few minutes until the cheese is bubbling and the nuts are lightly browned.

Ladle the hot soup into shallow bowls. Slice the brie toasts and serve on the side.

312

cream of sweetcorn
soup

SERVES 4–6

40 g (1½ oz) butter
1 onion, chopped
2 potatoes, diced
25 g (1 oz) plain flour
900 ml (1½ pints) milk
1 bay leaf
2 x 325 g (11 oz) cans sweetcorn, drained
6 tablespoons double cream
salt and pepper
fried bacon, crumbled, to garnish

Melt the butter in a large saucepan, add the onion and potatoes and fry gently for 5 minutes without browning, stirring frequently.

Stir in the flour, then gradually add the milk, stirring constantly, and bring to the boil. Add the bay leaf and season to taste with salt and pepper. Stir in half the sweetcorn, then reduce the heat, cover and simmer for 15–20 minutes.

Remove and discard the bay leaf. Leave the soup to cool slightly, then purée in the pan with a stick blender or in batches in a blender or food processor until smooth, returning to the pan. Add the remaining sweetcorn and heat through, then stir in the cream.

Pour the soup into bowls, sprinkle over the bacon and serve immediately.

313

next time...

For cream of sweet potato & sweetcorn soup, make the soup as in the previous recipe, but replace the potatoes with 425 g (14 oz) sweet potatoes, diced. Serve the finished soup sprinkled with a little diced and fried chorizo instead of the bacon.

314

country bean & vegetable broth

SERVES 4

25 g (1 oz) each dried kidney beans, pinto beans and black-eyed beans, soaked in cold water overnight
25 g (1 oz) dried porcini mushrooms (ceps)
1 tablespoon olive oil
2 shallots, finely chopped
2 garlic cloves, crushed
125 g (4 oz) button mushrooms, diced
2 tablespoons chopped mixed herbs, plus extra to garnish
50 g (2 oz) dried small pasta shapes
1.2 litres (2 pints) hot beef stock (see page 9)
salt and pepper

Drain the soaked beans in a colander, rinse under cold running water and drain again. Put the beans into a large saucepan with water to cover. Bring to the boil and boil vigorously for 10 minutes, skimming off any scum that rises to the surface with a slotted spoon. Reduce the heat, cover and simmer for 1 hour, or until all the beans are very tender.

Meanwhile, put the dried mushrooms into a heatproof bowl, cover with boiling water and leave to soak for 15 minutes, then strain through a fine sieve, reserving the liquid.

Heat the oil in a large saucepan, add the shallots and garlic and fry, stirring frequently, for 3 minutes. Stir in the fresh mushrooms, then add the herbs and pasta shapes.

Drain the beans and add them to the saucepan with the hot stock and reserved mushroom liquid. Season to taste with salt and pepper. Bring to the boil, then reduce the heat and simmer for 12 minutes.

Serve the soup immediately in bowls, sprinkled with extra chopped herbs to garnish.

315

next time...

For country bean & tomato broth, make the soup as in the previous recipe, adding 400 g (13 oz) tomatoes, skinned and chopped, and 1 tablespoon tomato purée along with the herbs and pasta shapes, then continue as before.

316

moroccan mint soup

SERVES 6

25 g (1 oz) mint
300 ml (½ pint) boiling water
150 ml (¼ pint) chilled water
200 g (7 oz) green seedless grapes
1 round lettuce, roughly torn into
pieces
50 g (2 oz) baby spinach leaves
2 teaspoons clear honey
a few pomegranate seeds, to garnish

Reserve a few tiny mint leaves for garnishing in a small bowl of cold water. Strip the remaining mint leaves from the stems and put into a larger bowl, then cover with the measured boiling water. Leave for 15 minutes to infuse and cool.

Tip the infused mint water and leaves into a blender or food processor, then add the measured chilled water, grapes, lettuce, spinach and honey. Blend until smooth and frothy.

Serve the soup in bowls, sprinkled with the pomegranate seeds and reserved, drained mint leaves.

317

red lentil & spiced coconut soup

SERVES 6

1 tablespoon sunflower oil
1 onion, chopped
2 garlic cloves, finely chopped
4 teaspoons tikka masala curry paste
1 teaspoon ground turmeric
200 g (7 oz) dried red lentils, rinsed and drained
250 g (8 oz) carrots, diced
1 litre (1¾ pints) vegetable stock (see page 10)
2–3 tablespoons mango chutney
salt and pepper
toasted coconut shavings, to garnish (optional)

Heat the oil in a saucepan, add the onion and fry over a medium heat for 5 minutes, stirring occasionally, until softened. Mix in the garlic, curry paste and turmeric and cook, stirring, for 1 minute.

Add the red lentils, carrots and stock. Season with a little salt and pepper and bring to the boil. Reduce the heat, cover and simmer for 40 minutes, or until the lentils are soft.

Mash the lentils and vegetables for a coarse texture or, if preferred, leave to cool slightly, then purée in the pan with a stick blender or in batches in a blender or food processor until smooth, returning to the pan. Reheat, then taste and adjust the seasoning if needed.

Ladle the soup into bowls, top with spoonfuls of the mango chutney and garnish with toasted coconut shavings, if liked.

318

creamy bubble & squeak soup with crispy bacon

SERVES 6

1 tablespoon sunflower oil
150 g (5 oz) rindless smoked streaky bacon rashers
1 leek, halved and chopped, white and green parts kept separate
500 g (1 lb) potatoes, diced
750 ml (1¼ pints) chicken stock (see page 9)
1 teaspoon English mustard
large pinch of grated nutmeg, plus extra to garnish
100 g (3½ oz) Brussels sprouts, thinly sliced
75 g (3 oz) outer leaves from a Savoy cabbage, thinly sliced into bite-sized pieces
125 ml (4 fl oz) double cream
salt and pepper

Heat the oil in a large saucepan, add the bacon and fry over a medium heat until the fat is golden on both sides. Lift out of the pan with tongs, put on to a plate lined with kitchen paper and set aside.

Add the white leek and potatoes to the pan and fry for 5 minutes, stirring. Pour in the stock, add the mustard and a little nutmeg and season to taste with salt and pepper. Bring to the boil, then reduce the heat, cover and simmer for 35 minutes until the potatoes are very soft.

Roughly mash the potatoes in the stock with a fork, then add the sprouts, cabbage and green leek. Cook for about 5 minutes until the green vegetables are softened but still bright green.

Stir the cream into the soup, reheat gently, then taste and adjust seasoning if needed. Ladle into bowls. Chop the bacon and sprinkle on top with a little extra nutmeg and pepper.

319

thai gingered chicken **broth** with noodles

SERVES 6

900 ml (1½ pints) vegetable stock (see page 10)
2 tablespoons dark soy sauce
2.5 cm (1 inch) piece of root ginger, peeled and
 finely chopped
1 red chilli, finely chopped
6 spring onions, thinly sliced
300 g (10 oz) ready-cooked rice noodles or soba
 noodles
150 g (5 oz) cooked roast chicken, pulled into
 shreds
2 teaspoons sunflower oil
200 g (7 oz) ready-prepared stir-fry vegetables
1 garlic clove, finely chopped

TO GARNISH
sesame oil
chopped coriander

Pour the stock and soy sauce into a large
saucepan and add the ginger, chilli and spring
onions. Bring to the boil and add the cooked
noodles and shredded chicken. Bring back to
the boil and cook for 2–3 minutes until the
noodles and chicken are heated through.

Meanwhile, heat the sunflower oil in a frying
pan, add the ready-prepared vegetables and
garlic and stir-fry for 2 minutes.

Ladle the broth and noodles into bowls. Top
with the stir-fried vegetables and garnish
with a drizzle of sesame oil and a generous
sprinkling of chopped coriander.

320

next time...

For soya bean, chilli & ginger noodle broth,
pour the stock and soy sauce into a large
saucepan, then add the ginger, chilli and spring
onions as in the previous recipe. Bring to the
boil, then add 300 g (10 oz) ready-cooked rice
noodles or soba noodles and 200 g (7 oz) frozen
soya (edamame) beans. Bring back to the boil
and cook for 2–3 minutes until the noodles
and soya beans are heated through. Ladle into
bowls and top with a drizzle of sesame oil and
chopped coriander.

321

tuscan bean
& truffle soup

SERVES 4

2 tablespoons olive oil
1 onion, chopped
2 garlic cloves, sliced
400 g (13 oz) can cannellini beans, rinsed and
  drained
400 g (13 oz) can butter beans, rinsed and
  drained
400 g (13 oz) can chopped tomatoes
½ Savoy cabbage, shredded
½ tablespoon chopped rosemary
850 ml (1½ pints) vegetable stock (see page 10)
1 teaspoon truffle oil
25 g (1 oz) grated Parmesan cheese
salt and pepper

Heat the oil in a saucepan, add the onion and
fry over a medium heat for 1–2 minutes until
slightly softened. Stir in the garlic and all the
beans and cook for 1 minute.

Add the tomatoes, cabbage and rosemary to the
pan, then pour in the stock and the truffle oil.
Mix together well, season to taste with salt and
pepper and bring to the boil. Reduce the heat
and simmer for 10–12 minutes, or until the
cabbage is just cooked.

Ladle the soup into shallow bowls, sprinkle
with the Parmesan and serve immediately.

322

next time...

For Tuscan bean soup with herb butter,
mix 75 g (3 oz) butter with 2 teaspoons
chopped capers and 2 tablespoons chopped
flat leaf parsley. Roll the butter up in clingfilm
or foil into a log and chill in the refrigerator
until firm. Make the soup as in the recipe
above, ladle into bowls and top with slices of
the herb butter.

323

beetroot &
horseradish soup

SERVES 6

1 tablespoon olive oil
1 onion, chopped
3 raw beetroot, about 400 g (13 oz), peeled and
  coarsely grated
600 ml (1 pint) hot vegetable stock (see page 10)
400 g (13 oz) can chopped tomatoes
3 teaspoons horseradish sauce
75 g (3 oz) fat-free natural yogurt
salt and pepper
chopped dill or parsley, to garnish

Heat the oil in a saucepan, add the onion and
fry over a medium heat for 5 minutes, stirring
occasionally, until softened. Stir in the
beetroot, stock, tomatoes and 2 teaspoons of
the horseradish sauce. Season with a little salt
and pepper.

Bring to the boil, then reduce the heat, cover
and simmer for 10 minutes. Leave the soup
to cool slightly, then purée in the pan with a
stick blender or in batches in a blender or food
processor until smooth, returning to the pan.
Reheat, then taste and adjust the seasoning
if needed. Meanwhile, mix the the remaining
horseradish sauce into the yogurt.

Ladle the soup into bowls, top with spoonfuls
of the yogurt and garnish with chopped dill or
parsley and a grinding of pepper.

324

next time...

For beetroot soup with goats' cheese, fry the
onion in oil as in the recipe above, then stir
in the beetroot, stock and tomatoes, omitting
the horseradish sauce, and season. Continue
making the soup as above, then ladle into
bowls, top with 100 g (3½ oz) goats' cheese,
crumbled and serve immediately.

325

roasted celery soup

SERVES 6

1 head of celery, base trimmed, sticks
    separated, tiny inside sticks with leaves
    reserved for garnishing and larger sticks
    thickly sliced
1 courgette, about 200 g (7 oz), sliced
½ small onion, roughly chopped
2 tablespoons light olive oil
25 g (1 oz) butter
25 g (1 oz) plain flour
300 ml (½ pint) semi-skimmed milk
300 ml (½ pint) vegetable stock (see page 10)
2 egg yolks
150 ml (¼ pint) double cream
salt and pepper

Put the celery, courgette and onion into a
roasting tin, drizzle with the oil and toss
together. Roast in a preheated oven, 180°C
(350°F), Gas Mark 4, for 20–25 minutes until
softened and only just beginning to colour.

Meanwhile, melt the butter in a saucepan and
stir in the flour to make a paste. Gradually
whisk in the milk over a medium heat and cook
for a few minutes, stirring, until thickened and
smooth. Season with a little salt and pepper.

Transfer the roasted vegetables to a blender or
food processor, add the stock and purée until
smooth. Pour into a large saucepan and mix in
the white sauce.

Beat the egg yolks with 4 tablespoons of the
cream in a bowl. Mix in a ladleful of the warm
soup, then pour the mixture into the saucepan.
Bring the soup just up to the boil, stirring, but
don't allow it to boil, or it will curdle. Taste and
adjust the seasoning if needed.

Ladle into cups set on saucers, then swirl
1 tablespoon of the remaining cream over the
top of each serving. Garnish with the reserved
tiny celery sticks.

326

next time...

**For chilled celery soup with candied pumpkin
seeds**, make the soup as in the previous
recipe, then leave to cool. Cover and chill in the
refrigerator for 3 hours before serving. Toast
3 tablespoons pumpkin seeds in a dry frying
pan until hot, spoon over 2 tablespoons maple
syrup and cook for 1 minute until bubbling.
Scoop out on to a baking sheet lined with
nonstick baking paper and leave to cool. Break
into pieces and sprinkle over the soup as you
serve it, omitting the swirls of cream.

327

roasted garlic & parsley soup

SERVES 6

2 garlic bulbs
pinch of dried thyme
2 tablespoons olive oil
1 large onion, finely chopped
2 rindless smoked back bacon rashers, cut into
    small dice
500 g (1 lb) potatoes, diced
400 g (13 oz) can cannellini beans, rinsed and
    drained
1 litre (1¾ pints) chicken stock (see page 9)
3 tablespoons chopped parsley
3 tablespoons chopped chives
salt and pepper

Line a small ovenproof dish with foil, then place the whole, unpeeled garlic bulbs on the foil. Sprinkle with the thyme, a little salt and pepper and 1 tablespoon of the oil. Wrap the foil around the garlic and roast in a preheated oven, 180°C (350°F), Gas Mark 4, for 30–35 minutes, or until the garlic is soft.

Remove from the oven and leave the garlic until cool enough to handle, then separate the cloves, squeeze the flesh from its skins and chop.

Heat the remaining oil in a saucepan, add the onion and fry over a medium heat for 5 minutes, stirring frequently, until softened. Add the bacon and fry for 5 minutes until the bacon and onion are pale golden. Stir in the potatoes, beans and chopped roasted garlic with any juices from the foil. Pour in the stock and bring to the boil, then reduce the heat, cover and simmer for 30 minutes.

Taste and adjust the seasoning if needed, then stir in the chopped herbs. Ladle into bowls and serve with warm crusty bread.

328

next time...

For roasted garlic, chicken & leek soup, roast the garlic as in the previous recipe. Thinly slice 1 leek, keeping the white and green parts separate. Fry the white leek in 1 tablespoon of the oil in a large saucepan for 5 minutes until softened. Add bacon and fry as before, then add the chopped roasted garlic with any roasting juices, omitting the potatoes and beans, and pour in the stock. Bring to the boil, then simmer for 20 minutes. Add the green leek and 200 g (7 oz) leftover roast chicken, cut into small pieces, and cook for 10 until the chicken is piping hot. Stir in the chopped herbs as before and serve.

329

eight treasure soup

SERVES 4–6

1.2 litres (2 pints) chicken stock (see page 9)
   or water
50 g (2 oz) frozen peas
50 g (2 oz) frozen sweetcorn
1 small skinless chicken breast fillet, about
   100 g (3½ oz), cut into very thin strips
75 g (3 oz) shiitake mushrooms, stems
   discarded, very thinly sliced
3 tablespoons soy sauce, or to taste
2 tablespoons rice wine or dry sherry
1 tablespoon cornflour
50 g (2 oz) cooked peeled prawns, defrosted
   and thoroughly dried if frozen
50 g (2 oz) cooked ham, thinly sliced
150 g (5 oz) firm tofu, thinly sliced
50 g (2 oz) baby spinach leaves, very finely
   shredded
salt and pepper (if needed)

Bring the stock or water to the boil in a large
saucepan. Add the frozen peas and sweetcorn,
reduce the heat and simmer for 3 minutes.
Stir in the chicken, mushrooms, soy sauce and
rice wine or sherry and simmer for 3 minutes.

Blend the cornflour to a paste with a little cold
water, then pour into the soup and stir to mix.
Simmer, stirring, for 1–2 minutes, or until the
soup thickens.

Reduce the heat to low and add the prawns,
ham, tofu and spinach. Simmer for about
2 minutes, or until the spinach has just wilted,
stirring once or twice; take care to stir gently so
that the tofu does not break up. Taste and add
salt and pepper if needed, and more soy sauce,
if liked. Serve piping hot.

330

next time...

For eight treasure vegetable soup, make
the soup as in the previous recipe, replacing
the chicken stock with 1.2 litres (2 pints)
vegetable stock (see page 10) and adding a
2.5 cm (1 inch) piece of fresh root ginger, peeled
and finely chopped, and 100 g (3½ oz) frozen
edamame (soya) beans with the frozen peas and
sweetcorn. Then replace the chicken with 150 g
(5 oz) broccoli, cut into small florets, and add
50 g (2 oz) sugar snap peas, halved, instead of
the prawns and ham with the tofu and spinach,
simmering for 2 minutes as before. Adjust the
seasoning and serve.

331

331

thanksgiving turkey, pumpkin & cranberry
soup

SERVES 6

25 g (1 oz) butter
1 tablespoon sunflower oil
1 onion, chopped
300 g (10 oz) deseeded, peeled and diced
    pumpkin
200 g (7 oz) carrot, diced
2cm (¾ inch) piece of fresh root ginger, peeled
    and finely chopped
1 litre (1¾ pints) turkey stock (see page 9)
4 tablespoons cranberry sauce
large pinch of ground allspice, plus extra
    to garnish
150 ml (¼ pint) double cream
150 g (5 oz) cooked turkey, cut into shreds
salt and pepper

Melt the butter with the oil in a saucepan,
add the onion and fry over a medium heat for
5 minutes, stirring occasionally, until softened.

Stir in the pumpkin, carrot and ginger and
fry gently for 5 minutes. Pour in the stock,
add 1 tablespoon of the cranberry sauce and
the allspice and season with a little salt and
pepper. Bring to the boil, then reduce the heat,
cover and simmer for 40 minutes.

Leave the soup to cool slightly, then purée
in the pan with a stick blender or in batches
in a blender or food processor until smooth,
returning to the pan. Reheat, then taste and
adjust the seasoning if needed.

Ladle the soup into shallow bowls. Swirl the
cream over the top, sprinkle with the turkey
and add spoonfuls of the remaining cranberry
sauce. Garnish with a sprinkling of allspice and
serve immediately.

332

chilled spinach, kiwi & chia seed soup

SERVES 6

100 g (3½ oz) baby spinach leaves
½ cucumber, diced
2 kiwi fruit, peeled and diced
300 ml (½ pint) cold vegetable stock
  (see page 10)
150 g (5 oz) fat-free natural yogurt
4 teaspoons chia seeds
6 teaspoons maple syrup
a few tiny edible flowers, such as
  viola, pansy, nasturtium, sage
  or rosemary flowers, to garnish
  (optional)

Put the spinach, cucumber, kiwi fruit and stock into a large jug and purée with a stick blender or add to a blender or food processor and purée until smooth.

Add the yogurt and chia seeds to the puréed soup and mix briefly together until an even colour.

Pour the soup into teacups or small glass dishes, drizzle each serving with a teaspoon of maple syrup and garnish with some tiny edible flowers, if liked. Serve immediately, as if left to stand the chia seeds will give a jelly-like set to the soup.

333

chunky chorizo, chickpea, tomato & red pepper soup

SERVES 6

1 tablespoon olive oil
1 onion, finely chopped
100 g (3½ oz) chorizo, diced
100 g (3½ oz) carrot, coarsely grated
1 red pepper, cored, deseeded and diced
400 g (13 oz) can chopped tomatoes
400 g (13 oz) can chickpeas, rinsed and drained
600 ml (1 pint) chicken stock (see page 9)
1 teaspoon dried oregano
75 g (3 oz) kale, shredded
salt and pepper

Heat the oil in a saucepan, add the onion and fry over a medium heat for 5 minutes, stirring frequently, until softened. Add the chorizo and fry for 5 minutes.

Stir in the carrot, red pepper, tomatoes, chickpeas and stock, then add the oregano and season with a little salt and pepper. Bring to the boil, then reduce the heat, cover and simmer for 25 minutes.

Stir in the kale, re-cover and simmer for 3–5 minutes until it has just wilted. Taste and adjust the seasoning if needed.

Ladle the soup into bowls and sprinkle with pitta bread croûtons (see page 13) or serve with garlic bread.

334

chicken, leek & black pudding soup

SERVES 6

1 tablespoon sunflower oil
375 g (12 oz) skinless chicken thigh fillets, diced
25 g (1 oz) butter
1 leek, thinly sliced, white and green parts kept separate
375 g (12 oz) potatoes, diced
1 small dessert apple, quartered, cored and diced
100 g (3½ oz) black pudding, diced
1 litre (1¾ pints) chicken stock (see page 9)
2 rosemary sprigs, leaves stripped from the stems and chopped
salt and pepper
chopped parsley, to garnish

Heat the oil in a saucepan, add the chicken and fry over a medium heat for 5 minutes, stirring, until lightly browned. Stir in the butter until melted, then add the white leek and potatoes and fry for 5 minutes, stirring.

Mix in the apple, black pudding, stock and rosemary, then season with a little salt and pepper. Bring to the boil, then reduce the heat, cover and simmer for 45 minutes.

Stir in the green leek, re-cover and simmer for 5 minutes until softened. Taste and adjust seasoning if needed.

Ladle the soup into bowls and sprinkle with chopped parsley to garnish. Serve with warm crusty bread.

335

cream of celeriac soup with porcini dumplings

SERVES 4–6

50 g (2 oz) butter
2 shallots or 1 onion, chopped
1 garlic clove, crushed
500 g (1 lb) celeriac, peeled and cut into small dice
900 ml (1½ pints) vegetable or chicken stock (see pages 10 and 9)
300 ml (½ pint) single cream or milk
salt and pepper

DUMPLINGS

5 g (¼ oz) dried porcini mushrooms (ceps)
25 g (1 oz) butter
1 shallot, finely chopped
175 g (6 oz) ricotta cheese
25 g (1 oz) Parmesan cheese, finely grated
2 egg yolks, beaten
2 tablespoons plain flour, plus extra for dusting and rolling
1 tablespoon chopped flat leaf parsley

Put the porcini for the dumplings into a small bowl and pour over warm water to cover. Leave to soak for 30 minutes. Strain through a fine sieve, reserving the liquid. Rinse the mushrooms well in cold water, chop finely and set aside.

Melt the butter in a small saucepan, add the shallot and fry gently for 5–6 minutes, or until softened but not browned, stirring frequently. Spoon into a bowl, add the remaining dumpling ingredients and mix to form a soft dough. Season to taste with salt and pepper. Cover and chill in the refrigerator for 30 minutes–1 hour. Shape the mixture into about 30 small balls with lightly floured hands, then roll in flour and put on to a tray.

Meanwhile, to make the soup, melt the butter in a saucepan, add the shallots or onion and garlic and fry over a medium heat for 5 minutes without browning, stirring frequently. Stir in the celeriac, cover and cook for 5–10 minutes, or until it begins to soften. Pour in the stock and bring to the boil, then reduce the heat and simmer for 10–15 minutes.

Leave the soup to cool slightly, then purée in the pan with a stick blender or in batches in a blender or food processor until smooth, returning to the pan. Stir in the cream or milk and season to taste with salt and pepper. Reheat gently without boiling.

Bring a saucepan of lightly salted water to the boil. Add the dumplings and simmer for 3–4 minutes. Drain well and add to the soup just before serving.

336

next time...

For cream of carrot soup with porcini dumplings, make the soup as in the previous recipe, replacing the celeriac with 500 g (1 lb) carrots, cut into small dice. Serve the soup with the dumplings as before.

337

smoked haddock & sweetcorn soup with wild rice and bacon croûtons

SERVES 4

75 g (3 oz) wild rice
250 g (8 oz) smoked haddock fillet
600 ml (1 pint) milk
1 bay leaf
50 g (2 oz) butter
1 large onion, chopped
1 leek, sliced
1 celery stick, chopped
1 garlic clove, crushed
1 tablespoon thyme leaves
900 ml (1½ pints) chicken stock (see page 9)
pinch of grated nutmeg, or to taste
125 g (4 oz) sweetcorn, defrosted if frozen
salt and pepper

BACON CROÛTONS
3 tablespoons olive oil
4 rindless pancetta slices or streaky bacon rashers, cut into strips
2 slices of bread, crusts removed, cut or broken into 1 cm (½ inch) pieces

Put the rice into a small saucepan and cover with cold water. Bring to the boil, then reduce the heat and simmer for 40–45 minutes, or until tender. Drain and set aside.

Put the haddock, milk and bay leaf into a saucepan and bring to the boil, then reduce the heat and simmer for 8–10 minutes, or until just cooked. Lift the fish out with a slotted spoon and leave to cool, then break the flesh into flakes, discarding the skin and any stray bones. Strain the milk through a sieve and reserve.

Melt the butter in a large saucepan, add the onion, leek, celery and garlic and fry gently for 8–10 minutes, stirring frequently, until the vegetables are softened but not browned.

Add the thyme, stock and reserved milk. Season to taste with salt and pepper and the nutmeg. Bring to the boil, then reduce the heat and simmer for 10 minutes. Add the sweetcorn and simmer for a further 5 minutes. Stir in the cooked rice and flaked haddock and heat through for a few minutes. Taste and adjust the seasoning if needed.

Meanwhile, heat the oil for the bacon croûtons in a large frying pan, add the pancetta or bacon and fry over a medium heat for 5–6 minutes, or until crisp. Remove with a slotted spoon and drain on kitchen paper. Add the bread to the pan and fry for 4–5 minutes, turning frequently, until crisp and golden brown. Drain on kitchen paper.

Ladle the hot soup into bowls and serve sprinkled with the bacon croûtons.

338

next time...

For smoked haddock & sweetcorn soup with cannellini beans, poach the smoked haddock in the milk with the bay leaf added, then strain as in the previous recipe. Fry the onion, leek, celery and garlic in the butter, then add the thyme, stock and reserved milk as before, along with a rinsed and drained 400 g (13 oz) can cannellini beans. Season and simmer as before, then add the flaked haddock, omitting the rice, and stir in 2 tablespoons finely chopped parsley. Serve with the bacon croûtons as before.

339

velvety fennel & parmesan soup

SERVES 6

25 g (1 oz) butter
1 tablespoon olive oil
4 spring onions, sliced
2 fennel bulbs, trimmed and green feathery
    fronds reserved, cored and chopped
200 g (7 oz) potato, cut into small dice
750 ml (1¼ pints) chicken stock (see page 9)
100 g (3½ oz) wedge of Parmesan cheese
    including the rind
salt and pepper

Melt the butter with the oil in a saucepan, add
the spring onions, fennel and potato and fry
over a medium heat for 5 minutes, stirring,
until softened but not browned.

Pour in the stock and bring to the boil. Coarsely
grate 50 g (2 oz) of the Parmesan and reserve,
then add the remaining Parmesan and rind to
the pan. Season with a little salt and pepper,
cover and simmer for 25 minutes.

Meanwhile, line a baking sheet with nonstick
baking paper, arrange the grated Parmesan into
6 well-spaced mounds on it, then spread each
into a roughly shaped circle about 7.5 cm
(3 inches) in diameter. Bake in a preheated oven,
200°C (400°F), Gas Mark 6, for 5–6 minutes until
bubbling and golden brown. Leave to cool on the
paper.

Lift the Parmesan rind out of soup with a
slotted spoon, cut away any soft cheese and
return to the pan, discarding the rind. Leave
the soup to cool slightly, then purée in the pan
with a stick blender or in batches in a blender
or food processor until smooth, returning to
the pan. Reheat, then taste and adjust the
seasoning if needed.

Pour the soup into cups, garnish with any
reserved snipped green fennel fronds and serve
each with a Parmesan wafer, breaking it into
pieces and scattering over the top of the soup,
if liked.

340

aubergine & harissa
soup

SERVES 6

2 tablespoons olive oil
1 onion, finely chopped
1 aubergine, diced
2 garlic cloves, finely chopped
400 g (13 oz) can chopped tomatoes
900 ml (1½ pints) vegetable stock (see page 10)
2 teaspoons harissa paste
1 tablespoon tomato purée
50 g (2 oz) giant couscous
150 g (5 oz) Greek yogurt
salt and pepper
chopped mint, to garnish

Heat the oil in a saucepan, add the onion and aubergine and fry over a medium heat for 5 minutes, stirring frequently, until softened. Stir in the garlic and fry for 3 minutes.

Pour in the tomatoes and stock, then mix in the harissa and tomato purée. Season to taste with salt and pepper and bring to the boil. Reduce the heat, cover and simmer for 20 minutes.

Stir in the couscous, re-cover and simmer for 10 minutes, then taste and adjust the seasoning if needed.

Ladle the soup into bowls, top with spoonfuls of the yogurt and sprinkle with chopped mint to garnish.

341

next time...

For the curried aubergine & chickpea soup, fry the onion and aubergine, then add the tomatoes and stock as before. Omit the harissa and couscous, stir in 1 tablespoon medium–hot curry paste with the tomato purée and season to taste with salt and pepper. Bring to the boil and add a rinsed and drained 400 g (13 oz) can chickpeas. Cover and simmer for 30 minutes. Serve the soup topped with the yogurt and garnished with mint as before.

342

chicken bredie

SERVES 6

1 tablespoon sunflower oil
1 onion, finely chopped
250 g (8 oz) skinless chicken thigh fillets, diced
1 garlic clove, finely chopped
½ teaspoon ground turmeric
½ teaspoon ground cinnamon
½ teaspoon chilli powder or hot smoked
    paprika
large pinch of chilli flakes
1 bay leaf
200 g (7 oz) sweet potato, cut into small dice
1 carrot, cut into small dice
400 g (13 oz) can chopped tomatoes
1 litre (1¾ pints) chicken stock (see page 9)
1 tablespoon dark brown soft sugar
salt and pepper

Heat the oil in a saucepan, add the onion and fry over a medium heat for 5 minutes, stirring frequently, until softened. Add the chicken and garlic and fry for 5 minutes, stirring frequently, until the chicken is lightly browned.

Sprinkle the ground spices and chilli flakes over the chicken, then mix together. Add the bay leaf, sweet potato and carrot, then pour in the tomatoes and stock. Add the sugar and a little salt and pepper and bring to the boil, stirring. Reduce the heat, cover and simmer for 40 minutes until the chicken is cooked and the sweet potato is tender, stirring occasionally.

Ladle the soup into bowls and serve with warm crusty bread.

343

next time...

For peppered bredie, fry the onion in the oil as in the previous recipe, then add 1 orange and 1 red pepper, cored, deseeded and diced, in place of the chicken, and fry for 5 minutes. Continue making the soup as before.

344

mushroom multigrain
soup

SERVES 6

100 g (3½ oz) shop-bought dried pea and barley
    soup mix, soaked in cold water overnight
10 g (¼ oz) dried mixed mushrooms
150 ml (¼ pint) boiling water
1 tablespoon olive oil
1 onion, chopped
25 g (1 oz) butter
250 g (8 oz) chestnut mushrooms, sliced
2 garlic cloves, finely chopped
1.2 litre (2 pints) vegetable stock (see page 10)
2 rosemary sprigs, leaves stripped from the
    stems and chopped, plus extra chopped
    leaves to garnish
1 teaspoon Dijon mustard
4 tablespoons sherry
salt and pepper
chopped parsley, to garnish

Drain the soaked pea and barley mix and
set aside. Put the dried mushrooms into a
heatproof bowl, pour over the measured boiling
water and leave to soak for 15 minutes.

Meanwhile, heat the oil in a saucepan, add
the onion and fry over a medium heat for
5 minutes, stirring occasionally, until softened.
Add the butter and stir until melted, then mix
in the fresh mushrooms and garlic and fry for
5 minutes, stirring.

Pour in the stock and add the rosemary,
mustard and a little pepper (don't add salt here,
as it can toughen the soaked dried peas). Strain
the mushroom soaking liquid through a fine
sieve into the pan, then finely chop the soaked
mushrooms and add to the pan. Bring to the
boil and boil rapidly for 10 minutes.

Stir in the sherry, then reduce the heat, cover
and simmer for 40–50 minutes until the peas
and barley are tender. Season to taste with salt.

Ladle the soup into bowls, sprinkle with
chopped rosemary and parsley and serve with
warm crusty bread.

345

next time...

For mushroom, kale & multigrain soup, make
the soup as in the previous recipe, adding 75 g
(3 oz) kale, shredded, and 3 tomatoes, chopped,
for the last 10 minutes of cooking.

346

beef tom yum soup

SERVES 4

2 tablespoons sunflower oil
1 onion, finely chopped
250 g (8 oz) mushrooms, sliced
4 teaspoons ready-made tom yum paste
3 teaspoons light brown soft sugar or
    palm sugar
1.2 litre (2 pints) chicken stock (see page 9)
250 g (8 oz) flat iron or rump steak
300 g (10½ oz) pack ready-prepared stir–fry
    vegetables with bamboo shoots and water
    chestnuts
4 tablespoons chopped coriander

TO SERVE
fish sauce
lime wedges

Heat 1 tablespoon of the oil in a saucepan,
add the onion and fry over a medium heat for
5 minutes, stirring frequently, until softened.
Mix in the mushrooms and curry paste and
cook for 2 minutes, stirring.

Stir in the sugar and stock and bring to the boil.
Reduce the heat, cover and simmer gently for
10 minutes.

Meanwhile, heat the remaining oil in a frying
pan, add the steak and fry for 6–8 minutes,
turning once or twice, until browned and
medium rare. Remove from the heat and leave
to rest for 2–3 minutes.

Add the ready-prepared vegetables to the broth
and cook for 3 minutes. Stir in the coriander.

Ladle the soup into bowls. Thinly slice the
beef and arrange on top of the soup. Serve with
fish sauce and lime wedges so that diners can
season the soup to taste.

347

celeriac soup with chorizo croûtons

SERVES 6

1 tablespoon sunflower oil
1 onion, roughly chopped
25 g (1 oz) butter
625 g (1¼ lb) celeriac, peeled and diced
750 ml (1¼ pints) vegetable or chicken stock
    (see pages 10 and 9)
300 ml (½ pint) milk
2 tablespoons dry sherry (optional)
salt and pepper

CHORIZO CROÛTONS
3 tablespoons olive oil
100 g (3½ oz) chorizo, cut into small dice
3 slices of white bread, crusts removed, cut into
    small dice

Heat the oil in a saucepan, add the onion and
fry over a medium heat for 5 minutes, stirring
occasionally, until softened but not browned.
Add the butter and stir until melted, then
mix in the celeriac. Cover and fry gently for
5 minutes, stirring occasionally.

Pour in the stock and bring to the boil, then
season to taste with salt and pepper. Reduce the
heat, cover and simmer gently for 40 minutes
until the celeriac is tender.

Leave the soup to cool slightly, then purée
in the pan with a stick blender or in batches
in a blender or food processor until smooth,
returning to the pan. Stir in the milk, add the
sherry (if using) and reheat, then taste and
adjust the seasoning if needed.

Heat 2 tablespoons of the oil for the croûtons
in a large frying pan, add the chorizo and diced
bread and fry over a medium heat, stirring,
until golden and crisp, adding the remaining
oil as needed.

Ladle the hot soup into bowls. Sprinkle some of
the croûtons over the soup and serve the rest in
a small bowl for diners to help themselves.

348

next time...

For Jerusalem artichoke soup with chorizo
croûtons, peel 625 g (1¼ lb) Jerusalem
artichokes and quickly slice, dropping them
into a bowl of cold water mixed with the juice
of 1 lemon as you prepare them to prevent
discoloration. Fry the onion in the oil as in
the previous recipe, then add the butter and
the drained sliced artichokes. Add the stock,
season to taste with salt and pepper and
bring to the boil, then cover and simmer for
40 minutes. Purée, then add the milk as before
with 2 tablespoons dry white wine instead of
the sherry, reheat and check the seasoning.
Serve with the chorizo or plain croûtons.

349

wheat noodle soup with marinated chicken

SERVES 4–6

1 teaspoon ground turmeric
2 teaspoons salt
300 g (10 oz) skinless chicken breast fillets, cut into 2.5 cm (1 inch) cubes
3 tablespoons skinned roasted, unsalted peanuts
3 tablespoons long-grain white rice
2 tablespoons vegetable oil
1 onion, chopped
2 lemon grass stalks, bruised
3 garlic cloves, crushed
5 cm (2 inch) piece of fresh root ginger, peeled and finely chopped
¼ teaspoon paprika
2 red bird's eye chillies, chopped
900 ml (1½ pints) water
2–3 tablespoons Thai fish sauce, plus extra to serve
250 g (8 oz) dried wheat noodles

TO SERVE

3 hard-boiled eggs, shelled and halved
2 tablespoons chopped coriander leaves
3 spring onions, finely chopped
chilli flakes
1–2 tablespoons balachaung (optional)

Mix the turmeric with the salt and rub into the cubes of chicken in a dish. Cover and leave to marinate in the refrigerator for 30 minutes.

Crush the roasted peanuts finely in a food processor or using a pestle and mortar. Heat a dry frying pan, add the rice and toast over a medium heat until golden brown. Grind to a powder in a food processor or spice grinder. Mix with the crushed peanuts and set aside.

Heat the oil in a large saucepan, add the onion and fry for a few minutes until just softened. Stir in the marinated chicken with the lemon grass, garlic, ginger, paprika and chillies.

Pour in the measured water and fish sauce and bring to the boil, then reduce the heat to a gentle simmer. Stir in the crushed peanut and ground rice mixture and simmer for 10–15 minutes, or until the chicken has cooked through and the broth thickened slightly.

Meanwhile, bring a saucepan of water to the boil, add the noodles and cook for 3–4 minutes, or until just tender. Drain and refresh under cold running water, then divide among large soup bowls.

Ladle the chicken soup over the noodles and serve topped with the hard-boiled egg halves, coriander and spring onions. Add an extra splash of fish sauce and a sprinkling of chilli flakes and balachaung to taste, if liked. Eat the soup with a spoon and fork.

350

next time...

For wheat noodle soup with marinated tofu, crush the peanuts and toast the rice as in the previous recipe. Fry the onion in the oil, then add the flavourings as before along with 1 teaspoon ground turmeric, omitting the chicken. Then add the water and fish sauce or vegetarian alternative and continue as before. While the noodles are cooking, stir-fry 2 x 160 g (5½ oz) packs marinated tofu pieces in 2 tablespoons sunflower oil for 3–5 minutes until hot. Divide the cooked noodles between the serving bowls, ladle over the soup and top with the tofu, along with the hard-boiled eggs, coriander and spring onions as before.

351

chickpea, lemon & parsley soup topped with black olive tapenade toasts

SERVES 6

1 tablespoon olive oil
1 onion, finely chopped
1 courgette, about 200 g (7 oz), diced
2 garlic cloves, finely chopped
400 g (13 oz) can chickpeas, rinsed and drained
900 ml (1½ pints) vegetable stock (see page 10)
grated zest and juice of 1 lemon
salt and pepper
chopped chives, to garnish (optional)

TAPENADE TOASTS
6 teaspoons ready-made black olive tapenade
1 baguettine or ½ thin French stick, sliced and toasted

Heat the oil in a saucepan, add the onion and fry over a medium heat for 5 minutes, stirring occasionally. Add the courgette and garlic and cook for 2 minutes. Stir in the chickpeas and stock and season with a little salt and pepper. Bring to the boil, then reduce the heat, cover and simmer for 10 minutes.

Leave the soup to cool slightly, then purée in the pan with a stick blender or in batches in a blender or food processor until smooth, returning to the pan. Stir in half the lemon juice, then add more to taste, and adjust the seasoning with salt and pepper if needed.

Reheat the soup, then ladle into soup bowls. Spread the tapenade over the toasted French bread and float on top of the soup. Sprinkle with the lemon zest and chopped chives, if liked.

352

next time...

For **chickpea, tomato & pepper soup**, fry 1 red onion, chopped, in 1 tablespoon olive oil in a saucepan for 5 minutes until softened. Stir in 1 red pepper, cored, deseeded and diced, 3 plum tomatoes, diced, and 2 garlic cloves, finely chopped, and fry for 2 minutes. Mix in the chickpeas, stock and a little salt and pepper as in the previous recipe and bring to the boil, then cover and simmer for 10 minutes. Purée until smooth and reheat as before, then ladle into bowls and top with a drizzle of olive oil.

353

barbecue sausage, bean & tomato soup

SERVES 6

1 tablespoon sunflower oil
1 onion, chopped
150 g (5 oz) mushrooms, sliced
¼ teaspoon chilli powder or hot smoked
    paprika
400 g (13 oz) can chopped tomatoes
400 g (13 oz) can mixed beans, rinsed
    and drained
600 ml (1 pint) chicken stock (see page 9)
2 teaspoons tomato purée
2 tablespoons brown sugar
2 tablespoons sherry vinegar or cider vinegar
1 large bay leaf
250 g (8 oz) Cumberland pork chipolata
    sausages
salt and pepper

Heat the oil in a large saucepan, add the onion and fry over a medium heat for 5 minutes, stirring occasionally, until softened. Stir in the mushrooms and fry, stirring, for 3 minutes, then mix in the chilli powder or paprika.

Pour in the tomatoes, beans and stock, then stir in the tomato purée, sugar, vinegar and bay leaf. Season to taste with salt and pepper and bring to the boil. Reduce the heat, cover and simmer for 30 minutes.

Meanwhile, cook the sausages under a hot grill for 10–12 minutes, turning frequently, until evenly browned and cooked through.

Cut the sausages into slices and stir into the soup. Re-cover and simmer for 10 minutes. Remove and discard bay leaf, then ladle the soup into bowls and serve with garlic bread.

354

next time...

For barbecue mixed bean & tomato soup, make the soup as in the previous recipe, replacing the chicken stock with 600 ml (1 pint) vegetable stock (see page 10). Once the bean and mushroom mixture has simmered for 30 minutes, add 75 g (3 oz) green beans, thickly sliced, and 75 g (3 oz) runner beans, shredded, instead of the sausages. Re-cover and simmer for 10 minutes, then ladle into bowls and serve.

355

tasty bean soup

SERVES 4

375 g (12 oz) dried haricot beans, soaked in cold
    water overnight
2 litres (3½ pints) water
1 carrot, chopped
1 onion, quartered
1 bouquet garni
125 g (4 oz) cooked smoked ham, diced
40 g (1½ oz) butter
2 shallots, finely chopped
1 garlic clove, crushed
1 tablespoon chopped parsley, plus extra sprigs
    to garnish
salt and pepper

Drain the beans in a colander, rinse under cold
running water and drain again. Put them into
a large saucepan with the measured water and
bring to the boil. Reduce the heat and simmer
for 1½ hours, or until the beans are just tender.
Add the carrot, onion, bouquet garni and ham
and simmer for 20–30 minutes. Remove and
discard the bouquet garni.

Leave the soup to cool slightly, then purée
in the pan with a stick blender or in batches
in a blender or food processor until smooth,
returning to the pan. Reheat gently.

Melt the butter in a heavy-based saucepan, add
the shallots and garlic and fry gently for a few
minutes, stirring frequently, until golden but
not browned. Add the chopped parsley and mix
together quickly.

Add the shallot mixture to the puréed soup,
mix well and season well with salt and pepper.

Pour the soup into bowls. Garnish with parsley
sprigs and sprinkle with croûtons (see page 13).

356

jamaican pepperpot soup

SERVES 6–8

1 kg (2 lb) boneless lean stewing beef, cut into
    small cubes
250 g (8 oz) boneless lean pork, cut into small
    cubes
2.5 litres (4 pints) water
24 okra, conical stalk end discarded and
    roughly chopped
500 g (1 lb) kale, roughly chopped
500 g (1 lb) spinach leaves, tough stems
    discarded and leaves roughly chopped
2 green peppers, cored, deseeded and roughly
    chopped
2 spring onions, roughly chopped
1 thyme sprig or ¼ teaspoon dried thyme
¼ teaspoon cayenne pepper
500 g (1 lb) yellow yams, thinly sliced
1 large potato, thinly sliced
1 garlic clove, crushed or finely chopped
salt

Put the meat into a large saucepan and pour
over the measured water. Bring to the boil, then
reduce the heat, half-cover and simmer for
about 30 minutes.

Stir in the okra, kale, spinach, green peppers
and spring onions with the thyme and cayenne.
Half-cover and simmer for 15 minutes.

Add the yams, potato and garlic to the pan and
simmer for a further 20 minutes, or until the
yams and potato are tender. Add more water if
the soup is too thick. Season to taste with salt.

Serve the soup hot in a warmed soup tureen.

357

spiced chickpea & lamb soup

SERVES 6

50 g (2 oz) dried chickpeas, soaked in cold water
  overnight
50 g (2 oz) dried black-eyed beans, soaked in
  cold water overnight
50 g (2 oz) trahana or bulgur wheat
500 g (1 lb) boneless neck of lamb, cut into
  4 pieces
4 tablespoons olive oil, plus extra for drizzling
1 onion, chopped
2 carrots, chopped
425 g (14 oz) can chopped tomatoes
4 small red chillies
4 thyme sprigs
1 teaspoon each ground coriander, cumin and
  cinnamon
½ teaspoon each dried mint and oregano
salt and pepper

Drain the soaked peas and beans separately in
a colander, rinse under cold running water and
drain again. Put them into separate saucepans,
cover with plenty of cold water and bring to the
boil. Reduce the heat and simmer for 1 hour.
Drain, reserving the cooking liquid.

Put the cooked pulses into a casserole dish, add
all the remaining ingredients and cover with
the reserved cooking liquid, adding extra water
to cover if necessary.

Cover the casserole dish with a tight-fitting lid
and bake in a preheated oven, 180°C (350°F),
Gas Mark 4, for 1½ hours, or until the meat
and vegetables are tender.

Ladle the soup into bowls, drizzle with olive oil
and serve with crusty bread.

358

next time...

For spiced chickpea & citrus beef soup, cook
the soaked pulses as in the previous recipe.
Drain and add to a casserole dish with the
trahana or bulghar wheat, 500 g (1 lb)
boneless lean stewing beef, diced, the pared
rind of ½ lemon and ½ orange, cut into strips,
and the remaining ingredients, then continue
making the soup as before.

359

fennel & lemon
soup with black olive gremolata

SERVES 4

75 ml (3 fl oz) olive oil
3 fat spring onions, chopped
250 g (8 oz) fennel bulb, trimmed and any green
   feathery fronds reserved, cored and thinly
   sliced
1 potato, diced
finely grated rind and juice of 1 lemon
750 ml (1¼ pints) vegetable or chicken stock
   (see pages 10 and 9)
salt and pepper

BLACK OLIVE GREMOLATA
1 small garlic clove, finely chopped
finely grated rind of 1 lemon
4 tablespoons chopped flat leaf parsley
16 Greek-style black olives, pitted and chopped

Heat the oil in a large saucepan, add the onions
and fry for 5–10 minutes, or until beginning
to soften, stirring occasionally. Add the fennel,
potato and lemon rind and cook for 5 minutes.

Pour in the stock and bring to the boil, then
reduce the heat, cover and simmer for about
25 minutes, or until the vegetables are tender.

Meanwhile, for the gremolata, mix together the
garlic, lemon rind, parsley and any reserved
green fennel fronds, finely chopped, in a bowl,
then stir in the olives. Cover and chill in the
refrigerator until ready to serve.

Leave the soup to cool slightly, then purée in
batches in a blender or food processor until
smooth. Pass the purée through a fine sieve
to remove any strings of fennel back into the
rinsed-out saucepan. The soup should not be
too thick, so add more stock if necessary. Taste
and season well with salt and pepper, and add
the lemon juice, then reheat.

Pour into warmed soup bowls and sprinkle
each serving with a portion of the gremolata.

360

next time...

**For fennel & watercress soup with citrus
gremolata**, make the soup as in the previous
recipe, adding 50 g (2 oz) watercress, roughly
chopped, to the pan for the last 3 minutes
of cooking until just wilted but still bright
green. Make the gremolata as before, adding
1 teaspoon finely grated orange rind along with
the lemon rind. Purée and strain the soup, then
season and reheat as before. Serve topped with
the citrus gremolata.

361

smoked aubergine & tomato soup

SERVES 6

2 large aubergines
2 tablespoons olive oil
1 large onion, roughly chopped
2 garlic cloves, finely chopped
500 g (1 lb) plum tomatoes, skinned and chopped
½ teaspoon smoked paprika
1 teaspoon caster sugar
600 ml (1 pint) vegetable or chicken stock (see pages 10 and 9)
salt and pepper

ANCHOVY TOASTS

50 g (2 oz) can anchovy fillets in oil, drained and finely chopped
2 tablespoons chopped chives
75 g (3 oz) butter
1 small baguette or ½ french stick, sliced

Prick each aubergine just below the stalk and cook under a hot grill for 15 minutes, turning several times, until the skin is blistered and blackened. Transfer to a chopping board and leave to cool.

Heat the oil in a large saucepan, add the onion and fry for 5 minutes, stirring, until softened. Meanwhile, cut the aubergines in half and use a spoon to scoop out the soft flesh from the blackened skins.

Add the aubergine flesh and garlic to the onion and fry for 2 minutes. Mix in the tomatoes, smoked paprika and sugar and cook briefly, then stir in the stock and season to taste with salt and pepper. Bring to the boil, then reduce the heat, cover and simmer for 30 minutes.

Leave the soup to cool slightly, then purée in the pan with a stick blender or in batches in a blender or food processor until smooth, returning to the pan. Mix together the

anchovies, chives, butter and a little pepper. Toast the bread and spread with the anchovy butter. Reheat the soup, then ladle into bowls and float the anchovy toasts on top. Serve immediately.

362

next time...

For smoked tomato soup, make the soup as in the previous recipe, but omit the aubergines and add 875 g (1¾ lb) skinned and chopped plum tomatoes to the fried onion with the garlic. Flavour with the smoked paprika, then simmer with the stock, sugar and salt and pepper to taste and purée as before. Serve the reheated soup with a drizzle of chillied olive oil instead of the anchovy toasts.

beef & flat noodle soup

SERVES 4–6

500 g (1 lb) chuck steak
1.8 litres (3 pints) beef stock (see page 9) or
　water
4 star anise
1 large cinnamon stick
1 teaspoon black peppercorns
2 sweet onions or 4 shallots, thinly sliced
4 garlic cloves, crushed
7 cm (3 inch) piece of fresh root ginger, peeled
　and finely sliced
125 g (4 oz) bean sprouts, plus extra to serve
250 g (8 oz) dried flat rice noodles
6 spring onions, thinly sliced, plus extra to
　serve
handful of coriander leaves
250 g (8 oz) fillet of beef, thinly sliced
2 tablespoons fish sauce
salt and pepper
red bird's eye chillies, to serve

NUOC CHAM SAUCE
2 red chillies, chopped, plus 1, sliced, to serve
1 garlic clove, peeled
1½ tablespoons caster sugar
1 tablespoon lime juice
1 tablespoon rice vinegar
3 tablespoons fish sauce
4 tablespoons water

Heat a large, dry frying pan until very hot and
sear the chuck steak on all sides until brown
and charred.

Transfer the beef to a large saucepan and add
the stock or water, whole spices, 1 onion or
2 shallots, the garlic and ginger. Bring to the
boil, skimming off any scum that rises to the
surface with a slotted spoon, and continue to
boil for about 10 minutes. Reduce the heat,
cover and simmer for about 2 hours, or until
the beef is tender.

Blanch the bean sprouts in a separate saucepan
of boiling water for 1 minute, then drain well.

Cook the noodles in boiling water for 3–4
minutes, or until just tender; don't overcook
them. Drain well and divide among large
soup bowls. Sprinkle the bean sprouts, spring
onions, coriander and the remaining onions or
shallots over the noodles.

Pound the chillies, garlic and sugar for the
nuoc cham sauce until smooth using a pestle
and mortar. Add the lime juice, vinegar, fish
sauce and measured water and blend together
well. Transfer the mixture to a small bowl.

When the beef from the broth is tender, lift
it out with a slotted spoon on to a chopping
board, slice it thinly and divide among the
bowls with the slices of raw beef fillet and
garnish with the red bird's eye chillies.

Strain the broth through a sieve, return it to
the pan and season with the fish sauce and
salt and pepper to taste.

Ladle the hot broth over the contents of the
bowls and serve immediately with the nuoc
cham sauce and a plate of extra bean sprouts,
spring onions and the sliced red chilli.

364

vegetable soup with bacon dumplings

SERVES 6

50 g (2 oz) butter
1 onion, finely chopped
1 leek, diced, white and green parts kept
    separate
300 g (10 oz) swede, diced
300 g (10 oz) parsnip, diced
300 g (10 oz) carrot, diced
2 celery sticks, diced
3–4 sage sprigs
2.5 litres (4 pints) chicken stock (see page 9)
salt and pepper

DUMPLINGS

100 g (3½ oz) self-raising flour
½ teaspoon English mustard powder
2 teaspoons finely chopped sage
50 g (2 oz) vegetable suet
2 rindless smoked streaky bacon rashers,
    finely chopped
4 tablespoons water

Melt the butter in a large saucepan, add the onion and white leek and fry for 5 minutes until just beginning to soften. Stir in the other vegetables and sage sprigs, cover and cook gently for 10 minutes, stirring occasionally.

Pour over the stock, season to taste with salt and pepper and bring to the boil. Reduce the heat, cover and simmer for 45 minutes, stirring occasionally, until the vegetables are tender. Remove and discard the sage, then taste and adjust the seasoning if needed.

Make the dumplings by mixing the flour, mustard powder, sage, suet, bacon and a little salt and pepper together in a bowl. Gradually stir in the measured water and mix first with a spoon, then squeeze together with your hands to make a smooth dough. Cut into 18 slices and roll each slice into a small ball.

Stir the remaining green leek into the soup. Add the dumplings, re-cover and simmer for

10 minutes until the dumplings are light and fluffy. Ladle into bowls and serve immediately.

365

next time...

For creamy winter vegetable soup, make the soup as in the previous recipe, but using 1.5 litres (2½ pints) stock. Omitting the dumplings, add the green leek after simmering the soup for 45 minutes, re-cover and simmer for a further 10 minutes. Leave the soup to cool slightly, then purée in the pan with a stick blender or in batches in a blender or food processor until smooth, returning to the pan. Stir in 300 ml (½ pint) milk and reheat gently. Ladle into bowls, then swirl 2 tablespoons double cream into each serving and garnish with a little chopped sage and some diced crispy bacon.

index

picture credits

Additional picture credits:

Octopus Publishing Group Adrian Lawrence 152, 156, 163, 167, 168, 177, 179, 182, 186, 189, 191, 194, 196, 200, 201, 202, 204, 205, 207, 210; David Loftus 158; Diana Miller 39, 175; Ian Wallace 173, 213; Lis Parsons 70, 76, 122, 134; Sean Myers 26, 164; Simon Smith 38, 184; Stephen Conroy 94, 138, 215; Will Heap 54, 90, 140, 145; William Lingwood 27, 30; William Reavell 16, 28, 108; William Shaw 6, 11, 12, 14, 18, 22, 24, 34, 40, 42, 46, 48, 50, 59, 62, 63, 66, 72, 80, 82, 84, 89, 96, 98, 100, 104, 112, 116, 120, 124, 128, 130, 139, 148, 217

acknowledgements

Publishing Director: Stephanie Jackson
Assistant Editor: Nell Warner
Contributor: Sara Lewis
Copy-editor: Jo Richardson
Proofreader: Jane Birch
Indexer: Isobel McLean

Senior Designer: Jaz Bahra
Design: Jeremy Tilston
Special Photography: Adrian Lawrence
Home Economist: Amy Stephenson
Prop Stylist: Cynthia Blackett
Production Controller: Katie Jarvis